SUNRAY

SUNRAY

THE DEATH AND LIFE OF CAPTAIN NICHOLA GODDARD

■ ■ ■

VALERIE FORTNEY

KEY PORTER BOOKS

Library and Archives Canada Cataloguing in Publication

Fortney, Valerie
      Sunray : the death and life of Captain Nichola Goddard / Valerie Fortney.

ISBN 978-1-55470-300-5

1. Goddard, Nichola, 1980-2006. 2. Afghan War, 2001- —Participation, Canadian. 3.
Canada. Canadian Armed Forces—Officers—Biography.
4. Women soldiers—Canada—Biography. 5. Canada. Canadian Armed Forces—
Women—Biography. 6. Afghan War, 2001- —Casualties—Canada.
I. Title.

DS371.43.G64F67 2010   958.104'7092   C2010-901802-8

ONTARIO ARTS COUNCIL
CONSEIL DES ARTS DE L'ONTARIO

The publisher gratefully acknowledges the support of the Canada Council for the Arts and
the Ontario Arts Council for its publishing program. We acknowledge the support of the
Government of Ontario through the Ontario Media Development Corporation's Ontario
Book Initiative.

We acknowledge the financial support of the Government of Canada through the Book
Publishing Industry Development Program (BPIDP) for our publishing activities.

Key Porter Books Limited
Six Adelaide Street East, Tenth Floor
Toronto, Ontario
Canada M5C 1H6

www.keyporter.com

Text design and electronic formatting: Alison Carr

Printed and bound in Canada

10 11 12 13 14 5 4 3 2 1

FSC
Mixed Sources
Cert no. SW-COC-001271
© 1996 FSC

For Shelley Marie Louise Fortney
sister, friend, guiding spirit

Contents

Introduction

"I'M PROUD OF YOU GUYS—you got to do it, and you did it very well."

Captain Nichola Goddard placed one hand over her headset's microphone as she spoke these words to her fellow soldiers. Her compliment wasn't meant for the various radio frequencies tuned in by hundreds of other soldiers scattered around Afghanistan, at the main base, forward observation bases and command posts. There would be plenty of time to share in the accomplishment with others, but this was a private moment.

It was May 17, 2006—a victorious day for the twenty-six-year-old forward observation officer (FOO) in the Canadian Forces, and the pinnacle experience of a journey that had begun eight years earlier, when as a teenager she'd entered the Royal Military College of Canada in the hopes of emerging an educated, competent officer. In this fight with the Taliban in Afghanistan's Panjwayi District, just outside of Kandahar City, it was Nichola, supported by her FOO team, who executed high-explosive and illumination fire missions in support of Canadian troop manoeuvres against a known enemy. Nichola was the first soldier to do this since the Korean War, more than a half century earlier. While those in the civilian world might not readily grasp the importance of the day, it was not lost on Nichola, her team or any of the other two hundred Canadian soldiers on the battlefield: they were finally doing exactly what they had spent years being trained to do.

Lieutenant-Colonel Hope, the commander of Task Force Orion—the name of the Canadian battle group sent to Afghanistan in January 2006—understands well why spirits were so high: on that day, says Hope, "so many soldiers for the first time in their careers were in a situation which not only gave them the opportunity to fight, but demanded it of them." For Nichola, it was a double victory. She wasn't the first *female* soldier in fifty years to execute a fire mission—she was the first soldier. She had truly overcome the gender divide.

But the capable leader, who along with another junior officer had led this battle, knew she couldn't have done it alone. She and the boys, her FOO team, were going down in the military-history books, and they all knew it. A few hours after their momentous achievement, during a lull in the day-long fighting, Nichola, known to the four members of the team as "Boss," snapped pictures of Master Bombardier Jeff Fehr, her gunner, as he held up the mission and sported a big grin. After exchanging high-fives and laughter with fellow team members Bombardier Chris Gauthier and Bombardier Clint Gingrich, they went back to work. Clint settled back into his driver's seat while Chris ducked out via the back ramp for a cigarette. Nichola and Jeff, their heads and shoulders sticking out of the turret of their light armoured vehicle (LAV), scanned the lush Panjwayi landscape: the leafy vines of the grape fields and the twenty-foot-high grape-drying huts, mulberry trees with thick overhanging branches, and mud compounds and high village walls. They were looking for signs of enemy activity, and also to determine where to direct the army's new M777 howitzers for maximum Taliban destruction and minimal risk to civilians and coalition soldiers.

"Ka-boom!" is all Jeff, a twenty-three-year-old from rural southern Manitoba, remembers of the moment that changed all of their lives forever. Three rocket propelled grenades (RPGS) simultaneously hit the body of their double-armour-plated LAV. The impact threw him and Nichola into the vehicle, knocking him unconscious. When he came to a few seconds later, Jeff was blinded by a white cloud: the LAV's fire-suppression system had been set off by the blast. It took him a minute or two to see Nichola, who was lying back as though asleep. Several minutes passed while Jeff and Chris desperately tried to engage their damaged guns as the ambush continued to rage, and driver Clint struggled to extricate them from their vulnerable position. It was only another several minutes later, while still under attack from the Taliban, that they discovered the gaping wound at the back of their leader's head. Shrapnel from the grenade—one that might have been Soviet-made, left behind when that country retreated in defeat in 1989 after nearly a decade of fighting— had torn through Nichola's helmet, killing her instantly.

Jeff cried into the radio, relying on the military term for a commander, or boss, to convey his message: "My Sunray's down! My Sunray's down!"

With that chance ricochet of shrapnel at just before 7:00 p.m. Afghanistan time, as the sweltering sun set on the battlefield, Captain Nichola Goddard entered the history books for the second time that day. Over the next twenty-four hours, Canadians would be informed of the sixteenth Canadian soldier to die in Afghanistan. The young captain, whose job at the front of the front line was one of the most dangerous in the military, had become the highest-ranking soldier to die since Canada had joined the United States and the North Atlantic Treaty Organization (NATO) in a counter-insurgency fight against the Taliban four years earlier. But there was one thing that would overshadow all others: Nichola was the first female Canadian soldier to die in a combat role.

But it wasn't Nichola's destiny to serve merely as a symbol of the final frontier of Canadian military gender parity: being remembered only as the "first female," say those closest to her, would have horrified the young woman whose entire life was a refutation of gender stereotypes. And it was an extraordinary life, marked by a wide variety of people, places and influences far beyond the scope of a conventional Canadian childhood. Nichola's parents, Tim and Sally Goddard, have spent their adult lives helping to build and rebuild education systems in some of the most remote corners of the planet. From Canada's First Nations reserves to post-war Kosovo and Lebanon, the self-described hippies have put their "books not bombs" philosophy into practice. Toting their daughter from pillar to post—she was born in Papua New Guinea and grew up in every corner of Canada—the peripatetic but headstrong academics instilled in Nichola a desire to make a difference in the world. Yet the daughter who shared her father's gap-toothed smile and rigorous intellectual curiosity chose a wildly divergent route to achieve that end.

Nichola spent a lifetime becoming acquainted with foreign cultures. While her parents worked to build a high school on the remote Trobriand Islands, a place where even in the twenty-first century people live an almost Stone Age existence, Nichola was taken in by the local tribeswomen and taught to wield a machete, develop a taste for the exotic local food staples and build bonfires to cook the daily catches of fresh fish. As her nomadic family made its way through various parts of Canada, she spoke Dene with the First Nations children of Black Lake, Saskatchewan, explored the natural wonders of Baffin Island and made lifelong friends from the prairies to the East Coast. The woman who as a child had dined on taro, caribou and seal had no trouble sitting down to a meal of goat soup with Afghan village elders. Mentors both predictable and unorthodox shaped her world view, from top-notch military leaders of both genders to authority-challenging, civilian liberal arts academics in a military university.

If Nichola's family background doesn't wholly answer the question of why this modern-day, educated woman would choose the profession of warrior, the honours English graduate has left us with perhaps the most detailed account—her observations, philosophical arguments and sometimes tangled emotions—of the Canadian soldier's experience in this twenty-first-century war.

Throughout her time in Afghanistan, Nichola wrote prolifically, to family, friends and even strangers, about her observations and experiences in this foreign land. Her private, far more intimate letters to Jason Beam, her husband of three years, reveal the maturity and complexity of a woman who, while struggling with so many aspects of the gruelling tour in Afghanistan, never wavered in her belief that she was doing the right thing. These remarkable letters, reflecting Nichola's keen intellect and awareness of the danger she faced, offer many insights into why, with all of life's choices laid out before her, she might choose to kill and risk being killed in a conflict halfway around the world.

More than eighty people contacted for this book—Nichola's family, friends, colleagues and mentors—have helped to further paint a vibrant, in-depth portrait of this multifaceted young woman who is now an important figure in Canada's military history. Reading her words, hearing her stories, one can come to know Nichola as much as one can know a person one has never met, and understand, if not always agree with, the convictions and overwhelming sense of duty she took to her grave.

Sunray is the tale of one soldier's ultimate sacrifice, and of the impact just one death can have on a multitude of people around the world. It also serves as a reminder that our country has now been at war for going on a decade, and that our comforting stereotype of the blue-beret-wearing, non-violent Canadian peacekeeper is an antiquated notion at best. As of this writing, more than 150 Canadian soldiers and 4 Canadian civilians have joined the more than 800 Americans and soldiers of other NATO countries who have died in the war against the Taliban, in a country that no one has ever been able to conquer.

For good or bad, Nichola died believing that the Tim and Sally Goddards of the world needed warriors like her, to do the advance dirty work before the rebuilding could begin. Or, as she once put it to her father, "I do what I do, so you can do what you do."

PART I

FROM SEA TO SEA TO SEA

ONE

Islands of Love

THE "PEARL OF THE PACIFIC" is a magical place, famed for its bats that fly in daylight, hundreds of species of orchid and brilliant red bougainvillea as plentiful as prairie dandelions, not to mention its crocodile-filled waters and the alluring scent of fragrant frangipani trees that constantly hangs in the air. On the first day of May 1980, Tim Goddard found himself in the Pearl, also known as Madang, a pretty port town in Papua New Guinea. He wasn't there as a tourist. As he paced around a palm-treed courtyard under a blanket of shimmering stars, counting the sidewalk cracks and struggling to keep his fears at bay, the twenty-six-year-old tried to distract himself from the events unfolding just a stone's throw away: inside one of the sorbet-hued buildings that looked like a run-down vintage motel in Miami's South Beach, his twenty-eight-year-old wife was about to give birth to their first child.

Only two days earlier, Sally Goddard had heard the words "breech birth" from a doctor in Wewak, the town on the main island's northern coast where she and her husband worked as educators. While Sally knew that if she were back in Canada, she would be facing a relatively minor birthing complication, the expectant mother understood the grave implications of her condition. She was 14,000 kilometres from home, in a country that the twentieth century had left behind. Most parts of Papua New Guinea had no electricity, let alone doctors trained to perform Caesarean sections. Her family physician had discovered the breech by performing an X-ray on her abdomen, a procedure a Western doctor would take great pains to avoid, but the only diagnostic tool he had on hand. He'd never performed a caesarean alone: she needed to be near a hospital. His pronouncement set off a forty-eight-hour scramble, in which Tim and Sally had to make their way to Madang on the once-a-week flight, a white-knuckle ride over jagged mountain peaks, rainforest and active volcanoes. They'd had to bump a Japanese tourist to make that flight, but when they arrived in Madang, they discovered, as Sally would say with a sardonic laugh, "no rooms at the inn." In the end, it didn't matter: Sally—who doctors said was still a month away from giving birth—went into labour hours after touching down.

As his wife waited in Madang Hospital for the arrival of members of the surgical team—it was a Friday night, so they were rounded up via ambulance from dinner parties, local bingo halls and movie theatres—Tim contemplated this new life chapter. He also had plenty of time to think about how he got here in the first place, when on a wintry day in 1976 he'd hopped a plane at London's Heathrow airport and headed to a remote cluster of islands on the other side of the planet.

■ ■ ■

From an outsider's perspective, it's not surprising that Tim Goddard and Sally West set their sights on one another from practically day one. They shared many things in common, including British passports, a passion for teaching and a devilish sense of humour. Both had chosen Papua New Guinea out of a desire to escape predictable lives and plunge themselves into the wholly unknown, a primitive country that few back home could point out on a map, let alone know was a complex place made up of more than a thousand, often-warring, tribes, with more than eight hundred languages.

Their so-called regular lives, though, were vastly different. Sally, the second of five daughters of a British internist and his nurse wife, had come to Canada as an infant. She'd grown up in near-idyllic circumstances in Sault Ste. Marie, Ontario, spending her leisure time swimming, rowing and playing tennis in the summer, her winters downhill and cross-country skiing. Her father, Michael West, had constantly encouraged the wiry athlete and her sisters to try their hand at new things, with the understanding that he and wife, Kathleen, were always there to rescue a stranded traveller or repair a bruised knee or a broken heart. By the time 1974 rolled around, Sally's path was tidily laid out: she'd head to Papua New Guinea for a two-year volunteer stint with the Canadian University Services Overseas (CUSO), then likely return to Trent University in Peterborough, Ontario, where she'd just graduated with a degree in history, to pursue a master's.

Across the Atlantic, Tim wasn't enjoying such a carefree existence. As Sally was packing her green Samsonite for Papua New Guinea in late summer 1974, Tim, the eldest son of a Leeds police inspector and his staff-nurse wife, found himself in a rut. He had just started his first job after graduating from teachers' college, assigned to a school in Harlow, England. The town that was mostly rebuilt after World War II and a half hour's train ride from London was distinguished by grey tenement high-rises, a far cry from the lush dales of Tim's native Yorkshire. He spent his days trying to excite the intellects of the children of blue-collar workers from the nearby biscuit factory; in his cramped one-bedroom apartment, he devoted evenings and weekends to poring over the *Times of London Educational Supplement*, always on the lookout for new opportunities.

One Sunday in the fall of 1975, an ad caught his eye: Papua New Guinea had just declared its independence. The Australians who had governed it for the better part of the twentieth century were packing their bags and heading home, creating a brain drain of skilled workers in every sector; among the most desperately needed were teachers. What the job lacked in remuneration would be made up for in adventure. Tim's thoughts immediately wandered back to his primary-school teacher, Miss Scarborough, who one day simply up and left Leeds. She joined the Voluntary Service Overseas (vso), the British version of cuso, and later sent her students a postcard from Peru. When he arrived at his interview in London a few weeks later, Tim told the recruiter he didn't want to hear about the malaria-carrying mosquitoes, lack of modern amenities or any other drawbacks. "Where do I sign?" was all he asked.

■ ■ ■

When the pair finally met in January 1976, sparks literally flew. Tim had arrived at the teachers' compound in Alotau, a relatively peaceful coastal village on the northern shore of Milne Bay, where many inhabitants still practised witchcraft but also enjoyed such rare modern-day conveniences as electricity. Tim was on a high: he'd just spent his first week in a remote village where he'd fished for his supper in an outrigger canoe and slept in a thatched hut perched on stilts. He felt as though he'd been thrust onto the pages of Robert Ballantyne's *Coral Island*, the nineteenth-century boys' own adventure; trading in the concrete jungle for the real one had brought him back to vibrant life.

On that first day at the compound, a storm blew in and downed a power line in front of his small teacher's house. As he stood in front of the wire, contemplating the best way to get around it, Tim heard a female voice scream out an expletive-filled warning. "I'm not a complete idiot!" he barked back in a thick Yorkshire accent to the slender, pretty young woman sporting long, braided pigtails. The stocky, dark-haired new-comer walked the long way around the power line and introduced himself to his new neighbour, Sally West.

That inauspicious introduction was quickly forgotten as Tim's charms were made apparent to Sally. A week after his arrival, he returned to school from town on his red Honda 70 motorcy-cle, a live turtle the size of a throw cushion tied to his back. Tim was a passionate shell collector who hadn't been able to resist the promise of a turtle shell on sale at the Alotau market. No one had told him the turtle was still alive; he bought it anyway. It was the first, but certainly not the last, time the townsfolk would refer to Tim as "that crazy dim-dim"—"dim-dim" being the term used to describe foreigners. His arrival at the school elicited convulsive laughter from many of the six hundred students gathered outside for assembly, not to mention Sally West.

Tim was immediately drawn to the athletic teacher whose soft-spoken manner thinly concealed a mischievousness and confidence that he found irresistible. One evening, as several teachers sat around chatting after dinner, Sally told a story that sealed the deal. In the early summer of 1974, she took a cross-Canada journey with a group of Quebec fishermen's children in a school bus, as part of an effort to open their eyes to all the country had to offer. That's the sort of crazy thing I'd do, Tim thought. From that day on, he did his best to woo Sally, who, to his relief, didn't require arm-twisting. She couldn't resist the fiery Brit, a man whose childlike enthusiasm for just about everything energized her, and whose love of a good laugh matched her own.

Like any love story worth its salt, there were obstacles. Dating between dim-dims caused a sensation in these parts, so the pair kept their budding romance under wraps. Public displays of affection were out of the question; for weeks, they made sure to travel in groups to fellow teachers' homes and the local movie house. Constantly looming over their heads was the winding down of Sally's two-year CUSO stint: she was scheduled to return home in late summer, and was already enrolled at Trent University. Undaunted, Tim suggested one evening they take their motorcycles out for a ride to the town's airstrip. When Sally arrived at his house on her green Honda 70 bike, her hot-pink helmet atop her head, Tim presented her with a ring and a necklace. "Will you marry me?" he asked. Sally didn't say no, but Tim's surprise proposal didn't change her plans, either. She put the ring on the necklace, and fastened it around her neck. She had to go home, if only to make sure that what they felt for one another was genuine and not just the by-product of two Westerners being thrown together in a strange land.

The following spring, Sally was back. The quiet university campus in the town of Peterborough was no match for the South Pacific, or that Brit with the gap-toothed grin. She missed the "sing-sing" traditional dances by natives in full body paint, the white sand beaches that stretched beyond the horizon—but mostly, she missed Tim. Not that he didn't provide a nudge or two. Over those long, miserable ten months, he sent Sally regular letters proclaiming his love, amusing her with a Papua New Guinea newspaper of his own making entitled *The End of the World Gazette and Citizen*, which detailed the gossip and daily exploits of the villagers and expats. Just after Christmas, Tim sent her money for a one-way plane ticket; Michael West, fearing his daughter might stay and marry Tim just because she didn't have a way back home, provided the return airfare. "You don't have to fly 26,000 miles just to jump in bed with somebody," was his grumpy but loving admonishment.

On July 9, 1977, under threatening grey skies in the midst of the rainy season, the pigtailed flower child and the self-described "mercenary educator" were married before a crowd of two hundred, made up of the couple's colleagues, senior students of the school and friends they'd made in town. Sally wore a citron-hued polyester gown sewn by a local woman as a gift, her long, wavy brown hair pulled back and adorned with a rainbow cluster of orchids; Tim sported a cream-coloured linen suit, his wild black curls and full beard making him look as though he'd just emerged from weeks in the rainforest. Clare Chidgey, Sally's Welsh friend who came to Papua New Guinea as a nutritionist, was the maid of honour; Arty Morson, a fellow Brit educator who'd arrived with Tim nineteen months earlier, was best man. The elderly Father John Bodger, an expat Brit who had been an Anglican priest in Papua New Guinea for fifty years, presided over his first dim-dim wedding. He made an impromptu speech about the Wars of the Roses and uniting the houses of York and

Lancaster, the provenance of Tim and Sally's families, while the giddy pair tried not to laugh. The crowd feasted on roast pig, sweet potato and yam while their students performed the Tapioca Dance. The newlyweds did their best to feign surprise as they unwrapped no less than eight identical metal serving trays, one of the few precious items on offer at the local trade store.

■ ■ ■

As the clock struck midnight, ushering in May 2, 1980, Tim continued to pace, his brow furrowed by both worry and the unrelenting humidity of the tropics. Initially, having a baby had been Sally's idea. The fall prior, she'd sat on the stoop of their house at their new school in Wewak, and watched Tim play with the three-year-old son of a fellow teacher. As the two tinkered with Tim's train set—he'd lamented to Sally he never had one as a child, so she'd bought him one for his twenty-sixth birthday— she realized then and there it was time. Perhaps after five years here, she had absorbed some of the local beliefs, one being that a child's spirit first finds its way into its mother, in the form of a thought. Later that day, for the first time since they'd met over a live power line, she broached the subject of a baby.

Tim, waiting outside the hospital nearly nine months from that day, thought about the arrival of Nicholas. Or maybe it would be a she: then, Nichola would do nicely. Sally had been reading a book about Nicholas and Alexandra, the last crowned czar of Russia and his wife, and fell in love with the name. She also loved its Greek origins: "victory of the people." Tim approved. On the flight to Madang, he'd told Sally that it sounded "strong and beautiful at the same time."

Somewhere between 1:00 and 2:00 a.m. on May 2, 1980, Nichola Kathleen Sarah Goddard let out her first cry. The tiny newborn was placed in a wheeled trolley, which a nurse pushed into the warm night air, presenting the girl to her father. As tears filled his eyes, Tim was at once elated, relieved and horrified. The trolley, he thought, looked like a meat safe. How was that little metal box—surrounded by screen wire to keep out the mosquitoes, and with a procession of ants climbing up its legs—going to protect his daughter?

He couldn't have imagined that this four-pound miracle would one day be a five-foot-five-tall officer in the Canadian army, who would not only match her fellow soldiers in mental and physical strength, but lead them into a historic battle against the Taliban of southern Afghanistan.

TWO

Coconuts to Caribou

"Give me a child until he is seven, and I will give you the man."
— old Jesuit saying

ON CHRISTMAS EVE, 1979, elite Soviet forces began flying into Kabul airport and the military airbase at Bagram, farther north. Three days later, the main telephone exchanges of Afghanistan's capital were destroyed and the radio station was taken over, along with several government buildings. Within a week, 50,000 Soviet troops would be on Afghan soil. In an impressive display of modern military might, the Red Army swept into the country of seventeen million mostly illiterate souls and immediately choked off major roads. Afghanistan's latest invaders had moved thousands of tanks and combat vehicles into the country and had already secured bases for supplies.

By early May 1980, Soviet troops had occupied most of the country's main cities, while the Basmachi (bandits), as the Soviets called the Muslim and Turkic peoples rising up against their rule, began waging a guerrilla war in the mostly forgotten countryside. It was an atmosphere the citizens of the impoverished, medieval country knew only too well. For centuries, conflict had been a way of life, from the tribal warlords fighting one another for supremacy to foreign would-be conquerors drawn to the land-locked country's attractive location on the crossroads between Iran, the Arabian Sea and India. Genghis Khan, Alexander the Great and a host of others, at one time or another, had set their sights on Afghanistan. In the nineteenth century, the British, fearful of an expanding Russian empire, made three attempts to conquer the region. Its actions began "The Great Game," in which Afghanistan would serve as a buffer state between Russia and Britain's Indian empire. The endless state of war and invasion developed in the Afghans a fierce fighting mentality, and an impermeable defiance against all comers: not even the world's most powerful rulers could wrestle the Afghans into submission. "No outsider has ever captured them or claimed their soul," wrote Pakistani journalist Ahmed Rashid in his seminal book *Taliban*, of the country described as the heart of Asia. The Soviets, though, were confident they would change the course of history.

The Western soldiers who would find themselves in Afghanistan nearly a quarter of a century later were, in 1980, either small children or not yet born. Their parents were too busy with the care and feeding of young children to take much notice of events unfolding nearly 10,000 kilometres away, in a country few people, outside of the worlds of academia or geopolitics, were familiar with. This applied even more to Sally and Tim Goddard, who were living where news from other parts of the world was often weeks late, if it came at all. As she departed the quaint coastal town of Madang with her husband, their tiny daughter bundled up in a borrowed blanket, Sally's chief concern was how she would settle in without a single baby necessity. The crate of infant supplies they had shipped from England—where

Tim had taken his pregnant wife to meet her new in-laws several months earlier—had been lost en route to the South Pacific. They were without diapers, bottles and infant clothes. Tim had run out and bought an outfit for Nichola he'd found at a local trade store. "It'll fit her perfectly—when she turns three," said Sally, sighing as she held up the toddler-size dress.

If Wewak had its inconveniences—a cardboard box on the floor of their truck cab, for instance, served as Nichola's car seat—it was nothing compared to the Goddards' next Papua New Guinea teaching stint. With their infant daughter in tow, in late 1980 they landed on Kiriwina, the main island of the Trobriand Islands, one of the most mysterious, remote parts of the planet. It was a place few Westerners had ever been to, but was internationally known as the Islands of Love, thanks to its inhabitants' curious sexual practices: premarital sex was not only accepted, but encouraged, and tales of gang rape of males by females, part of the bacchanalian rituals that accompanied the celebration of the annual yam harvest, had received sensational reporting in the Western media. In the early twentieth century, one of the world's leading anthropologists, Polish-born Bronislaw Malinowski, had spent time in the Trobs, as the locals referred to the islands, conducting groundbreaking field research.

These newcomer dim-dims found themselves on the receiving end of careful study when they disembarked from the small twin-engine plane and stepped onto Kiriwina's dusty airstrip. While Nichola nervously sucked on the end of her mother's pigtail, the trio was transported in the back of a truck along a road lined with hundreds of fascinated tribes people, most of whom had never seen a white baby. The scrutiny only grew as they realized the outsiders were staying. Over the first week, a constant procession of the island's ten thousand citizens sauntered past Tim and Sally's house, smack dab in the centre of a busy crossroads of Losuia, its main village. "We're in a fishbowl," a disconcerted Sally said as she peered out her window and saw scores of eyes peering back. Looking out at the daily commotion, Tim, who'd brought his family here after being hired to help build and establish the island's first high school, would shake his head and crack jokes, usually succeeding in making his more private spouse laugh along with him over the spectacle.

The people of the Trobs possessed softer Polynesian features than the rugged main islanders of Melanesian descent. Their skin was paler, and they were more diminutive in stature and delicate in bone structure. But these famed lovers became warriors when faced with an assault on their cultural sensibilities, a lesson Tim and Sally learned one evening. The couple had been sitting out on their front stoop sipping gin and tonics when Nichola's cries rang out from inside. Her wailing prompted a typical parental debate: Tim thought he should go in and calm her; Sally, whose mum, Kathleen, believed that a constantly held baby grew into a spoiled child, thought it better to let Nichola settle in. She needed to learn her parents wouldn't drop everything and come running at the first sound of a cry. "If we do that," she told Tim, "we'll be holding her the rest of her life." Almost before Sally was finished speaking, a village woman silently strode past the pair and through their front entry. Seconds later, still silent but with a disgusted expression on her face, the stranger emerged with a now-quiet Nichola swaddled in her arms. She sailed past the Goddards, down the lane and into another house. Exchanging guilty glances, Sally and Tim calmly finished their cocktails before getting up to go face the new neighbours. They walked up to the door of the house into which they'd seen the woman and their daughter disappear, finding inside a group of agitated village women gathered around a contented Nichola. "We don't let babies cry on the island," one informed them. "Do that again, and we'll take her away from you for good."

Tim and Sally were quickly forgiven. Sally knew it had everything to do with Nichola. She was the centre of attention everywhere she went, not seeming to mind the constant stroking of her wispy ringlets, the kisses planted on her soft, chubby thighs. You can never get too much love, thought Sally, even if at times she worried that her daughter, whose feet hardly ever touched the ground, might never learn to walk. Nichola quickly dispelled such concerns. In the summer of 1981, while Sally's back was turned in the kitchen, the one-year-old gave her the slip. Both parents tore out of the house, their worst fears flashing through their minds. They lived only steps away from the sea, and parts of the shoreline had the consistency of quicksand. "Nichola! Nichola!" they screamed in unison, racing down the gravel road. They found her about 50 metres from the house under a tree in the town's centre. Within seconds, Nichola had stripped herself naked and was running and squealing with the other bare-bummed village toddlers, a handful of women on the sidelines laughing and cheering them on. Nichola's first words, naturally, were in Kiriwina, the language of her first home. By age three, she was adept in both this language and Creole-based Tok Pisin.

In time, the dim-dim baby became, in the eyes of the islanders, a Trobs child. Her caregivers Mispah and sister Rose soon had her eating boiled and mashed taro, a nutrient-rich root vegetable with the taste and consistency of potato. She never turned down the Trobriand staples of yams, tapioca, sweet potato, bananas, passion fruit, coconut and fish. Nichola also liked starfruit, which her father introduced to the island after bringing back a box of seeds from the main island, and later convincing some Kiriwina farmers to add it to their crops. Rose's husband, Ernest, was a former ground engineer for Air Niugini, who returned home in his thirties after becoming disillusioned with the hustle and bustle of the main island. "What I really wanted, what I really needed, was all here," the always-barefoot Ernest Goweli told Sally when they first met. "To make enough to live on, to look out at the sea from this beach every day." The thirty-six-year-old father of three indulged Nichola's every whim, prompting his fifteen-year-old daughter, Susan, to tease, "You're spoiling that cheeky little girl. Whatever she wants, you just give her." At two years of age, Nichola began accompanying Ernest on fishing expeditions. He taught her how to hold a rod, gather wood and stack it to create a bonfire. Nichola delighted in helping "Uncle" get the fire ready, clapping as he cooked the newly caught fish over the flames. One evening, as they sat together on the beach at sunset looking out at the turquoise-hued, pearl-rich Solomon Sea, Ernest looked at his chubby little companion and took a mental photograph, hoping never to forget Nichola. "She's really a Trobs girl," he thought. "Like one of my own children."

The toddler also found another adult friend in Sister Helen, a Catholic nun who had been posted to Kiriwina a year before the Goddards. It was only natural that the feisty five-foot-tall Australian nun, as one of the few white people on the island, would be drawn to Sally, whom she'd first met back in Alotau but hadn't had time to form a bond. On lazy afternoons, the two women would sit on Sally's porch drinking tea and swapping stories of their joys and frustrations in this confounding country. The former Helen Warman, having resided in various parts of the country for two decades, certainly had those in abundance. She told Sally while she now loved the place and its people, as a young nun she'd been willing to go anywhere except Papua New Guinea: she'd seen a documentary, filmed by a missionary, showing the "filthy, desperate" natives famed for cannibalism and headhunting. Her regular visits from the Catholic mission a few kilometres away to Kiriwina, though, were as much for Nichola as for Sally. Whenever the little girl heard the unmistakable roar of Sister's Helen motorcycle coming up the road, she'd run to the front porch, her little arms wildly waving in greeting. The nun, who amused the locals by whizzing around on her bike in a starched white dress and with her white wimple firmly affixed to her head, always spent part of her visit counting and chasing geckos with Nichola. "You may be a girl of the Trobs," Sister Helen would tell the toddler as she stroked her hair, "but you'll always be my Nichola."

As with any other Trobriand child, conventional toys had no meaning for Nichola. There weren't any swing sets or soccer balls on the island, and playtime was about imitating grown-ups by pretending to cook, clean and do other household and garden chores. Sally could have sent for care packages filled with crayons and dolls, but that wouldn't have made sense; Nichola was quite content with her Trobriand childhood, not missing what she'd never had.

If her parents needed any further confirmation that their daughter's childhood was unconventional, Mispah proved herself indispensable in that regard. The middle-aged woman made sure Nichola was up to speed on all the lessons of a Trobs childhood, including learning how to wield a machete, an everyday tool as essential as a spoon in North America. With this survival skill mastered, a child could easily fend for herself. One day, on his way home for lunch, Tim spotted his daughter sitting under a rubber tree. She had a coconut in one hand and the large, cleaver-like knife in the other. He thought he was going to have a heart attack. "She's gonna cut herself," was all he could utter between short breaths as he grabbed the knife from her little hand. Sitting cross-legged on the grass, Mispah couldn't understand the fuss. "Why? Why would she do that?" she asked with a bemused expression. "She knows how to cut a coconut."

Though Tim was hired by provincial officials to start up the school, he was still required to navigate his way through the confusing tangle of often competing authorities on Kiriwina. After months of jumping through the island's political hoops—a feat accomplished with the help of Sister Helen and Ernest—in January 1981 headmaster Tim opened Kiriwina High School. His total teaching staff consisted of Sally and Charles Rato, a teacher who hailed from the main island's Highlands, charged with the schooling of seventy-four children. Twenty-five years later, the school would house, in several more buildings built over time, 240 children. Kids like Diana Pwaka were at first frightened by the dim-dims, until she realized "they didn't judge us." Serah Kalubaku, the first of her large family to stay on the island for high school, liked to get in on pranks against their good-natured headmaster, hand-delivering him parcels filled with spiders, "and laugh till we cried, while Mr. Goddard screamed."

The island's teenagers took turns babysitting Nichola and hitching rides in the Goddards' Mazda 929 station wagon, one of the only motorized vehicles on the island. Still, there were reminders that they inhabited very different worlds. Before one of the infamous Trobriand cricket matches, often involving up to two hundred players, along with brief sexual liaisons in the nearby bushes, Sally's students expressed dismay that she was interested in coming out to observe the event. "Please, Miss," they told her, "we don't care if the tourists see us, but you are someone we know. You're our teacher." She was welcomed in the village and the classroom, and at ceremonies where the girls and women would don the traditional grass skirts and perform sing-sings, but they preferred that she didn't know everything.

When Sally discovered she was pregnant again in the spring of 1982, she determined there would be no repeat of the life-and-death drama of her first child's entrance into the world. That fall, she left Tim to his duties at Kiriwina High School, and headed with her toddler to her parents' home in Sault Ste. Marie.

Nichola donned her first pair of shoes for the trip: Sally had traced the two-year-old's feet on a piece of paper a month earlier, and had an Australian visitor send for shoes that fit. The shiny red Mary Janes had to be custom made to accommodate the wide feet Nichola had developed from going barefoot. The pair overnighted at a hotel in San Francisco, which gave Nichola her first glimpse of the conveniences of modern life. She made the most of it, standing over the toilet for an entire evening, repeatedly flushing and squealing with delight as the water swirled down into the bowl, her mother too tired to put up a fight.

The next day, Sally arrived at the Canadian border without the proper paperwork for Nichola. A customs officer escorted the pair into an interview room. He couldn't quite understand the unusual circumstances. Because Papua New Guinea had strict laws governing citizenship, Nichola wasn't considered a PNG citizen merely by right of birth; had she lived out her life there, it would take two more generations born in Papua New Guinea before any of her descendants could claim citizenship. The customs officer told the seven-months-pregnant mother she'd have to get the documentation sorted out before Nichola could enter Canada. Exasperated and bleary-eyed from three days of almost non-stop travel, Sally plunked her smiling toddler onto his desk and said, "Why don't you keep her until tomorrow, then, and I'll come back for her when this is all sorted out?" He let the pair go, with the understanding Sally would complete the paperwork to make Nichola, who one day would don a soldier's uniform to fight on behalf of her country, a Canadian citizen.

■ ■ ■

In the spring of 1983, the Goddard family—now counting four with baby Victoria—headed to the main island's Eastern Highlands, where Tim took a job as a department head at Aiyura National High School. While Sally worked at the school, the children often headed with their babysitters to the nearby coffee plantations, where Nichola joined the other children in picking beans. "She didn't need the money," Tim would say in an amusing speech on his daughter's wedding day twenty years later. "It was where all the kids were, so she wanted to be part of the action." Nichola also made a good friend in Jacqueline Patterson, her fifteen-year-old babysitter. Jacqueline hailed from the Trobs; she spoke Kiriwina with Nichola, and liked to dress her up in a grass skirt, paint her face and take her to sing-sings. One day, Jacqueline snapped a photograph of Nichola wearing one of those grass skirts. She had a big pout on her face; Sally had forgotten the skirt at home, and had to run back to retrieve it. Even though Nichola got her way, she was still angry when Jacqueline took the picture. "Nichola," said Jacqueline through tears of laughter, "you can stop pouting now, you have your grass skirt on just like all the other village girls."

This life was the only one her three-year-old child had ever known, but Sally knew there was an easier way for a mother with two young children. Trying to raise two in a place where few amenities existed had worn her down. Not long before her eldest child's fourth birthday, the family left Papua New Guinea for Canada, a place they'd decided would offer them, and their children, the most opportunities. Their long journey to their new home included a stop in England, so Betty and Tony Goddard could see their grandchildren. At Heathrow airport, the group popped into an atrium café in one of the terminals. As Tim regaled his parents with tales of their travels—which included a stop in Singapore's Tiger Balm Gardens, where the preschooler had posed for Japanese tourists with a giant snake in her hands— Nichola slid out of her seat and began to wander the café. Betty looked up to see her granddaughter standing before a large tree. The blond-haired girl dressed in a navy pea coat was picking off the leaves and eating them. The proper Englishwoman let out a shriek equal parts horror and amusement. "Nichola, you can't eat the trees!" she cried out to the little girl who firmly believed she was doing nothing out of the ordinary.

■ ■ ■

Walking by her daughter's classroom one chilly fall day, Sally Goddard poked her head inside. It was a habit of hers—partly because she was there every day, working as a grade three teacher at the same school her grade one child attended—but also because she wanted to be assured that Nichola was settling in well. Her good-natured six-year-old, her once-wheat-coloured curls now a light brown mane falling past her shoulders, was usually sitting at her desk listening to her teacher or scribbling in her notebook. On this day, however, Sally was startled to see Nichola standing upright, straight as a razor, one hand thumping her chest and yelling out with her classmates, "I am a Chipewyan Indian!" Sally's first impulse was to put her hand over her mouth so Nichola and the others wouldn't hear a laugh from the hallway.

She really shouldn't have been surprised. From the moment they'd arrived at the Black Lake Dene First Nation, a fly-in reserve just a few kilometres from Saskatchewan's border with the Northwest Territories, Nichola had jumped head first into the culture of her new home. Despite a shocking introduction to fifty-below Celsius weather on a walk to church on Christmas morning, 1984, Black Lake was a wondrous place for the active preschooler. She didn't flinch when the parents of her playmates offered her a bowl of caribou stew, or bannock, the local version of fry bread. As in Kiriwina, there were more children than grown-ups here, and like Nichola, they loved to play outside until sunset. She picked up the local Dene language almost overnight, and in grade one would win a class speaking contest.

Nichola was settling in nicely, Sally thought. It really didn't matter if she lined up with the other kids in the assembly hall on Treaty Day, hoping to get five dollars from the Royal Canadian Mounted Police. When she came home empty-handed, Tim and Sally simply gave her five dollars and made a mental note to sit her down at some point and explain how she descended from the houses of Lancaster and York, not the nomadic hunters of the Beverly caribou.

The Black Lake job had been a godsend after several months of bunking with Sally's parents in Sault Ste. Marie, as Tim applied all over the country for teaching positions. It had been a stressful time: Tim's Papua New Guinea credentials didn't hold much sway in Canada. That is, until his résumé landed on a desk at the Black Lake First Nation in northern Saskatchewan. Rick Sullivan, a consultant with the band, called Tim one night to offer him the job of principal of the Black Lake Band School. He was impressed with his experience in such a foreign culture, and the fact his wife was also a teacher. He told Tim that the community had just taken control of its own schools, and was looking for someone with his unique skills and experience to get things up and running. The job suited Tim perfectly, and not just because it would mark the first time he was making a salary befitting a professional educator with more than a decade's experience. Sullivan tried to describe to the British expat where Black Lake was located. Tim grabbed an old school atlas off a nearby bookshelf and flipped to the page featuring Saskatchewan, a place he'd never set foot in. "Can you see Saskatoon?" asked the man on the other end of the line. "Yeah," said Tim. "Well, look north of there. Can you see Prince Albert?" "Yeah," Tim said, growing more confused. "Well, it's north of there."

Like his daughter, Tim preferred to notice the similarities, not the differences, between him and his new neighbours. Though he had only known Canada's indigenous peoples from books, he too loved to fish in Black Lake's crystalline waters and hunt for caribou and other game in the nearby forests, a practice the Dene liked to say was part of their lives long before the ancient pyramids of Egypt were built. He also shared their reliance on the snowmobile as a prime form of winter transportation. His tomboy eldest daughter joined him on ice-fishing expeditions, cheering him on as she'd once done for Ernest Goweli on Kiriwina. Riding with Tim on the snowmobile, clutching on to her dad for dear life, she would scream with delight as he navigated the high snowdrifts. He and Sally joined their daughters in making snow angels in the newly fallen snow as Winston, their new St. Bernard puppy, tried to lick their faces; after supper, they'd all don their parkas and snowmobile suits to dance under the brilliant northern lights. At bedtime, Tim would read to his daughters from books such as J. R. R. Tolkien's *The Hobbit*, taking on the voices of characters like the fantastical Gollum, complete with its horrifying swallowing noises, and Tolkien's coined words like "birdses" and "tricksey." Victoria, so enamoured with her father's animated performances that she herself began reading at age three, would later remember such evenings as the beginning of a lifelong love of fantasy and science fiction.

Black Lake opened Tim's eyes to his need for more academic credentials. He also knew that heading back to school would mean his family would likely spend the next few years bouncing around the country. "It's nothing different from what we've always done," Sally told him stoically. "We'll figure it out." They packed up the family again in 1987 and headed to the Saskatoon area, where Tim enrolled at the University of Saskatchewan. Over the next two years, he'd earn his bachelor of education, followed quickly by a master's degree. The modest house he chose in nearby Dundurn was only twenty minutes from the university. Their outdoorsy seven-year-old and five-year-old daughters settled in nicely. When Sally thought it was time her girls learned how to cross-country ski, she bought them their first skis and took them to a local park with groomed trails. Nichola took to the sport like a natural—after a few months on skis, she was already catching up to her mom—although the same couldn't be said for her brief foray into figure skating. "It was probably the only time we ever went out of our way to fit in," says Victoria. "We failed miserably."

Two years later, the Goddards were on the move once again. Tim, now with both a bachelor's and master's in education, accepted a job as principal for both the Attagoyuk and Alookie schools in Pangnirtung, Baffin Island. Pangnirtung, which means "the place of the bull caribou" in the Inuktitut language, was simply irresistible. Tim, an avid amateur photographer, couldn't wait to snap images of sunsets on the waterfalls, glaciers and snow-capped peaks and to see the bowhead whales in the waters of Cumberland Sound. He headed there in late summer of 1989, his two daughters in tow but his wife absent: Sally, having just given birth to third daughter Kate, was recuperating in hospital in Sault Ste. Marie after a bout of post-partum complications. Tim's mother, Betty, who had spent a few weeks in Papua New Guinea not long after her son's wedding, flew from England to the Arctic to help take care of Nichola and Victoria until Sally was well enough to travel with the new baby. When she arrived and surveyed her surroundings, Betty had to shake her head. Back when she had been pregnant with Tim, her firstborn, Betty had been reading a book about the Hudson's Bay Company's dominance in Canada's Far North. It was the first time she'd encountered words like "igloo" and "Eskimo," the once fashionable but now politically incorrect outsider's term for those residing in the world's Arctic regions. While nursing Tim, she had moved on to another book. It was 1954's *A Pattern of Islands*, in which British civil servant Sir Arthur Grimble recounted his time among the people of the South Pacific's Gilbert and Ellice Islands. For the first fifty years of her life, the mother of five had considered a caravan, or motor home, holiday in Wales to be the epitome of adventure. Now, here she was with a passport stamped with some of the world's most exotic locales, babysitting her granddaughters in a house 50 kilometres away from the Arctic Circle. Was it destiny? Betty wondered as she dined on caribou. Or is life just filled with these strange coincidences?

Yet, Pang, as the locals called it, would offer a much harsher initiation for even those accustomed to the new and novel. The Inuit had suffered more than their fair share of exploitation over the centuries, and had long memories. Explorers like Martin Frobisher—who in 1557 brought back to England three Inuit, all of whom died shortly thereafter—treated the inhabitants more like museum pieces than human beings. Some had even been placed in European zoos, and Tookolito, a female Inuit from Cumberland Sound, was put on display in the nineteenth century at P. T. Barnum's American Museum in New York. This wasn't like Black Lake, where the people's warmth made up for its remoteness and spartan conditions; those who ventured in to Pang felt the crushing weight of the sins of their forefathers.

The Goddards' daughters were on the front lines of the frosty reception. The simple act of stepping outside their door became a test for the girls, who'd never learned how to form a proper fist. When school was out, Tim would call Sally so she could stand watch and make sure no one tried to pick a fight with her two young outsiders. "What am I doing wrong?" said a confused Nichola to her mom one day after being shoved into a snowbank. Sally didn't know how to tell her innocent ten-year-old, who was used to being the fairest-skinned child in the crowd, that she'd finally come to a place where such things mattered. Being the principal's daughter made the target on her back that much bigger. Their social isolation was compounded by the imprisonment of winter: the thermometer often dipped to sixty degrees below Celsius, and the houses had to be tied down with cables to offset winds that regularly swept in at 150 kilometres an hour. The girls holed up in their house, doing homework, reading and watching television, a habit they took to out of sheer desperation. "We go to school, it's dark, we come home, it's dark," said Victoria, also tired of the daily taunts. "It's too lonely here." It was also expensive. After reviewing her first grocery bill, which included a pail of ice cream that cost twenty-eight dollars and navel oranges at three dollars each, Sally quipped to Tim: "That nice big salary is fool's gold."

Tim tried to make things exciting, taking his daughters out on snowmobile rides. However, one dogsled excursion with a friend and their two eldest children had nearly tragic results. Tim, with Nichola riding behind, ventured out with high hopes. At one point in the day, while the group explored the area on foot, Tim attempted to jump over a crevasse in the ice, but fell short by a few inches. Nichola stood by helpless as her father flailed about in the icy waters before the other adult pulled him out and helped him take off his drenched clothes. Nichola stripped off her clothes and wrapped herself behind her half-naked father in the hopes of saving him from hypothermia, the pair enveloped in blankets for the long sled journey home. Years later, Nichola would tell friends that seeing her father nearly die was the worst moment of her life.

The couple considered sending the girls to their maternal grandparents' home in the Soo for the remainder of the school year, but couldn't bear the thought of not seeing them for several months. Tim promised his wife and children they wouldn't stay in Pang. But their spirits remained low until the return of daytime sunlight in February. Tim took both girls on a snowmobile ride so they could share in witnessing the late-morning sun emerge over the top of a mountain peak. As the pink hues overtook the grey sky, Nichola and Victoria flung off their snowsuits and danced. And laughed.

By the summer of 1990, they were back in familiar, comfortable territory. Tim took a job as superintendent of education for the Lac La Ronge Indian Band in La Ronge, a rough-and-ready town in northern Saskatchewan on the Precambrian Shield, about 250 kilometres north of Prince Albert. With its hundreds of nearby lakes and forested wilderness, the town of La Ronge was paradise for avid hunters and anglers, and for kids who preferred fort-building to watching the small television that sat in the family's cold basement. When they weren't outside, Nichola and Victoria were curled up on the couch reading their weekly supply of books from the La Ronge Public Library. The family camped, hiked and fished together, and Nichola joined the local cross-country-ski club. On weekends, she prepared for local competitions by strapping on her skis and gliding along the 61 kilometres of groomed trails at Lac La Ronge Provincial Park.

While she pursued a bachelor's degree in education, Sally led a Girl Guides troop, giving her two eldest girls even more opportunities to get out into the world and socialize. While Kate took her first baby steps, Nichola and Victoria indulged their love of languages by learning Cree, which was spoken by the local band. Nichola even took her Anglican Church confirmation lessons in Cree. Two more dogs were added to the family: Charlie, a blue-eyed mutt, was Nichola's, while Petra, an overweight black Lab, became Victoria's.

Just after Nichola celebrated her thirteenth birthday, Tim had another surprise for his family. He'd been accepted into the PhD program at the University of Alberta, in Edmonton. Victoria wasn't sure she'd like a big city, but Nichola assured her they'd have a great time. Sally added in the promise that once they had settled into their new home, she'd finally fulfil Victoria's wish to take horseback-riding lessons. While Tim focused on his studies at the university, Sally worked in places like Black Lake and Norman Wells, Northwest Territories, helping to develop First Nations curricula. The job kept her away from home for long stretches, but they needed the income to support Tim's schooling and the girls' many extracurricular activities. Besides, it was what Sally loved to do and what she was good at.

Nichola had some ready-made friends waiting for her arrival: Edmonton had a large cross-country-ski community, and she had met many of her fellow athletes at various competitions. Vernon Barford Junior High focused on the needs of children excelling in both academics and athletics. Because of its specialized nature, each year the school attracted a new batch of students from across the city. For the first time, Nichola walked onto a level playing field: she was a newcomer, but so were a lot of the other kids. It was her first big city, and the possibilities seemed endless for a teenager with unstoppable energy. "I might want to become a doctor one day," she told her mother after receiving a stellar report card.

Edmonton was also where Nichola's athletic abilities had a chance to fully blossom. Rowing soon joined cross-country skiing as a favoured sport. Her friends in the Edmonton Nordic Ski Club, girls like Tara Whitten, who one day would become an international-level cyclist, shared her love of pushing the limits of physical endurance. During the summer, Tara and Nichola joined a rowing club together. Nichola took on the role of nurturer with Tara and the other girls, but was also the life of the party. "I can't believe that at fifteen, you've already lived in twelve different places," Tara told Nichola. Her fellow athletes would long remember her for an incident that took place at a major cross-country skiing competition. In the middle of the race, a fellow competitor had an asthma attack and nearly collapsed. Nichola stopped in her tracks and accompanied the distressed skier down the hill, forfeiting her race. Her teammates laughingly called her "Care Bear"—a nickname that would stick, and that Tara thought applied "to her whole character."

Just days after junior-high graduation, where Nichola, wearing an inexpensive purple cocktail dress purchased from a street vendor on Whyte Avenue, joined her girlfriends in a limousine, the family began packing once again. "I don't want to move, I like it here," Nichola confided to Victoria, who shared her feelings. Her parents didn't have much choice. Their dad had a newly minted PhD, and it was time for a proper university posting. Besides, the school that wanted him was right by the ocean. He knew that once his daughters caught sight of beautiful Ballantyne's Cove, any objections would soon be put to rest.

THREE

"Come From Away"

AUTUMN IN THE TOWN of Antigonish, Nova Scotia, arrives not subtly but with an eye-popping explosion of brilliant gold, copper and crimson. From the forests filled with oak, spruce, pine and maple, to the weeping willows lining quiet streets with names like Chestnut and Pleasant, it's a Nova Scotia picture postcard brought to vivid life.

On one of those crisp days in early September 1995, a convoy roared into the county, transporting a quintet of "Come From Aways"—or CFAS—the local name for anyone not from this pleasant but deeply entrenched town a two hours' drive from the bright lights of Halifax. Behind the wheel of the lead vehicle, a tightly packed U-Haul truck, was the new education professor at St. Francis Xavier, Tim Goddard, his passenger his twelve-year-old daughter Victoria. Following closely behind was Sally Goddard in her trusty Isuzu Trooper, her eldest daughter, fifteen-year-old Nichola, helping to navigate from the passenger seat, while six-year-old Kate entertained herself in the back with a hand-held computer game.

They roared into the Catholic region not knowing all that much about its insular ways, nor particularly caring: Antigonish certainly couldn't be more challenging territory than what had come before. Besides, come September each year, the town of four thousand souls was invaded by an equal number of outsiders, to both teach at and attend the university.

Fifteen-year-old Krista MacEachern knew otherwise. The child of a native Antigonisher, she was well acquainted with the town's ethereal beauty—its charming statues, grand Romanesque cathedral and Gothic church, the quaint lace-curtained teahouses and ramshackle lobster joints. She was also aware of the cautious attitudes of this place, where nearly everyone's name started with a "Mac," and which bestowed upon its residents assorted nicknames to distinguish the scores of John MacDonalds and MacNeils from one another. Forty-eight hours after the Goddards' arrival, Krista was sitting down to breakfast in the kitchen of her new home, a farmhouse nestled on the banks of pretty Livingstone Cove. As she stood to peer out the kitchen window, the teenager was gripped by a dread only another adolescent could understand. Not knowing that the school bus that would soon arrive to transport her to Dr. John Hugh Gillis High School would also change her life, she sat contemplating her predicament. It didn't matter that her family's Scottish roots went back several generations in Antigonish County; she hadn't let out her first cry at St. Martha's Regional Hospital, so she was always going to be a CFA. Even worse, she was a "hick" instead of a "townie."

For Krista, the CFA sticker was a fair trade-off for a life she was happy to put behind her. A few months earlier, her dad, Bernie, a scaffolder in Halifax, had fled his turbulent marriage and returned to the place of his youth with his only child in tow. The last few years had been rocky ones, living under the same roof with a mother who had far too many problems of her own to focus on the needs of a child. The farmhouse overlooking the ocean on the outskirts of her dad's hometown was the first bit of peace and quiet Krista had known in years. Still, she wasn't thrilled about stepping off that school bus to curious stares from the three hundred other kids at her new school. There couldn't be a worse year to be a newcomer than grade ten. Her fellow students had forged their friendships in junior high, and, to add to her troubles, she was a bookish introvert. When the orange school bus rolled up and stopped in front of the farmhouse, Krista shuffled in and found a seat, careful to avoid eye contact with the other young passengers. Midway through the long, winding ride along the narrow routes with ocean views, the bus pulled over on the side of Highway 337. Krista looked up at the grand two-storey house perched at the edge of a cliff overlooking the lapping waves of Ballantyne's Cove. Wow, they must be rich, she thought.

What Krista didn't know was that the house was a rental, a romantic but impractical choice the new professor had found on an earlier reconnaissance visit, a good half hour out of town. Two teenage girls, dressed in school clothes their panicked mother had found the night before, after tearing open a series of unmarked cardboard boxes, stood at the side of the road. "Hi, I'm new here, my name's Nichola, and this is my sister Victoria," the older girl said with a beaming, far-too-enthusiastic smile. "Um, hi," Krista responded reluctantly. Who is this person, and why is she picking on me? she thought. Maybe if she just ignored her, the overly effervescent teen would get the hint. "What's your name?" Nichola asked, seemingly oblivious to the rebuff. "Krista," she replied through clenched teeth. The next few minutes were a blur for the Halifax transplant as Nichola regaled her with tales of her previous homes, her dad's new job at the university, how much she loved being near the ocean and so on. Krista couldn't believe anyone could be so clueless. The last thing she needed was to hitch her wagon to someone who was even more of an outsider than her; that would definitely not help in her quest to fly under the radar over the coming weeks. Yet she almost felt sorry for the poor kid. "Do you, like, talk on the phone?" Nichola asked between breathless accounts. "No, I never talk on the phone," said a by-now-panicked Krista, surprising herself with her rudeness. "Me and phones don't mix." Undaunted, Nichola scrawled something on a piece of paper. "Okay," said the still-cheerful girl. "But I'll give you my number anyway. Call me if you ever want to talk."

Krista had done her darnedest to deflect the newcomer's friendly gestures, and in a matter of days she was questioning her own judgment. She eyed Nichola carefully when the two were seated next to one another in geography class. She noticed her fellow student didn't share her tendency towards introversion: she wasn't loud and brash, but when asked her opinion she didn't flinch. She even seemed to enjoy getting into debates. Krista was intrigued with this girl who possessed a poise and polish she hadn't encountered before, and found herself becoming increasingly drawn into her orbit. She watched Nichola find quiet corners during the lunch hour and bury her head in a book. A voracious reader herself, Krista decided that, yes, they should be friends. Once she let her guard down, Krista revealed herself to be a boiled egg: tough shell on the outside, mushy in the centre. The girls exchanged their library of books, everything from highbrow literature to racy novels by Danielle Steel. Nichola snuck those into her backpack. "I need to read a little smut once in a while," she joked to Krista. "But if my father found it, he would not be amused." One evening, Nichola dug out from deep in her closet *Fancy Pants*, a steamy bestseller written by Susan Elizabeth Phillips. "This is the best smut I've ever read," she whispered as she handed it over to her friend. The book had "La Ronge Public Library" stamped on an inside page. "Nichola, you devil!" she yelped in mock horror.

While Krista worried she was a corrupting influence on her otherwise virtuous friend, as hellions the pair failed miserably. One warm fall day, the two straight-A students decided to play hookey. They had Krista's dad's car, but not enough money to fill a gas tank, so a two-hour drive to Halifax was out of the question. They headed east instead, to the nearby industrial town of Port Hawkesbury. When they arrived at 7:30 a.m., not even the local Walmart was open. Sitting in the car, Krista flung her arms up in defeat. "What a couple of nerds," she said to Nichola. "We can't even properly skip school." After sitting in the store parking lot for about a half hour, they turned around and were back at school in time for the first bell.

Nichola and her family proved to be powerful influences upon the motherless teenager. In a place where hospitality is a point of civic pride, the Goddard family fit right in. What was routine for Nichola—an evening filled with Sally's delicious home cooking and storytelling around the table, interspersed with frequent bursts of raucous laughter—was a revelation for her new pal. The Goddards had rituals, table manners she'd never before experienced. At first, she was "scared to death to eat with them," but quickly learned which fork went with which course. She started getting in her two cents' in the vigorous family debates, even studying current affairs so she could keep up. Krista had a chance to show some expertise of her own when

Tim came home one day with a crate of live lobsters that he didn't know how to cook. The native Nova Scotian took over, pulling a giant pot out of the cupboard and filling it with salted water. "You might want to cover your ears when we put them in," she told a horrified Tim as she turned the burners on full tilt. "They tend to scream a bit when they hit the water."

When the Goddards moved into a house in Maryvale later that year, the two friends who shared a gap-toothed smile were only a 10-kilometre bike ride apart. They cried on one another's shoulders when a teen romance hit the skids, and they had their own song, "Cumbersome," by indie band Seven Mary Three, which they sang in unison. Nichola shared her stories of a childhood in the tropics, near the Arctic Circle and on Native reserves, and confided to Krista that sometimes she envied those with a sense of history and roots in just one place, who "belonged" somewhere. Krista disagreed. "I wish I had your life. I feel like I haven't done anything, or seen anything."

The CFA status didn't stick to Nichola the way it did to other newcomers. Her classmates were drawn to her easygoing, often-times flirtatious manner. She'd inherited her dad's gregarious nature, and both her parents' mischievous sense of humour. She charmed her teachers, and she became part of the "smart kids" pack of academic achievers. English teacher Eleanor Mutimer loved to sit in on the spirited debates in their lunchroom club, a casual gathering in her classroom over the lunch hour that was always filled with spirited chatter. Soon Nichola and Krista were part of a clique that included Heather MacIsaac, a bagpipe player, Shanon Archibald, a downhill-ski competitor, and Zeph Williams, who worked backstage in theatre productions at St. Francis Xavier University. Nichola signed up for a variety of school clubs, ran for student council and made it on to the provincial cross-country-skiing team. She even tried her hand at acting, playing the part of the mother-in-law of Charles VII in *The Lark*, based on the life of Joan of Arc. Eleanor, who cast her in the role, was mesmerized by this good-humoured girl who "had experienced a life different from the rather comfortable, materialistic environment of many of her contemporaries at the school; one where pain and struggle are normal." Sally, who worked at the school part-time as a sociology teacher, had long abandoned the habit of peeking her head into a classroom to make sure her daughter was fitting in. Nichola was doing more than that: she had become a leader.

The only time anyone can remember Nichola getting into any kind of trouble became something of a Dr. John Hugh Gillis High legend. In a more graphic nod to Alice Munro's famed coming-of-age book, *Lives of Girls and Women*, in which one teenage girl convinces another to touch a dead cow, Nichola and her friends dared another student to eat a cow's eye they were dissecting in biology class. He said, predictably, "No way." So the kids upped the ante and offered him money. Egged on, the boy—who also happened to be the principal's son—ate the cow's eye to a roar of cheers and shrieks. With mad cow disease at its height, the teacher sent the boy to hospital, and Nichola and a handful of her peers to the principal's office. "If one of us is going down, we're all going down," Nichola muttered to the group as they shuffled into the office. The principal gave them a stern lecture, and then announced he was going to suspend a young man fingered as the ringleader. "If you suspend one of us, you have to suspend us all," Nichola said politely but firmly. The students were ultimately sent packing with no more than a verbal warning.

■ ■ ■

A couple of months after the school career fair in her senior year, Nichola showed up at the door of Bonnie Picard, the school's student services manager, with a startling announcement. "Mrs. Picard, I want to go to Royal Military College in Kingston, and then into the armed forces." Bonnie was new to her job at J. H. Gillis, but she'd come to know Nichola well over the past few months. The idea of military service hardly fit with everything she had gleaned about this well-mannered girl with high marks in advanced English, chemistry and French. Bonnie's first thoughts were, What are your mom and dad's feelings on this? It's such a dangerous occupation. But she held her tongue. She saw a certainty in Nichola's face that told her the decision had been made and the teenager simply needed guidance about how to put together a winning application to the Royal Military College of Canada (RMC).

Nichola's family was already aware of her plans. A recruiter from RMC had come to the school earlier in the year, and his pitch had intrigued the girl. She told her mother about the visit, about this school that offered free tuition and a monthly stipend, for all who could make the cut, in exchange for five years of military service. "They'll pay all my expenses," she told Sally, "and when I graduate, I'll do so without being in debt." Her mother already knew a little about RMC, having briefly dated a student from there during her undergraduate years at Trent University, accompanying him to a Christmas ball. "It was like something out of a movie," Sally said to Nichola about the pomp and pageantry of colourful military uniforms and women in ball gowns.

"It was quite spectacular." But she didn't know much else about it. Why not? Sally thought when her daughter said she wanted to throw RMC into the mix.

"Are you sure you want to do this, be a peacekeeper?" Tim asked his daughter. "Yes, I have thought it out—this is what I want to do." Tim didn't put up much of a fight; like his wife, he saw peacekeeping as an honourable profession, and he could empathize with Nichola's desire to serve society, even if it was in a form he wouldn't have chosen himself.

Still, neither of her parents could understand Nichola's insistence on a free education; while money had been tight as both Tim and Sally pursued post-secondary degrees, they'd made sure the kids never felt deprived. There weren't a lot of savings in the bank, but Tim and Sally were determined to help their eldest daughter in any way they could. To make sure she had options, Sally had sent a thousand dollars to Trent University to reserve a room in one of the school's residences; Trent had accepted Nichola and offered her a thousand-dollar scholarship.

But it was RMC that captured Nichola's interest. She and Victoria had heated debates about her decision to apply there: Victoria couldn't imagine her strong-willed sister developing a military mindset, and asked her if she really wanted to enter into a lifestyle "that would put you into a hierarchy." Nichola tried to explain that it was the perfect fit for her. "I can be athletic and intellectual at the same time," she told Victoria. "It'll be a great adventure." Victoria, who over time gravitated more to scholastics than sports, was well familiar with Nichola's passion for physical fitness, having spent many a Saturday morning reading in the car while her sister inline-skated along the side of the highway. It hadn't occurred to either sister to bring up the possibility that her choice could one day send Nichola to war. "Canadian soldiers were peacekeepers," says Victoria. "There were risks, but not more than if she wanted to be a police officer, which is a tradition in my father's family."

Sally thought back to her own upbringing, how "my parents would support me always, whatever smart or stupid decision I made." She believed in this child-raising approach: having spent eighteen years under the same roof as the headstrong girl, she also knew well enough that Nichola was going to do what she wanted. Like her dad, the teenager displayed from an early age an independent, stubborn streak.

Sally and Tim had long joked with one another that Nichola would rebel against their peripatetic lifestyle by marrying a banker and running off to live in the suburbs. It had never entered their minds she might run off and become a soldier. But if she was serious about the school, a couple of years of peacekeeping in a place like Cyprus, they reasoned, didn't seem like a terrible exchange for a free education. In between the rare overseas peacekeeping posting, Canadian soldiers could be found helping out in natural disasters, doing things like putting out forest fires and building walls of sandbags in flood zones. This desire to make a difference, Sally thought, must run through their veins.

■ ■ ■

The Goddards were far from alone in their view of a Canadian soldier as a blue-beret-wearing peacekeeper. Aside from some isolated incidents in Bosnia in 1993 and 1995, when the 2nd Battalion of the Princess Patricia's Canadian Light Infantry engaged in combat in Croatia's Medak Pocket, the Canadian military hadn't

faced protracted incidents of direct contact with an enemy combatant since the Korean War. News of a member of the Canadian
Forces being injured or dying on the job was a rarity; even though
more than a hundred Canadian soldiers had been killed since the
country had become part of the United Nations' peacekeeping
forces nearly a half century earlier, their sacrifices hadn't made so
much as a dent in the consciousness of the country.

To add to that, few had noticed developments taking place in
Afghanistan, which would soon not only set Canada's antiquated
peacekeeping notion on its ear, but also involve the country in the
first major conflict of the twenty-first century. The Soviet Union
had pulled out of Afghanistan in February 1989, leaving the
Western-backed mujahideen (freedom fighters) victorious and
bringing the once-mighty superpower to its knees. Afghanistan
had become the Soviet Union's Vietnam. Its mistake was even
more catastrophic, though, than the Americans' disastrous foray
into Southeast Asia: by late 1989, the Berlin Wall had fallen, and
within two years, so too would the Soviets' entire empire.

Still, the invaders had done considerable damage, leaving
behind tens of thousands of brightly coloured landmines, so
attractive to children, along with other assorted weaponry. The
Soviets also left Afghanistan a country that was essentially a
failed state. The various mujahideen, no longer unified by a cause,
fought one another for supremacy in protracted battles that
incurred horrific civilian slaughter. Afghanistan, which had
been for the preceding four decades a place of relative peace and
prosperity—a must-see for Western travellers drawn to its
flourishing culture, beautiful scenery and majestic ancient
monuments—was again a hellish place of internecine conflict.
A once-interested America, its aid to the country helping to

guard against other comers, was now focusing on places like Iraq. With the Cold War over, this Cold War pawn was soon forgotten. By 1996, a new incarnation of mujahideen had wrested control of the country. Called the "Taliban," or "students" in Arabic, it was led by Mullah Omar, an Islamic studies teacher from Sangesar, a village in the Zhari-Panjwayi districts near Kandahar. Young men from refugee camps along the Pakistan border, orphaned by the war and with little hope for their future, now had a cause to believe in and fight for. Omar had witnessed the corruption and lawlessness of the years following the Soviet pullout, and decided to do something about it.

The weary citizenry initially saw Omar and his men as modern-day Robin Hoods who brought peace and stability to the country for the first time in decades. Backed by the Pakistani intelligence service, this new movement soon showed another, more sinister face. It introduced severe restrictions on daily life: kite flying, music and chess were banished; men were required to wear bushy beards; and women became nothing more than the property of their male relatives. Yet the most worrisome thing, at least to the rest of the world, was whom the Taliban chose to befriend. They offered their land as a sanctuary for extremist groups from more than two dozen countries, including one called al Qaeda ("the base"), headed by a charismatic Saudi. In July 1996, the man known as Osama bin Laden was part of a secret meeting in a remote region of Pakistan that brought together some of the most radical groups and individuals. Citing such examples as the Gulf War and the continuous presence of U.S. troops in Saudi Arabia, they accused the West of waging a war against Islam, and agreed to bring down their collective wrath against this new enemy.

■ ■ ■

Even though most had yet to awaken to the impact the growing unrest in a neglected country 10,000 kilometres away would have on the Western world in the coming years, others joined Victoria in feeling uneasy about Nichola's decision to pursue a military education. When Nichola approached her English teacher to write a letter of reference for her, Eleanor Mutimer, who saw her as a gentle, profoundly caring young woman, shook her head. The soon-to-retire educator had come by her pacifist views honestly, having grown up in England during World War II. Nichola's insistence that RMC was a great place for an athletic and academic achiever fell on deaf ears. Eleanor thought about Nichola and the other grade twelve grads who, over the years, had put her in this untenable position. In addition to learning about Shakespeare and world politics, they'd be taught how to kill. "Nichola, do you realize the implications of this choice?" she asked her point-blank. "I want the chance for a degree without incurring debt, and I want a challenge," Nichola told her teacher, and later, her fellow students. "And yes, I understand I'm embarking on a career that might put my life at risk." Eleanor knew Nichola wasn't the type to jump into something without thinking it through; she also knew it wasn't her place to try to stop her. With a heavy heart, she sat down to describe the student she could never imagine going to war, certain she was going to be a shoo-in. She's intelligent, thoughtful, imaginative, energetic . . . a leader of the best kind, thought the veteran teacher as she stared at the blank page. "Why wouldn't they want her?"

Krista, surprised at this sudden change in plans, was also less than thrilled by the news. Nichola had shared with her the dream of becoming a medical doctor; she was likely going to follow in her mother's footsteps and head to Trent. "I don't think it's your thing," she said bluntly of RMC. Krista knew Nichola was anxious to take the world head on, and to do it as a free agent. She was also fully aware that the gruelling physical challenges of a soldier-in-training were, for someone who thought nothing of jumping on her bike and cycling 40 kilometres up and down hills, the equivalent of waving a red flag in front of a bull. Yet she couldn't picture her inquisitive, tender-hearted friend in combat gear, falling into line in salutes—Nichola was too independent for groupthink, and far too gentle to ever shoot at someone. "I would be helping people. I'll be doing peacekeeping in a place where I'm needed," Nichola told her. Her friends Shanon and Zeph were skeptical, but they stopped arguing after Nichola offered up an impassioned speech at their lunchroom club about patriotism and service to Canada.

After going through the rounds of medical and psychological tests and fitness assessments, Nichola got word in the spring of 1998 that she'd made the cut. Sally and Tim were proud of their strong, smart daughter. They knew it wasn't easy to pass muster at RMC, yet Nichola had made it through with flying colours. She'd get the degree, do some peacekeeping and then maybe go back for a master's degree, just like her dad. Just before the start of Louise Loriface's global studies class, Nichola shared the news with some of her closest classmates. When her avowedly pacifist teacher walked into the room, one of the students said, "Nichola, tell Mrs. Loriface what you're going to do."

Nichola laughed, then turned to face her teacher. "I'm going into the armed forces." Louise couldn't believe what she was hearing from one of her favourite students. All she could do was let out a loud gasp. She was a card-carrying member of the New Democratic Party of Canada (NDP), the country's major left-of-centre political party: her students knew exactly how she'd react. Louise had former students who had gone to RMC, and thought that moment about a recent one who had dropped out during the first term at the notoriously difficult school. "Well, maybe you won't last," was all she could say on the spot, a glib response that betrayed her dismay. Later, Louise confronted her friend and colleague Sally Goddard. "What are we going to do about this?" she asked. "It's her decision, and we have to support her," Sally calmly responded.

Nichola's last weeks in Antigonish were filled with teary goodbyes, laughter at a barbecue with her gang at Arisaig Park, and her high-school prom. She wore a baby-blue cocktail dress and long white gloves, her friend Zeph Williams on her arm. On graduation day, when her name was called, Nichola walked up to the stage in her cap and gown to receive her diploma. This was followed by the announcement that the honours student had won a full scholarship to the Royal Military College of Canada. The gymnasium erupted into a deafening roar of cheers, applause and foot stomping. Nichola could barely contain her enthusiasm as she smiled and waved to the crowd. Less than twenty-four hours later, she was on a plane headed for Montreal, her ultimate destination the town of Saint-Jean-sur-Richelieu, where she would start her first day in the Basic Officer Training Course (BOTC) at the Canadian Forces Leadership and Recruit School. Within the next twenty-four hours, she'd shed the teenage skin of T-shirts and blue jeans to don military garb. Even more significant, she would trade in her easy-going civilian life for the rigours and restrictions endured by a soldier-in-training. She could hardly wait.

FOUR

Truth, Duty, Valour

"GODDARD."

"Beam."

"Goddard."

"Beam."

All morning long, the two young recruits engaged in a jovial duelling roll-call as they passed one another in the hallways of the school dormitory. Nichola figured if she repeated herself enough times as they knocked shoulders, by the end of the day her fellow student would have "Goddard" drilled into his head. They had been properly introduced earlier, but for some reason, Jason Beam kept forgetting Nichola Goddard's name. "It'll never happen again," he said with a laugh. "Now that you've told me a hundred times."

Jay—the nickname to which he answered—was oblivious to Nichola's flirtations. It never occurred to him that the pretty brunette whose dorm room was directly across from his was finding all sorts of creative excuses to engage him in conversation. Romance was not on his detailed checklist as he prepared to face the biggest challenge of his life. He'd worked hard to raise his grades to qualify for a scholarship to RMC, the venerable institution that produces many of the country's military leaders. The year before, he had dislocated and fractured his right kneecap playing rugby; after surgery and physiotherapy, he managed to get himself back in fighting shape just in time for his Canadian Forces evaluations. He and his fellow prospects underwent rigorous physical-fitness tests, interviews and security checks before making the final cut.

Jay's first stop en route to his new life was the town of Saint-Jean-sur-Richelieu, Quebec. Saint-Jean was a bedroom community for nearby Montreal, in a picturesque setting along the Richelieu River. The birthplace of the Formula One Villeneuve family and home of an annual international hot-air-balloon festival, the town also regularly churned out graduates of the Basic Officer Training Course at the Canadian Forces Leadership and Recruit School. Here, the newcomers were introduced to the insular world they were about to dive into at RMC. For eight weeks, they crawled under barbed wire, climbed rope and learned how to handle weapons in exercises fashioned to develop what Canada's National Defence website calls "a military state of mind and behaviour."

On day one of training, the recruits were put through their paces, in ways they would soon become accustomed to at RMC. "Get your boots and laces; go back and get your hat," the cadets were ordered at various times throughout the morning, creating a chaotic, Keystone Kops atmosphere of constant tearing up and down stairs and through cramped corridors, executing the tasks as best they could, standing at attention for inspections. At one point in the morning, Jay saw a couple of cadets having a laugh as Nichola practised a paltry salute in a corner. Jay, who had the basics down after years as an army cadet, took mercy on her. "This is how you do it," he told her, demonstrating the proper form. Nichola alternately flashed her gap-toothed grin at Jay and daggers at the offending cadets.

Call it love at first sight, infatuation or a mere crush. All Nichola knew was that she felt an immediate attraction to the quiet cadet with a tall, sturdy build tailor-made for his beloved sport of rugby. Not long after, she told her closest friends about the good fortune of being roomed across the hall from the great guy with the dreamy blue eyes. "Oh, wow," she emailed Krista MacEachern. "I really like this guy . . . I catch myself thinking about him all the time." Shanon Archibald knew Nichola jumped into things with passion, but she was still taken aback by her friend's uncharacteristic mushiness over this new prospect. "I know this sounds really cheesy," she wrote to Shanon, "but you know that film *An Officer and a Gentleman*? That describes Jay perfectly."

In typical forthright Nichola style, she soon made her intentions clear to the object of her affection. A couple of weeks into BOTC, cadets were given a leave pass for the weekend, with the exception of Jay, who was assigned sentry duty. Nichola volunteered to stay at the dorm and keep him company. Hmm, that's a bit strange, but whatever, the still-clueless Jay thought. It turned out to be fun for both. The pair spent the day talking about their lives and their likes and dislikes. About an hour before dinner, they retired to their respective rooms. Not long after, Jay heard a knock on his door. When he opened it, Nichola planted one on him, a lovely kiss right on the lips. Then she stood back and smiled. This is one forward woman, the inexperienced eighteen-year-old thought to himself as he finally cottoned on to the situation. But I'm not complaining. They walked to the mess hall together, not holding hands but smiling and exchanging conspiratorial glances, wordlessly agreeing that they were now dating.

Nichola and Jay arrived at RMC a few weeks later for the gruelling two-week Recruit Orientation Course, also known as ROC, or rook camp. First-year cadets know it's more of an initiation, or test, than a course, meant to weed out the weakest before Recruit Term begins. By then the pair were an item, albeit a discreet one. Like her mother, Nichola had met her man in the midst of a new and curious culture. The pair quickly formed a solid bond as they lived in a fishbowl with its own confounding code of conduct. Although PDAS, or public displays of affection, were ruled out, in temperament Nichola was like her no-holds-barred father; she was unabashedly enamoured of her fellow cadet. She later told her second-term dorm mate, Allison Clark, about her parents' romance, and her mother's initial fears that they had bonded because they were the only single white people at their school in a Papua New Guinean town. "I knew it from the start," she confided to Allison, who also met her husband, Hasan Alvi, that first year at RMC. "I'm going to marry him one day."

On paper, the two lovebirds seemed polar opposites. He was as reticent as she was gregarious. His almost Zen-like calm pegged him as a Type B personality, albeit one with enough get-up-and-go to meet the demands of military school. She was the type of person who had to try anything at least once and was determined to master all, unmistakable characteristics of a Type A. He was a computer geek training to be an electrical mechanical engineer (EME) officer, part of the military unit responsible for maintaining all of the army's equipment, from vehicles and weapons to optics, and everything in between. Video games were his escape from technical textbooks; she was a voracious reader with a love of the classics. Their upbringing, too, vastly differed. Nichola was from a demonstrative, warm family accustomed to dinnertime debates and laughter around a table of such favourite comfort food as roast beef and Yorkshire pudding. She was effusive in her praise of all members of her family. She told friends that Canadian singer-songwriter Jann Arden's song "Good Mother" and its lyrics—an homage to her beloved mom, Joan Richards—reminded her of Sally; home, she often said, was "wherever my parents, and all their stuff, happen to be." For Nichola, making it into RMC was a natural progression after the countless hours of high-school study, and her marathon runs and skis—a chance to keep testing her physical and mental limits.

For Jay, it was a new chapter in an altogether different story, the culmination of an escape plan hatched years earlier. His experience of growing up in a working-class district of Niagara Falls, Ontario, was rough enough to make Nichola's experience of living all over Canada seem smooth. Dad Norm was on a disability pension, which hardly brought in enough money to pay the bills. Mom Carol left when Jay was in his early teens, taking him and younger brother Matt with her. Jay turned to the 2835 Royal Canadian Army Cadet Corps, which offered programs to youths aged twelve to nineteen. It was a positive way to distance himself physically and emotionally from the upheaval. There he found direction, routine and a sense of belonging. Jay knew he was a boy from the proverbial wrong side of the tracks, with more baggage than the average teenager. Nichola was unfazed by this. Years later, she'd tell friends that her response to Jay was, "I'm strong, I'll help you carry the bags." His earlier struggles only further endeared him to her. She told Krista she had great admiration for the fact he'd sought out the cadets as a boy, that he "pulled it together" against all odds and won himself a scholarship to RMC. Krista wasn't surprised. She knew Nichola had a soft spot for the underdogs of the world. It wasn't so long ago that she herself had been the target of such boisterous affection. She was sure Jay didn't stand a chance against Nichola's charms.

In practice, the Nichola/Jay matchup was one made in compatibility heaven. The couple gradually discovered they shared a rare love for camping in all sorts of extreme weather conditions, long road trips and slapstick comedy. Both thumbed their noses at city-slicker luxuries. They dreamed of one day hiking the West Coast Trail on Vancouver Island, of driving the 671-kilometre Dempster Highway from Dawson City, Yukon, to Inuvik in the Northwest Territories. Best of all, they were both dog crazy. Nichola told Jay that her first plan upon graduation from RMC was to head to an animal shelter and pick out a dog she would name Sam. But all that would have to wait: if there was any environment capable of putting a damper on romance, it was RMC.

At first glance, the school spread out across the 41-hectare Point Frederick, a small peninsula just east of the pretty city of Kingston, Ontario, gives the impression of an impregnable, static fortress. The site alone, at the confluence of Lake Ontario and the mighty St. Lawrence River, has been part of Canada's military history for going on two centuries—a British Navy shipyard was located here from 1812 to 1814. The limestone facade of the imposing 132-year-old Mackenzie Building, with its grand clock tower, offers a rare sense of history for such a young country. But the school's appearance belies the constant evolution it has undergone since 1876, when it welcomed the Old Eighteen, students whose names are memorized by every first-year officer cadet. After almost closing its doors for good after World War II, in 1959 RMC became a degree-granting university; in 1976, it went fully bilingual; and in 1980, the year of Nichola's birth in Papua New Guinea, it admitted its first female students. The move was met, predictably, with resistance from many, both within the military and in civilian culture, and prompted that year's graduating students to dub themselves "The Last Class With Balls (LCWB)." In 1989, an even greater change came when Canada began admitting women into the combat, or soldiering, trades.

After a century filled with highs and lows, the years preceding the pair's first day of school were marred by chaos and growing cynicism. Under financial pressure, the country's two other military colleges, Royal Roads in Victoria, British Columbia, and Quebec's Collège militaire royal de Saint-Jean, both closed in 1995 (the latter reopened a decade later as a feeder school for RMC prospects); the Canadian Forces suffered major cutbacks; and the public's esteem for the country's military took a severe pummelling in 1993 in the wake of the Somalia Affair, in which a civilian died while in the custody of the Canadian Airborne Regiment. The scandal prompted a federal inquiry and the disbanding of the once-proud regiment.

As the twenty-first century approached, the institution was under increasing pressure to advance with the times. The Withers' Report, an examination of RMC's practices undertaken by the school and presented to the Department of National Defence (DND) in 1998, had made several recommendations on improving the school's offerings and strengthening its military connection. But such issues weren't the concern of these teenagers fresh out of high school and excited about their futures. They also had no time to look beyond their immediate horizon: over the next few months, every minute of their waking hours would be accounted for.

By the time they arrived and marched onto the campus and under the Memorial Arch inscribed with the motto "Truth, Duty, Valour"—a walk students perform only twice at RMC, on the first day and upon graduation four years later—the new recruits had already had a small taste of what made RMC a "university with a difference." All they needed now was to survive ROC. New recruits weren't considered part of the school until they had survived the entire first eight weeks, the two at ROC and the six of Recruit Term. Described rather euphemistically on RMC's official website as "a short period of familiarization and indoctrination" designed to mould the nation's future military leaders, rook camp is what separates RMC from any other degree-granting institution in the country: it's hard to imagine the students at nearby Queen's University being disciplined for an unmade bed, scuffed boots or poor marching form.

This unique combination of academic excellence and military indoctrination has not surprisingly had its detractors. Some psychologists have said that the sleep deprivation, daily room inspections and rules against leaving the school grounds have all the hallmarks of a cult. In his 2005 novel, *Bonk on the Head*, author and former RMC student John-James Ford described witnessing female recruits lying face down on the floor, "sputtering and being publicly humiliated and toe-tapped in the gut—all for training purposes," along with underground male-only clubs, where entry is gained after engaging in certain forms of exploitative sexual activity. While the book is presented as a fictional account of life at RMC, several professors there today will quietly admit to having read it, and, even more quietly, confide that such depictions are closer to reality than anyone would like to admit.

Get through rook camp, went the collective wisdom, and the rest will seem easier. Each morning at 5:00 a.m., Nichola and her thirty-member flight of first-years—the sub-group in each of the ten squadrons that made up the school's population—were jolted awake by a boom box in the hallway blaring Ozzy Osbourne's "Crazy Train," the British rocker's anthem to rebellion. It kick-started an eighteen-hour day jammed with physical workouts, drills on parade square, classes, study time and more discipline that ended only when recruits collapsed onto their three-inch-thick mattresses at 11:00 p.m., singing in unison as they lay in their beds the Billy Joel song "Goodnight Saigon." The poignant yet haunting lyrics from one of the most well known songs about the Vietnam War depict the U.S. Marines' training on Parris Island and combat experiences in Vietnam, along with their fierce fighting spirit and willingness to die together on the battlefield.

The long days included several checks of proper dress, stance and behaviour, with inspections and punishments doled out by rotating shifts of third-year students called section commanders (SCS), who in turn were managed by a fourth-year student known as a flight leader. Also known by their charges as the Nazis, these students were expected to help transform the rookies from lumpen, lazy souls to "keen" or top-notch officers. They barked out commands, made sure the recruits' rooms were in proper order and meted out punishment when an infraction was unearthed. Those doing room checks would see if suspenders had been rolled out exactly, and if socks were rolled properly and perfectly spaced in the small drawers provided for clothing. Improper spacing of hangers was cause for discipline. Every two weeks, recruits had to change rooms. Since they had only twenty minutes for the move, they'd simply grab their mattresses and take the entire bed with them. Hitting the showers after morning physical training (PT) also required some ingenuity. Nichola's flight had eight women, all of whom were allotted six minutes to disrobe, shower and be back at their dorm entrances, fully dressed and standing at attention. They would run in, get wet, and then step aside to soap themselves up while the others were getting wet. "We've got a real chain going," Nichola's roommate, Allison, joked. "I can't wait to go home at Christmas and take a long shower."

The combination of six hours a night of sleep, gruelling workouts and constant berating proved too much at times for some members of Rebel Flight, the ironic name given to Nichola and her twenty-nine fellow cadets. The muffled cries of both genders occasionally drifted through the dorm halls after dark. Nichola tried to approach the demanding training and discipline like Jay, who never seemed to get ruffled by the stress. One day, an SC yelled at her for her poor drill form: her feet, he said, were flopping around too much. Nichola flashed him a great big smile and tried again. "I guess not everybody can be a Wayne Gretzky," he said, shrugging his shoulders in defeat over her obvious lack of coordination.

There was little respite at the end of the two-week ordeal. Recruit Term for Nichola offered even more challenges and upsets. When she was suspended from the varsity team for failing a PT test—she could only do eleven of a dozen push-ups at the end of sweat-drenching workout—Nichola, knowing this meant she wouldn't be able to compete in the upcoming Canada Games as a biathlete, burst into tears. "Don't show your emotions," her section commander scolded her as she collapsed onto the floor in a puddle. She heeded the advice, and spent the next several nights crying quietly into her pillow. She was exhausted, she had strep throat, a stress fracture in one ankle and a partially dislocated shoulder. But she wasn't going anywhere. "All the bullshit will be worth it to be able to wear the RMC cap badge," she wrote to Krista in mid-September. "I'm the person they made up 'O Canada' for, little me . . ."

As Nichola fought to stay alert and keep one step ahead, her loved ones were also struggling with her new reality. Krista was disturbed by her friend's description of bayonet practice, "the most effective way to kill people with a knife." "Do you really think you could do that, Nichola?" Krista asked. Nichola had begun responding to such blunt challenges by simply changing the subject, a tactic that made Krista painfully aware they were now living in two very disparate worlds. Yet she felt it her duty to bring up such possible scenarios. Even though Nichola joked about the RMC "God Squad"—fellow students who were a little too pious for her liking—she was still an avowed Christian who attended regular Sunday church services in Kingston. "You've always been the kind of person who sits down and talks things out," Krista said to the woman who was one of the most compassionate people she'd ever met. "Violence isn't your thing."

For Sally and Tim, any illusions about what their firstborn had signed up for evaporated when they attended Recruit Term graduation in October. They proudly watched the elite athlete hold her own in the mud-splattered obstacle course, a rite of passage signifying acceptance into the cadet wing of RMC. She handily navigated her feet over a carpet of tires and helped her squadron team pull themselves by rope over 10-foot walls while her new friend Jay Beam was carted away after dislocating his right knee yet again. Afterwards, Tim and Sally watched as Nichola's squadron team, comprising fifty cadets, received their badges for completing Recruit Term. As the squadron sang along to those haunting "Goodnight Saigon" lyrics, Sally felt a shudder go up her spine. Despite her conviction that this was simply a phase in Nichola's life, that she'd soon be a civilian again, pursuing a safer career, the song unsettled her. Tim was similarly taken aback, but broke the tension with humour. "She's been brainwashed," he whispered to his wife with a nervous chuckle. At the ceremony later that evening, Nichola, wearing an RMC blue dress uniform—newbies don't don the famed scarlet uniforms until the end of their first year—strode up to her parents and greeted them with a professional handshake. She knows exactly what to do with her hands, Sally thought to herself. Our awkward teenager is gone.

Graduation from rook camp was no insulation from further psychological and physical torment. Because first-year cadets during Recruit Term had not yet earned the privilege of wearing full-fledged RMC uniforms, but rather the navy non-commissioned officers' black workpants and white shirt, they stood out like sore thumbs—all the better for others to spot them and inflict abuse. At Yeo Hall, the massive dining complex that fed the thousand or so students who lived on campus, there were designated seating areas for new recruits, along with taboos against looking directly at other members of the student population; doing so could result in a crusty dinner bun thrown in the direction of one's head, or some other humiliation. It was a scenario worthy of the wardens at the Tower of London: the second-year students, having not long ago been subjected to the test, paid it forward by doing their best to distract the recruits, calling out their names, making faces. Within days of arriving at RMC, Rebel Flight member Mitch Rivest made the grave mistake of passing only the salt when asked to pass the salt and pepper; his SC gave him "cock," the crude colloquialism for a public dressing-down, then banished him to a nearby table. Mitch grew up with the Victoria sea cadets and knew from a young age he was going to do his best to qualify for RMC. But he had underestimated the stress of ROC. He'd already been in trouble for having dessert with his meal. It wasn't technically an infraction, but the SCs had made his entire flight do an extra few push-ups to "work off" the additional calories. As he sat alone eating his dinner, it was all the ostracized recruit could do to keep from crying. Nichola strode across the room and plunked down her tray across from his. Mitch was dumbfounded. Who was this girl? Did she know that she too could get cock for such a brazen move? Instead of asking the questions floating around in his head, he simply looked at his fellow flight member and said, "You're a princess." Nichola responded with an ear-to-ear grin, then dug into her mashed potatoes.

If Nichola was already establishing herself as someone who stood out in the crowd, she wasn't all that different from her new friends in some important ways. Jay, Allison and Mitch had all signed up for the same reasons as she had: paid tuition, a monthly stipend and an opportunity to go to one of the best schools in the country. Laying down their lives for their country was still an abstract concept. Such twenty-first-century realities as 9/11, after all, still seemed like the stuff of science fiction novels.

Nichola and her cohorts quickly grew familiar with terms like "unlimited liability," which translates into an understanding that, in the line of duty, one may have to kill or be killed. Regardless, five years' mandatory military service was a good bargain for a free university education: she'd end up at a domestic base somewhere—they might get called to put out forest fires or evacuate people from another natural disaster, and maybe even do a stint in a place like Croatia. Peacekeeping was not without its casualties, but the odds were low. They'd yet to hear the term "peacemaking," used years later to euphemistically describe the life-and-death soldiering that would take place in Afghanistan. Nichola wasn't entirely naive, though. She knew that the rigors of RMC were shaping her up to be "tougher than the average person," she wrote to Krista in first term. "Otherwise, how can we possibly lead men, our men, into war where they might (and probably will) die? It's a huge responsibility."

The school did its best to remind the students that while their country hadn't been at war for some time, the job of soldiering was nevertheless one of the world's most dangerous professions. Within her first weeks of school, Nichola and her fellow first-years sat in on a fourth-year military class. A veteran soldier, a captain, visited the class to tell the story of his twenty-four days in captivity in Bosnia a few years earlier. The class was reminded that in Bosnia alone, sixteen soldiers had died since the Canadian Forces joined United Nations efforts in the former Yugoslavia seven years earlier—two of them in the last month, while the RMC recruits were in BOTC and rook camp. "That is a kind of scary wake-up call," Nichola wrote to her mom that evening.

While Nichola and Jay were finding their soldiers' legs during those first few weeks, events in Afghanistan were heating up. On August 7, 1998, two bombs went off within minutes of each other outside the U.S. embassies in Nairobi, Kenya, and Dar Es Salaam, Tanzania. By the time the dust settled, more than two hundred people were dead, and thousands more injured. In a chilling foreshadowing of the terrorist attacks of 9/11 on New York City and Washington, D.C., eyewitness Zachariah Chianda painted a picture of chaos and devastation in Nairobi to a *New York Times* reporter: "Everything was falling down. I found myself on the floor. People were screaming and some people were trapped in the elevators. We tried to get people out. There was glass and metal all over the place." An unknown group calling itself the Islamic Army for the Liberation of the Holy Places claimed responsibility and promised more attacks on U.S. and Western troops. But the Clinton administration believed someone better known to them was behind the attacks: Osama bin Laden, one of fifty children of a Saudi billionaire, an anti-U.S. dissident in exile in Afghanistan. On August 20, the Americans launched the ironically named Operation Infinite Reach, an ill-fated attempt to rout out bin Laden—a man described by the U.S. State Department as "one of the most significant financial sponsors of Islamic extremist activities in the world"—with a massive Tomahawk missile attack on his reported training camps in Afghanistan.

"The missile attacks exposed the inadequacy of American intelligence and the futility of military power," suggested author Lawrence Wright in the Pulitzer Prize–winning 2007 book, *The Looming Tower: Al Qaeda and the Road to 9/11*, "which rained down nearly three-quarters of a billion dollars' worth of armament on two of the poorest countries in the world." Wright went on to describe how bin Laden, said to be the head of the little-known terrorist network al Qaeda, gloated over the U.S. war machine's inability to capture one man, and used the opportunity to taunt American president Bill Clinton over his recently exposed dalliance with Washington intern Monica Lewinsky. Bin Laden was also aware of how the attack would offend Mullah Omar, and wrote to the Taliban leader acknowledging him as the leader of the faithful: "We consider you to be our noble emir, we invite all Muslims to render assistance and cooperation to you, in every possible way they can." From that day forward, Omar would protect bin Laden from all comers.

But the Clinton administration was in no hurry to march soldiers into Afghanistan. There was little to gain, and too much to lose, by upsetting the delicate balance of Central Asian politics for one renegade terrorist. As for Canada, there was scarce public or political interest in straying from its beloved peacekeeping image. Besides, resources were few, and the forces were already stretched in NATO peacekeeping exercises and missions in places like Haiti, the Balkans and central Africa. And those future officers enrolled in their first year of RMC? Most hadn't even absorbed the concept of unlimited liability. But some of those they encountered were well aware of the reality. Allison, the daughter of a North Bay doctor and stay-at-home mom, had been cautioned by one of her air cadet leaders not to admit to the army recruiter that she liked camping, a sure-fire way to get steered into the combat arms. "Do you really want to go into combat, to fight?" he asked the slight, five-foot-tall eighteen-year-old. "Definitely not," was her answer. "Then, whatever you do, don't admit that you like camping; don't put down infantry even as a fourth choice. It'll be nothing like camping at Algonquin Park." Nichola, who thoroughly enjoyed unrolling a sleeping bag amidst snowbanks and in below-zero-Celsius temperatures, was asked that same question at her interview at the recruitment centre in Halifax. She readily admitted to being an avid camper. She was put first into infantry, which was later changed to artillery. It didn't bother her because at that point she hadn't yet learned the difference between the two. Infantry, the army's primary war fighters, often referred to as foot soldiers, was the combat arm responsible for, according to the Canadian Forces literature, "closing with, and destroying, the enemy." Nichola would discover that artillery—the profession of Napoleon Bonaparte—was the combat arm that provides indirect fire support on the battlefield; or, as her future mentor Major Anne Reiffenstein would later try to put in layman's terms to an inquiring journalist, "all the stuff where you're not actually the person pulling the trigger, where you're not actually looking" at the target "and pointing at it."

"The thought of actually fighting hadn't entered either of our minds at that point," says Jay, who admits he and Nichola never had a conversation about such a possibility until after the 9/11 attacks, nine months before RMC graduation.

Both Jay and Nichola flourished under the strict regimen, despite the fact that during those first weeks their assignment to different flights meant virtually no contact. They weren't yet allowed computers in their rooms, so couldn't communicate by instant messaging. But neither was going to let zero-quality time get in the way of their budding romance. Every evening during study period, each scribbled a quick note telling the other about their day. When they passed one another in the halls, they'd stealthily exchange paper. If it was a day when they wouldn't be crossing paths, they made sure to pass the note to a fellow student who could then deliver it. One day in the middle of Recruit Term, Nichola walked past Jay in the mess hall and slipped him an envelope. "Dear Jay, I have fallen in love with you," was her opening in an effusive, heartfelt love letter several pages long. That night, Jay pored over the letter, smiling as he took in each and every word from this passionate, eloquent young woman. She beat me to the punch again, he thought. A couple of weeks later, when he could finally be alone with her behind closed doors, he quietly let her know that the feelings were mutual.

Throughout that challenging first year, Nichola still managed to write weekly emails back home. During exam times these were brief, but others waxed long and lyrical about life at the college. She vented to her parents about being homesick and the frenetic daily schedule: "There is way too much to do, and virtually no time to do it . . . I am absolutely wiped." She longed for Sally's spaghetti Alfredo, relied on her educator father to critique her writing assignments and sought his counsel on course selection. She shared some of her exploits, like dyeing her hair red, and described the various movies she saw with her friends at the Empire Theatre on Princess Street, such as *Saving Private Ryan*. She also remained euphoric about her choice of RMC for a university education. Rather than dampening her spirits, the bone-jarring initiation of the first two months firmed her resolve. "You know what, Mom?" she told Sally at the end of Recruit Term. "I go to the most amazing school in the world, and it's so phenomenal to be here."

Never passing up a chance to see his daughter, in the spring of 1999 Tim made a three-hour detour from a working visit to Toronto to "pop by" his daughter's neighbourhood for a few hours. As they drove around the historic garrison town, past the sailboats moored in the harbour and the fruit vendors at the foot of the clock tower at Market Square, Nichola regaled him with stories about life at RMC and her growing love for the military. The pair eventually ended up by the student residences at Queen's University. As they slowed along a procession of town houses, Nichola pointed to its residents sitting on their stoops drinking beer and smoking. "You know, I think if I had gone to a civilian university, I'd be having a different experience," Nichola said with a laugh as she cast her eyes on the bare-chested young men in blue jeans and girls in miniskirts, oversized hoop earrings dangling from their ears.

For the first time in her life, though, Nichola was keeping a secret from her parents—and a big one. They had met Jay when Nichola brought her new "buddy" home for a weekend that summer. They liked the easy-going young man, but had no idea that he was anything more than a friend. Nichola had had close platonic friendships with members of the opposite sex throughout her childhood. The family didn't even suspect that the daughter who wore her heart on her sleeve was capable of masking her feelings. In her letters back home, Jay was often mentioned, but only as part of a close-knit gang of friends. At times, Sally suspected there might be a stronger connection between the two, but she decided that since she didn't really want to know the answer, it was best not to ask the question. An earlier high-school romance had ended badly, and Nichola hadn't taken her first broken heart well. Sally remembered those several weeks when her daughter moped around the house, her joyful spark extinguished thanks to a teenage boy. She knew Nichola felt things deeply, and, hoping to protect her from another disappointment, urged her to "keep things platonic" at this early stage in her adult life. Nichola felt that her parents would worry she was too young to be so serious about a boy, that they'd write it off as a case of puppy love or tell her that the start of a demanding academic career, at a school with a 20 per cent dropout rate for first-year students, wasn't the appropriate time for such diversions. She confided to friends that she was also concerned about Jay's rough background, that her parents might not be thrilled she'd chosen a boy from the so-called wrong side of the tracks. Krista responded half-jokingly: "I don't know if in their eyes, anyone would be good enough for you, Nichola." In time Nichola would be ready to break the news. But for now, the officer cadet had far too many other things to concern herself with, staying awake being at the top of the list.

FIVE

Wolf's Eyes

HIS PILLBOX HAT sits on his crown at a precise angle, its chinstrap firmly in place. His sure, steady gaze conveys the confidence of one much older. Since 1976, Brucie has offered a constant reminder to RMC's student population: this is how proper officer cadets bear themselves. This is the level of spit and polish to which one should aspire. But Brucie's sentinel position on Parade Square has served a dual purpose. The bronze statue of a young male cadet also nods to the mischievous side of human nature, which persists even in this last bastion of regimentation and discipline.

Having taught at the college for more than a decade, Michael Hurley was familiar with the various monuments and memorials dotting the well-tended gardens and green spaces of his beloved campus. He could point with eyes closed to the exact locations of the F-86 Sabre airplane, the 88-mm German anti-aircraft gun, the Centurion tank and the Memorial Arch that honours former students who died in the line of duty. But none of those captured his imagination like Brucie. At the beginning of each school year, he'd eagerly await Brucie's latest incarnation. Over the years, the slim-silhouetted statue had been adorned with the jerseys of various NHL hockey teams, dressed in rookie PT shorts and painted with the blue-and-white fleur-de-lys symbol. Here, they call such innocuous acts of youthful high jinks "skylarks," and like the sightings of the bird itself, they are a rarity within the constraints of a military education.

Brucie warmed the heart of the goatee-sporting professor. Michael Hurley, despite his wild mane of greying hair, was a black sheep, a poetry-loving former hippie who as a young man hitchhiked his way across Europe, Iran, Pakistan, India and Afghanistan. He never made it to the northern Afghan province of Bamiyan, to see two statues he'd heard about as a youth, and one of the world's great archaeological treasures: the 53-metre-high Buddha colossi carved into a cliffside. It was an opportunity that would never come again. In March 2001, the Taliban would use tanks and rocket launchers to blow up the two-thousand-year-old statues that had outlasted thirteenth-century Mongols and twentieth-century Soviet invaders. Taliban leader Mullah Omar's reported response to the outrage over the destruction of these longtime symbols of Afghanistan's history of cultural and religious diversity was widely quoted in newspapers around the world: "All we are breaking are stones."

Michael, a practitioner of yoga and meditation long before they were fashionable in the Western world, understood there was more to even simple statues like the one he passed by each day—he grasped the liberating power of art. For him, Brucie, that much-decorated soldier, was a nod to the wild heart that stirred underneath the epaulettes and squadron colours of the various uniforms dotting the campus.

Like many others in this mostly civilian faculty assigned to educate future military leaders, Michael had become an unlikely fixture within RMC's limestone walls. It was 1988, when, to his surprise, he was recruited by the English Department's chair.

Why they wanted to throw a longhaired individualist into a sea of tamed crew cuts didn't make sense at first, but the incongruity intrigued him. Teaching the works of Margaret Laurence, E. M. Forster and Walt Whitman to a roomful of young men and women groomed to lead soldiers into battle? Being handed the power to encourage independent thinking in the midst of a military training designed to instill obedience? Once he confirmed that RMC's instructors enjoyed the same academic freedom granted to professors at any other Canadian university, he realized it was an offer he couldn't refuse. He relished the opportunity to make cultured men and women out of warriors, to send them one day into potential battle "as whole a person as possible." Adding to the tantalizing prospect of questioning the establishment in an authority-driven subculture were other immensely attractive benefits: the lowest teacher-student ratio of any degree-granting university in the country, and an academic policy that required all RMC graduates to have a well-rounded education in everything from the sciences and engineering to the arts. In other words, no future officer in the Canadian military who hoped to walk twice under the Memorial Arch could escape the radical clutches of its English Department.

Michael Hurley quickly became a colourful thread woven into the starched fabric of daily life at RMC. Though some still vocally questioned the inclusion of a liberal education as part of training for military life, by the late 1990s it was becoming an entrenched part of the school's curriculum. The popular professor who would go on to win teaching awards from his students also thumbed his nose at such outmoded views with his office decor. The small space was crammed with the talismans of Michael's inner and outer journeys: a variety of large and small

Buddha statues mingled with Guatemalan blankets, Tibetan bowls and pictures and postcards of motorcycles, reggae singer Bob Marley and the Dalai Lama.

On a warm fall afternoon in 1999, Michael was hauling yet another Asian deity up the three flights of stairs to his office, along with a new South American wall hanging, when a student offered to help him carry the load. The second-year cadet had just signed on as an English major, and chatted to him about her love of fantasy fiction and characters like Frodo Baggins from J. R. R. Tolkien's *Lord of the Rings*. She would soon read Margaret Atwood's *The Journals of Susanna Moodie*, and become mesmerized by the concept of needing "wolf's eyes to see the truth." When she broke into a smile, the wide gap in her front teeth hinted at a childlike wonder. She was effervescent, with an infectious and endearing laugh and *Anne of Green Gables* energy.

Nichola Goddard was the kind of student Michael hoped each year to get in one of his group-study classes. Spending intense time with a dozen or so students, he'd have a stellar opportunity to get to know them and influence their way of thinking about themselves, the world and their own place in it. He spent hours, both in and out of the classroom, talking to the likes of Nichola about the lessons from books such as Robertson Davies's *Fifth Business*, which showed one need not be centre stage to have an instrumental role in life's drama; about how to use the critiques of Northrop Frye to find your own voice; and about the notion that the first law of life, according to American mythologist Joseph Campbell, "is that you and the other are one." Campbell, who believed that the childhood years laid the foundation of our later view of the world, fascinated the young woman who'd never met anyone with a childhood like hers. She also appreciated his insights into indigenous cultures and the role myth plays in our lives, revelations that led her to share with teachers and fellow students her experiences among the tribes people of Papua New Guinea and Canada's First Nations. Michael's goal each year was to get his students to think outside the box, or at least to shake up the one they inhabited. Having this young woman with such an unusual pedigree in the mix, he could hardly believe his luck.

Nichola soaked up the assigned literature, and then some: she burned her way through such Canadian literary greats as Margaret Laurence, Michael Ondaatje and Alice Munro. She knew that pursuing an English degree at a military school was a bit out of the ordinary, but over time she realized that this, and not medical school, was what she really wanted. All through her first year, she warned her parents that this might be the path she would choose. Tim, an avid photographer who loved to write, understood the appeal. By the time first-year graduation rolled around, Nichola told Sally that she had not only decided upon English, "but if my marks are high enough . . . an honours English degree."

Choosing an education in the arts might have been seen as rebellious in an academic institution that in its first sixty years focused almost solely on educating future officers in the fields of engineering and the sciences. Even at the start of the twenty-first century, nearly half of RMC's graduates would come from the engineering discipline. The school that graduated First World War flying ace Billy Bishop, Lieutenant General Romeo Dallaire (ret'd) and astronauts Marc Garneau and Chris Hadfield was famed for being the place where the scions of Canada's upper middle class would receive one of the best engineering educations on the continent. By the time Nichola and her contemporaries had arrived, the school was on a major push to emphasize a well-rounded education, something new principal John Cowan boasted had given RMC the distinction of being "the true home of a liberal education in Canada." Cowan, lured away from nearby Queen's University to usher RMC into the twenty-first century, hoped to develop the school according to the recommendations of the 1998 Withers' Report, which redefined how RMC would provide a liberal, yet technically robust, education to its students. A major contributor to the Withers' Report, Cowan was convinced of the necessity of such an evolution: young officers were being sent to places like the Balkans and East Timor, where they might be faced with making quick decisions that would affect hundreds of lives. He knew that a good officer needed to be not only an independent thinker, but also a person with a modicum of cross-cultural sensitivity.

Then again, only a decade earlier, merely being female would have marked Nichola as a true rebel. Those first twenty-one female graduates in 1984 paid a heavy price for their trailblazing. "There was a tremendous amount of tension and conflict," one of them told the *Kingston Whig-Standard* in 1999 at a fifteen-year reunion. "There were a lot of guys that just openly hated us—and everything in between." By the time Nichola was in her first year, one in four, or about 27 per cent of the school population, was female. She and her closest friends found that the combination of those early women blazing the trail along with changing attitudes in greater society made their experience of being a minority, if not entirely smooth, at least a lot less bumpy. "The guys we were going to school with were part of our generation," Allison Alvi (Clark) says. "They grew up in a society used to women doing these kinds of things. There were still a few that didn't like it, but it wasn't acceptable to be open about it anymore."

Nichola and Allison arrived before many of the Withers' Report's recommendations had been implemented: for example, eliminating the discipline system in which mistakes were punished by additional physical training and replacing it with a policy that allowed for such only where there was a real need to make corrections.

Still, pursuing an education that included works by Homer, Henry James and Buddhist author Sharon Salzberg, who advocated "a heart as wide as the world," might seem like a contradiction for a young woman who spent her summers in phase training in places like Gagetown, New Brunswick, learning how to fire a howitzer and handle ammunition. Sylvia Berg was skeptical at first that such polarities could coexist under one roof. The newly arrived academic had five university degrees to her name, a Killam Scholarship and a postdoctoral fellowship to England's Shakespeare Institute. Like Michael Hurley, she was attracted to the prospect of sending out Canadian military officers whose world view had been shaped by the works of the Bard and John Milton. Her choice to teach at RMC was also a practical one: even the most qualified academics in the country faced a dearth of tenure-track positions. She decided to sign on to RMC for a year or two. Sylvia had heard the stories of the ostracizing of the first female RMC academics in the early 1980s; those who preferred the status quo were said to have simply turned their backs when females entered a room. Within months of her arrival, though, a new, much more promising reality emerged. These students, thought Sylvia, shared her fierce passion for intellectual rigor. Her previous experience at three other universities hadn't been anything like this. The officer cadets in her class were already well on their way to becoming true Renaissance men and women: in addition to being attentive and hard-working in class, they spent their off-hours studying, pursuing sports and volunteering in the outside community of Kingston. She'd never encountered a place where, to a person, the students were at once so high achieving and idealistic. At her 8:00 a.m. class, the students were already wide-awake, having been up hours earlier running up and down hills and around Parade Square.

Before launching into the lives of Michelangelo, Henry VIII and Martin Luther, Sylvia asked the new pupils of her Renaissance Studies class to write a brief autobiography. It was her short cut to seeing beyond the military uniform and into the individuals before her. When she went through Nichola Goddard's three-page life story, she thought the young woman fit the RMC high-achiever profile to a tee. She came from a supportive family: she considered Calgary home, even though she had never lived there, simply because that is where Tim and Sally now lived. Like the others, she was an overly eager student with a crammed schedule. She competed on RMC's biathlon team and was co-president of the college's peer support assistance group, was a first-year section commander and a Scout leader in Kingston. And, like the others, she admitted to only a sketchy awareness of what she was getting into when she signed up for four years at RMC. She confessed that her initial interest was based on a series of misconceptions: "I had no money and lacked a concrete idea" about what to do after high school. "I thought I was making an educated decision when I chose my military occupation and degree; I now realize I made two very uninformed decisions," she wrote. "Fortunately, I ended up loving both choices."

What impressed Sylvia most was Nichola's impassioned account of the thoughts behind changing her career course from medicine to the study of literature:

> *In history we study wars and famine; in English literature we learn why people acted the way they did in times of war, why they made the decisions they did and how they felt in the process. In my summers I learn how to be an officer, to lead people in times of war and peace. Studying literature allows me to learn from those who have gone before me, from both their positive and negative experiences . . . I chose Renaissance literature because it's a topic about which I know very little. I heard the majority of names we discussed in class, but I have no connections with their actions and works with the Renaissance. The process of linking them with ideals and thoughts of the time is an interesting one.*

Sylvia came to know Nichola even better after reading her defence of literature, another regular exercise she put her students through in order to push them to thoroughly contemplate the relevance of an arts education. Once again, the talented student didn't disappoint. She waxed eloquent on the difference between knowing the bare facts and truly understanding the flesh-and-blood human beings behind the names—how they felt, understood and interpreted their environment; how literature "allows individuals to view the world around them in a new light" and understand "why we think and act the way we do in certain situations." For Nichola, the opportunity to "experience the adventures, romances, tragedies, and ironies lived by others" was a seductive lure. But she most impressed Sylvia with her arguments on why a literary foundation benefits an officer:

> One day we may have the opportunity to serve overseas; it is imperative we learn from the mistakes and experiences of those who have gone before us. Without English literature and the works of poets, such as Owen and Hardy, we would not be able to appreciate how immense the sacrifice made by soldiers in the past has been. . . . Finally, as young officers, it is vital that we be able to express ourselves both orally and in writing. The greater the clarity and conciseness of our words, the faster our troops will understand our orders and our superiors will approve requests.

Sylvia developed an intense fondness for Nichola, and not just for her writing abilities and desire to take in as much knowledge as time permitted. She saw the young woman as a leader for other female students. "It is not a place in which it's easy to be a woman, either a cadet or a professor," she says. "Tell me anything I can fight for on behalf of women here," Sylvia would ask the female students. Nichola was one she could rely upon for a ready answer. Not only that, she saw that Nichola possessed "the courage and the presence to fight on behalf of others as well." One day, Sylvia took Nichola aside. "I'd like to recommend you for the master's degree program in English," she said. Nichola was flattered, and told the professor she'd keep it in mind for the future.

While Nichola's life and outlook on it were changing and maturing rapidly over those years, her family still saw the care-free, laughing girl they knew at times like Christmas and Thanksgiving, those visits when she would bring along friends like Jay, never hinting that they were much more than great pals. Apart from this tacitly agreed-upon fiction, home was where she could truly relax, shedding her military clothing and attitude.

While youngest sister Kate showed her admiration by en-rolling in cadets in Calgary, others in Nichola's life were taken aback by their friend's inner and outer transformation. When Nichola told Victoria about the rigorous schedule at RMC and such punishments as being made to sit out in the hall, the mid-dle sister was "bewildered about why she'd enjoy that." Nichola insisted it was all, ultimately, necessary to achieve a higher aim. "It's another branch of helping people," she told her sister. Victoria was at Ottawa's Carleton University, pursuing a degree in hu-manities. She was brilliant in the sciences, and had struggled with her desire to take a more creative academic route. It was Nichola who had encouraged her to follow her heart. Wanting to be supportive in return, Victoria held her tongue. Maybe Nichola wants to lead more than I ever would, she thought.

Krista MacEachern wasn't as philosophical about the changes she witnessed in her best friend. Although she felt that the core of Nichola had remained intact, it seemed to her she was "almost brainwashed." Krista debated with Nichola the pros and cons of choosing the military life; some of her friend's argu-ments were plausible, but others just didn't make sense to Krista. Unlike Nichola, Krista wasn't so certain of anything. After two years at St. Francis Xavier University in Antigonish, she had dropped out and moved west. Her hopes of being one of the easterners who found their fortune in boomtown Calgary hadn't panned out. She worked as a grocery-store cashier, making minimum wage and, she felt, overstaying her welcome in one of Tim and Sally's spare rooms. "I think we're kind of growing apart," she blurted out after one particularly tense discussion. Nichola wouldn't hear of it. "You'll always be my best friend and I'll always love you." But Krista was growing increasingly concerned. Nichola had thrown her a lifeline back in high school. Would time and distance, not to mention the regimented life and mindset of the military, weaken and maybe even sever a bond they'd both once thought was unbreakable?

Despite the views of those outside the fortified walls of RMC, Nichola's fellow students came to know her as something of a nonconformist. During "civilian dress down day," she paid her two dollars to the United Way for the privilege of going a day liberated from military wear. Nichola put on what she deemed appropriate civvies: a dress shirt and pressed pants, finished off with a pair of hiking boots she'd just purchased from a sporting-goods store in town. As she headed out to class, a cadet squadron training officer intercepted her. "Go back and change. Those aren't dress shoes," he snapped at Nichola. "I bought these specifically because they are leather shoes. They are new, not dirty at all, and they meet all the standards," she blasted back. After a standoff lasting only a second or two, Nichola turned on her heel, defying his order as she marched off to her Shakespeare class. "I can't believe he told me to change," she later fumed to her roommate, Allison, who laughed out loud at the combination of her friend's boldness and firm conviction that hiking boots qualified as dress shoes. Allison was even more shocked when one evening Nichola busted up a "Chicken and Porn Night" in the room next door. The officially outlawed practice saw a group of male cadets getting together in one of the dorm rooms to watch a porn video, with a bucket of takeout fried chicken for sustenance and pillows on their laps for privacy. Because the paper-thin walls didn't reach up to the ceiling, female officer cadets were often treated to all of the highly evocative sound effects. One night, the boys got too noisy for Nichola's liking. She got out of bed, put on her housecoat and pounded on the door. "What would your mothers think if they knew you were doing this right next door to a couple of girls?" she asked the stunned cadets. After meeting fiery Nichola and laid-back Jay, Allison's future husband and fellow RMC student Hasan Alvi later joked, "Wow, she really wears the pants in that relationship."

But no one ever accused Nichola of being a mannish version of a female cadet. Fellow English honours student Mitch Rivest learned quickly that while she could hang with the boys, she was still very much a lady. She could keep up with the men in PT, hiking for 30 kilometres wearing a 50-pound backpack and hardly breaking a sweat. But she let Mitch know in no uncertain terms that she preferred he keep his X-rated jokes to himself. When one of the first-year cadets she was supervising collapsed in the middle of a race and was hospitalized for several weeks, Nichola, knowing he didn't have family nearby, went to the hospital every day to check in on him. The day of his collapse was the only time in those four years Allison saw her usually unflappable friend and dorm mate cry. She didn't know that Nichola had long ago perfected the art of stealth sobbing.

On the morning of September 11, 2001, twenty-one-year-old Nichola was in her room studying when she heard a hard knock on her door. "Turn on your TV right now," a shaking Mitch told her. "Oh my God, this is terrible," the friends cried out in unison as they looked at the flickering images of fireballs and people falling out of skyscrapers. Together they sat on Nichola's bed watching the chaotic live news of the terrorist attacks on New York City and Washington, D.C., unfold. It was a day in which nearly 3,000 Americans, most of them civilians, and nationals of ninety other countries died in circumstances almost too unimaginable to be believed. Moments later, Nichola received an instant message from Jay, telling her to turn on the television.

But even on that momentous day, life went on. Jay arrived at his software-engineering class to find four other students, about half of the class. He told his professor, an air force major, what had just occurred. He didn't believe Jay and kept on teaching. One of the students pulled out his Palm Pilot and showed the teacher a news report. He cancelled the class, and Jay later met up with Nichola at a computer lab, where they tracked the hour-by-hour drama of the day. They didn't talk about how this might impact their own lives and military careers, not then. They were simply too stunned.

No one yet knew that September 11 would result in NATO troops being sent to Afghanistan to rout out the Taliban. Events had been set in motion that would place the RMC graduating class of 2002 in circumstances the Canadian military had not faced in more than fifty years. On October 19, 2001, the first American ground troops landed near Kandahar. Less than a month later, the United States asked its coalition partners, a variety of NATO countries that included Canada, to provide ground support in order to ensure that humanitarian relief and supplies were getting into the hands of ordinary Afghans. On November 14, Prime Minister Jean Chrétien announced Operation Apollo, Canada's name for its support role in Afghanistan. In additional to air support to help deliver humanitarian aid, the Edmonton-based Third Battalion, Princess Patricia's Canadian Light Infantry (3 PPCLI), part of the UN forces in Korea in 1952, was put on forty-eight-hour deployment notice. "Our soldiers are amongst the best in the world and will complement our U.S. allies extremely well," said Canada's defence minister Art Eggleton. "This mission will serve as yet another example of the outstanding cooperation between U.S. and Canadian militaries."

The initial worldwide trauma of 9/11 and the months that followed didn't stir Nichola overnight to become what she would later describe as a military "lifer." There were too many things occupying her mind, and time, that final year of school. Jay and Nichola's relationship had weathered the early frosh phase, and then some. Over the past three years, they had spent every spare moment together, even if that meant nights filled with studying in one another's dorm rooms, Jay reading his textbooks on information technology, Nichola her novels by the likes of Douglas Coupland and Margaret Atwood. On weekends, they'd go into town for Nichola's beloved Thai food, or to one of the pubs popular with both RMC and Queen's students. More often, they stayed in and rewatched their favourite movie, *Wayne's World*, which would inspire convulsive laughter and snorts even after the umpteenth viewing. Together, they led a local Scout troop with the 4th Kingston Group, taking the kids hiking and on camping trips.

On Halloween, 2001, the pair sat on Jay's dorm-room bed for a serious discussion before heading off to a party. "We should get married," Jay said to Nichola. She responded matter-of-factly. "Yeah, it's a good idea, we should do it." The plan was that after college, they'd wed. The next weekend, the couple went down to Princess Street and bought an engagement ring for Nichola. The small diamond-clustered band had a $1,300 price tag, which represented just about all of Jay's savings, but it was the one Nichola had always pictured wearing on her left hand. That Christmas, Nichola brought Jay home to Calgary. After a day of cross-country skiing in nearby Kananaskis Country, Nichola insisted Jay ride back to the city alone with Tim, while she went with Sally and her sisters. Before they departed, she took her dad to one side. "Look, Dad," she said, "Jay will be riding with you and he wants to talk to you. But you need to know, what he says is for information only. I've already made up my mind."

As Tim drove back to the city along the winding foothills of the Trans-Canada Highway, Jay nervously spurted out his thoughts. "I want to marry your daughter, and I'd like to have your permission." Tim didn't say a word, letting his body language do the talking as he sped the car up to 130 kilometres an hour. By the time his car hit the city limits, he'd managed to say yes, Jay could marry his daughter. When everyone had assembled in the living room of Tim and Sally's suburban home not far from the university, the young couple shared the news with the rest of the family. Her parents would have time to get used to their new reality. Three months later, as they were preparing for graduation, Nichola and Jay set the date: December 28, 2002.

■ ■ ■

In the spring of 2002, near the end of Nichola's final year, Tim stopped in to RMC on his way home from a conference in Toronto. As usual, his life was overflowing with new opportunities. He had moved the family from Antigonish to Calgary in 1999 to work in the University of Calgary's Faculty of Education. When he returned home, he'd begin preparing for a trip to Kosovo. He had been chosen by his school's dean of education to lead the school administrator component of a major project funded by the Canadian International Development Agency (CIDA). Its ambitious aim was no less than helping to rebuild the educational infrastructure of the formerly war-torn area as it emerged from the Balkan wars of the late 1990s. He was excited to return to the place where he'd travelled as a youth in the early 1970s, to bring his expertise to a still-tense area where hostility between Kosovars of Albanian and Serbian descent was contained only by the watchful presence of NATO troops.

When he arrived at his daughter's dorm, Tim was surprised to see Nichola in full military garb. They went for a stroll down Princess Street, one of the city's bustling main streets for shopping and entertainment. A procession of young men and women in military uniform saluted as they walked past father and daughter. Tim was accustomed to deference from his students, but this was something altogether extreme. He stopped in his tracks and looked to his daughter with a quizzical expression. "It's okay, Dad; it's not for you," she responded with a soft laugh. He was in her territory now, a hierarchical world where the badge on one's uniform and number of "pips" on the epaulettes spoke volumes.

■ ■ ■

On a sunny May afternoon in 2002, Nichola, Jay, Allison and Mitch took their places among more than two hundred other

RMC graduates, standing proudly in their scarlet uniforms on Parade Square. The pomp and circumstance of the event befitted a school touted as a "nation builder." Actually spread over two days, the ceremonies included a parade with the school's marching bands and a fireworks display, along with a rifle salute. As they walked through the campus, Nichola and her fellow graduates passed through the Mackenzie Building, overlooking Parade Square, up the red-carpeted stairs and past the framed photographs of those former RMC students who'd died in battle. A couple of days earlier, Nichola had created her own visual image of her experience here: a collage on cardboard, filled with photographs cut from magazines of Canada's prairies, tundra, mountain peaks and coastal beaches, accompanied by a series of questions: "Who am I? How do I get to the other side? What is over there? How do I survive?" It was Nichola's parting gift to one of the teachers who had opened up her eyes to the power of literature. Holding it in his hands, Michael Hurley shook his head with pleasure. He couldn't help smiling as he thought how his lessons on "The Quest"—men and women heroes travelling a difficult road towards a goal that promises to transform their lives— were brought to vivid life in this collage. He found a spot on his cluttered wall and added this new talisman to his collection.

Their officers' commissions with the Canadian Forces in hand—Nichola, like all her fellow graduates, had moved up from officer cadet to second lieutenant, posted to the 1st Regiment, Royal Canadian Horse Artillery in Shilo, Manitoba, where she'd begin making her way under the ranks of artillery—the graduates' final act was to walk through the Memorial Arch one more time. Perhaps as she walked under the names of RMC's war dead inscribed on the arch, Nichola thought back to mythologist

Joseph Campbell. His words had taught her that by following her bliss, she was putting herself "on a kind of track that has been there all the while, waiting for you, and the life that you ought to be living is the one you are living." Or maybe she thought of Arthur Schopenhauer, one of Campbell's favourite philosophers, who mused on the curious feeling one can have, that an author somewhere is writing the story of our lives, "in such a way that through events that seem to us to be chance happenings, there is actually a plot unfolding of which we have no knowledge."

Half a world away, more than 800 Canadian ground troops had spent the spring finding their footing on unforgiving soil, joining the U.S.-led Operation Enduring Freedom to rout out the remaining members of the al Qaeda terrorist group and its Taliban supporters, and to find the remains of the 9/11 mastermind Osama bin Laden, a man the Western world assumed by now to be long dead. For the most part, the Canadians, stuck behind the gates at the coalition airbase in Kandahar, spent their six months there waiting for a fight that didn't come; the bulk of their days delivered only an exercise in frustration. One incident took a tragic turn. On April 18, 2002, an American pilot mistook a live exercise on the ground for Taliban activity. In Canada's inaugural twenty-first century encounter with the term "friendly fire," a laser-guided bomb killed four members of the famed Princess Patricia's Canadian Light Infantry battle group. A month later, Defence Minister Art Eggleton announced that the troops were coming home and wouldn't be replaced. The Canadian mission to Afghanistan was drawing to a close, and the final word was that it was not much more than a test to endure heat and boredom.

No one else can be entirely certain what courses through the heart and mind of a human being on a milestone day in that person's life. But as Nichola posed for photographs on the grounds of RMC, clutching the scarlet folder that held her university degree in her white-gloved hand, her smile beaming and her family at her side, it was obvious that this was a day of victory. With a certainty matched only by Brucie's confident gaze, the twenty-two-year-old graduate had found her bliss.

PART II

STRENGTH AND HONOUR

SIX

Paradise on the Packway

THE SOUTHERN MANITOBA PRAIRIES have long inspired intense feelings in the first-time visitor. For some, this land of sweltering summers and deep-freeze winters is a barren and unforgiving swath of pancake-flat horizons—often derisively referred to as "bald-ass prairie"—offering not much more than extreme weather and no respite from a monotonous vista devoid of forests, mountains or hills. Others point to the panoramic views of the infinite prairie sky, the shimmering amber reflecting off millions of acres of wheat fields, and declare it nothing less than God's country.

In her first twenty-four hours at Canadian Forces Base Shilo, in August 2002, Nichola Goddard wasn't in any position to make a snap judgment about her new home. She had yet to experience its famed plagues of mosquitoes and black flies that punctuate the summer air. She didn't explore the fields around this desolate base that began its life in 1932 under a Depression-era government-relief program. It was, thought many young soldiers, a world away from plum deployments like Petawawa, nestled along the Ottawa River near the Laurentian Mountains.

The reason Nichola wasn't exploring was that she didn't come out of the house until after sunset the next day. She had arrived late the night before, was given the keys to her new home and settled in, quickly emptying her car filled with clothes and a rolled-up sleeping pad and bag. The next morning she awoke to find two portable commodes on the front lawn of her two-storey PMQ duplex, the name given to the military's on-base housing quarters. No one on the Packway, the strip of street filled with junior officers and their spouses, had seen Nichola move in the night before. As they set up for their annual fare-well-to-summer Packway party, it seemed only logical to locate the toilets on the lawn of the vacant house. "There's Porta-Potties on the lawn!" Nichola, sitting on the dining room floor, wailed over the phone to Jay back in Kingston. "I can't go out. I don't know anybody and I don't want to meet them this way." Jay tried to get his crying fiancée to see the humour in the situation, but she wasn't buying it. She was an officer, she told him, and she wanted her debut at Shilo to be a more formal affair than a handshake with cut-offs-wearing, beer-toting guys in front of portable toilets. She'd wait out the party with the stack of books she'd brought from Kingston.

Nichola wasn't the only newcomer in hiding. Down the Packway, Liane and Andrew Nicholson were holed up in their new duplex watching the afternoon festivities unfold. The high school sweethearts, newlyweds from Cole Harbour, Nova Scotia, had been living the past three years on another street. But since Shilo was one of the last bases in the country to have segregated-by-rank PMQs they had to move when Andrew was promoted to officer in June. Earlier that morning, the pair had given their new living room a fresh coat of paint; they were covered head to toe in paint splatters. Like Nichola, Andrew wasn't comfortable meeting his fellow officer neighbours in such dressed-down fashion.

It was an unusual start for Nichola, a woman accustomed to being the new kid on the block. But this was a move unlike any other. She didn't have backup support: her parents and sisters were in Calgary, and she was far away from her good-humoured fiancé for the first time in four years. None of her officer-cadet friends were at her side, as they had been throughout her summers of training; a couple of fellow RMC graduates had been posted to Shilo, but she didn't know them. She was riding solo. Like so many other military couples before them, she and Jay were learning the harsh realities of a dual-military partnership. He was back at CFB Kingston, assigned to the base just a stone's throw from Royal Military College, and working as a lab assistant at the school. Even before Jay's military career started, it was already in jeopardy. His bum right knee had been giving him trouble all through university. In February 2001, he'd had a second surgery to try to repair the cumulative damage. It was only afterwards that the army doctor informed Jay he probably wouldn't be able to run again. After graduation, his higher-ups gave him an MOT, or medical occupational transfer, from the army to the air force, where he could train to be an air traffic controller. There was a silver lining to the change in plans: Jay would soon be posted to Winnipeg, to work under his new air force boss at 1 CAD (Canadian Air Division) HQ while he awaited his training.

"It's time for Operation Sam," Jay announced via email as he prepared for his first visit to Shilo that fall. He knew their separation would be easier to take if Nichola had the company of a pet. "I'm not into the designer thing," Nichola reminded him. "I want a homeless dog." The September weekend he arrived, the pair went out to Brandon, the small university city just west of CFB Shilo, where they found their new dog among a cluster of mangy mutts at the local animal shelter. The shepherd cross Nichola picked out was a reject of the worst kind, already returned once thanks to his predilection for chewing up socks and other various household items. "That's Sam," said Nichola. "That's how I've always pictured him." The following year, the family would welcome Bill, a long, skinny mutt with the colouring of a Rottie, along with cats Frank and Laura. "We call him Frank the Tank, or Shit Disturber Frank," Nichola told friends. "Laura does whatever she wants, and doesn't answer to anything." When she called her parents to boast of the new additions, Sally couldn't help teasing her daughter. "If you two have children, what are you going to call them? Spot and Rover?"

CFB Shilo was a far cry from picturesque Antigonish, the last true home Nichola had enjoyed. The fading PMQs cried out for a fresh coat of paint, and the strip mall on the base housing the CANEX supply store and other small convenience shops wouldn't have looked out of place in one of nearby Winnipeg's run-down Main street neighbourhoods. One could easily imagine the occasional tumbleweed endlessly somersaulting along the grey roads, driven by a howling prairie wind.

Despite her inauspicious start, Nichola, as always, had little trouble once she started making connections. The residents of the Packway had so much in common, it was impossible not to. Besides sharing the same rank, nearly every one of Nichola's fellow officers was newly married; they were all in their early to mid-twenties and had yet to start their families, and they hailed from all four corners of Canada. Like Nichola, the Nicholsons had been raised in Nova Scotia; Sonny and Chantal Hatton, who met while Sonny was on leave from a tour in Bosnia and were married just two weeks when Nichola moved onto the block, came from the Vancouver area; and Julianne and Andrew Charchuk, who'd be the last of the tight-knit group to arrive on the Packway in the spring of 2003, had met while both were political science students at the University of Calgary. They all had dogs, and were, like Nichola and Jay, dog fanatics.

Working full-time and living alone with a demanding canine proved easy: during the day, the women brought Sam along on their walks in the fields surrounding the base. Nichola had a support network of doggie day cares and kennelling; when one couple went away for a weekend, they'd simply leave their door unlocked so that fellow Packway neighbours could pop in to feed and walk their dogs. When they returned home, they often found a batch of still-warm cookies made by Julianne or Liane, or a bottle of wine and a "welcome home" card from Nichola or Chantal. The pets offered any excuse for a party or a Packway barbecue; whenever someone brought home a new puppy or a rescue dog from the pound, Nichola hosted a doggie shower. "We were all so young and starry-eyed, it was a magical time in our lives," Chantal says. "Nichola would call me up and say, 'Can you play?' Which was code for us going for a nice long walk with the dogs." The walks in the wide-open fields were always off leash, freeing up the hands and minds of the owners. At one point, the Packway had more dog residents than humans.

It was through her love of dogs that Nichola was lured to her own surprise wedding shower in late fall of 2002. Chantal announced she was having a birthday party for her dog, Lively. On cue, Nichola showed up at the appointed time with a wrapped squeaky toy in tow, only to find a roomful of soldiers' wives yelling out, "Surprise!" Over the course of the evening, the women played an assortment of what Chantal called "dumb-ass shower games," complete with making a hat out of bows for Nichola, who responded in her trademark style: slapping her knee in amusement, throwing her head back in hearty laughter.

Nichola was settling in well, too, in her new job as a junior officer in Shilo's A Battery. RMC had prepared her well for the daily morning PT, which usually included cardio and weight training, along with ruck marches: hikes often consisting of several kilometres, the soldiers weighted down with heavy kit or supplies. It gave her an invigorating start to the day, which she appreciated. As a commissioned officer, a large component of her work was administrative, completed during a regular nine-to-five work schedule. She wrote and corrected performance evaluations, processed special requests and performed other management and human resources–related tasks. Then there was the annual "refresher training" soldiers need to remain deployable: everything from personal weapons training and testing for their C7A2 assault rifles and C9 light machine guns, to updating first-aid training and chemical defence procedures. Nichola's favourite activities usually revolved around field exercises, which lasted anywhere from three days to several weeks and had her working with the infantry and armoured corps. A few times a year, she and her fellow artillery soldiers headed to CFB Edmonton, where they'd do computer exercises, practising tactics, techniques and procedures before going into the field.

While she juggled all her new work duties that fall, Nichola still made time for wedding planning, which included going with Julianne to Winnipeg one weekend to have her wedding dress fitted. Days before their December 28, 2002, wedding,

Nichola and Jay braved the prairie winter highway, as did so many of their Shilo friends, to be in Calgary. As they exchanged vows in St. Barnabas Anglican Church, the young couple was at turns giddy, teary-eyed and shaking with nervous joy.

Stepping into the church on her father's arm, Nichola was the embodiment of Princess Buttercup in *The Princess Bride*, her favourite romantic film as a young girl. Gone were the olive combat boots, replaced by white satin pumps. Her jewel-encrusted, strapless white gown sported a long train befitting royalty. Her long brown hair fell in ringlets from a loosely fastened bun, her lips shimmered with burnished red gloss, and her hands, which sported a fresh French manicure, clutched a bouquet of yellow roses. Around the twenty-two-year-old's neck was a simple choker-length string of pearls, a gift presented by grandfather Michael to her grandmother Kathleen on their wedding day more than a half-century ago. Nichola and her father flashed identical gap-toothed grins as they slowly marched up the red-and-cream-tiled aisle to the strains of "Oh Come, All Ye Faithful," past a bejewelled Christmas tree, a manger display and the smiling faces of Sally, her sisters and Nichola's grandparents. Following in their steps were maid of honour Krista and bridesmaids Victoria and Kate, all dressed in various styles of midnight-blue gowns, their hair swept up like the bride's. Krista, who'd almost been stranded en route from Nova Scotia, where she was now back in university, tried valiantly not to look frazzled by the panic of the past twenty-four hours as she glanced around at the crowd of about eighty friends and family; twenty-year-old Victoria, the most sensitive of the sisters, was already close to tears; and thirteen-year-old Kate, smiling shyly through her braces, bore the slightly embarrassed expression of a young girl not yet accustomed to playing dress-up.

Jay, sporting a buzz cut and a rented black tuxedo, with best man Mitch Rivest at his side and his mother and brother watching from the crowd, fastened his eyes on his extroverted bride as though breaking that gaze for even a split second might cast him adrift forever. As they entwined their hands, they recited their vows before the Anglican priest through trembling smiles and the occasional giggle. The radiant bride began to cry as she said the words "I, Nichola Kathleen Sarah Goddard, take you, Jason Beam."

The reception in the banquet hall of a nearby hotel was filled with all the typical wedding rituals: amusing anecdotes from a procession of relatives and friends, and the frequent clinking of wine glasses, which inspired Nichola and Jay to indulge in long, passionate kisses. The assembled throng egged them on with cheers, foot stomping and wolf whistles. And, of course, the toasts, which from this family of storytellers were much more colourful than most come to expect at weddings. Tim told the ever-popular stories of finding the future soldier with a machete in her chubby toddler hand, and of his little girl picking coffee beans in Papua New Guinea for "five cents a can"; Sally recalled meeting Nichola's new "friend" Jay just after their training at Saint-Jean-sur-Richelieu, and how their first visit home to Nova Scotia put her back nearly a thousand dollars after tallying the fuel costs of driving to and from Halifax, paying Nichola's airfare and feeding two athletic cadets with huge appetites; Krista related her fated encounter with the "friendliest person on the bus" on that first day of high school; and Sally's sister Alison talked about Nichola's pearl necklace, hoping that "maybe someday your children will wear it." Nichola told the crowd, "I'm having a great day," and promised not to cry. She thanked her bridesmaids and maid of honour. "Raise your glass with me in a toast to the two best sisters anyone could have, Victoria and Kate, and the bestest friend I could ever have, Krista." As the emcee, Mitch read out telegrams from friends and family who couldn't be there. "We wish you many years of happiness. And no wars—personal and international," went one of the messages, which prompted raucous laughter from all in attendance, "especially the latter."

After cutting through their three-tiered white wedding cake and tenderly placing a piece in one another's mouths, Nichola and Jay strolled arm in arm to the middle of the ballroom floor for their first dance together as a married couple. Smiling and sharing kisses with her new husband, Nichola swayed to the sounds of "Storybook Story," the theme song of the film *The Princess Bride* she had more than a decade earlier decided would play on her long-dreamed-of day.

The new bride returned home to Shilo, alone. It would be three long months before Jay was posted to Winnipeg, a two-hour drive from his wife. She kept busy with her military training, and relied on her new friends to stave off loneliness. Because the women on her street weren't soldiers, the rules that applied in her work life were thrown out: she could relate her most intimate thoughts with impunity. While she steered away from talking about the details surrounding work—her friends, after all, were the wives of her colleagues—she did occasionally drop hints that being a woman in a sea of men wasn't always a picnic. On one walk with Chantal, the one Packway female friend who had some soldiering experience from being in the reserves, she confessed to a stress-relieving exercise for those days when the military life took its toll. "When things get to me," Nichola said, harkening back to the stealth sobbing of her RMC years, "there's a bathroom I go to on a vacant floor, so I can cry without anyone seeing or hearing me."

On the day Jay arrived in Winnipeg in the spring of 2003, he dropped off his bags at his new post and within minutes was on the Trans-Canada Highway heading west. He did this every Friday afternoon, excited to see his exuberant new wife and their pets. They fell into a groove that, although unconventional, worked marvellously for them. While he awaited the start of his training, Jay's daily duties back at the base in Winnipeg largely consisted of surfing his favourite websites, filing papers and making the odd photocopy. The boredom of a job without much to do made the hours go by like days. But he liked his boss, who took pity on the groom-in-training and let him take off early on Fridays. When he arrived at Shilo, he was raring to go, while Nichola needed to kick off her combat boots and put up her tired feet. So he did the cooking while she relaxed, both of them revelling in the fact that they weren't just playing house anymore. This was the real, true-blue beginning of the rest of their lives as a married couple. Each time they said their good-byes, Nichola uttered the words that would become her mantra for the next few years. "What did I do to deserve you? I'm the luckiest girl in the world." And just to make sure he knew she meant it, she often called out, "I love you, with all of my heart," as he backed out the driveway.

As the veteran spouse on the Packway, Liane Nicholson had met her fair share of female officers over the two years she'd spent on the base. They were "as tough as nails," she told Andrew.

They hardly ever made gestures of friendship to the female spouses of soldiers, lest it weaken them in the eyes of their male colleagues. They generally had a "best-defence-is-an-offence" attitude. One of Liane's first encounters with Nichola suggested that the new resident was living up to her assessment of the stereotypical hard-shelled female soldier. A large group of soldiers and their spouses were enjoying drinks at the Double Decker pub in Brandon one Saturday night, when someone walked up and said, "Hi, Nichole." In a businesslike, slightly intimidating voice, the new officer said, "It's Ni-Ko-la, not Nicole, not Nicky. Nichola."

Liane made a mental note never to make the same mistake. She soon discovered, though, that Nichola—who in time allowed others to address her as "Nich," the gender-neutral nickname Jay and others mostly used—was in a class of her own. She was a tough soldier who quickly earned the respect of her comrades, both male and female. But she was also unabashed about letting her feminine side shine through. She was happy to sit and chat with Liane over a pot of tea on Sunday afternoons while Jay and Andrew tinkered on their cars in the driveway. Nichola insisted Liane watch the opening episode of each season of the reality TV show *The Bachelor* with her, because, she explained, "I just love to see what kinds of dresses the contestants will come out of the limousine wearing." Nichola tried to take up sewing so she could fix the dog beds Sam kept chewing up, but she didn't even know how to thread a bobbin. After being summoned on several occasions to perform the task, Julianne walked over to Nichola's house one Saturday and rethreaded it. Then she pulled it out. "Okay, now you do it," she told her dumbfounded friend. "Oh no, you did not just do that," said Nichola, who pouted as she threaded the bobbin under Julianne's watchful eye. When Liane and Julianne booked a pedicure appointment at Pantages salon in Brandon, Nichola asked if she could come along. As the razor was put to her heels, Nichola piped up. "Whoa, whoa, go easy on the calluses," she insisted to the esthetician. "I want to keep those. I worked really hard to get them and I need them for my boots." Julianne and Liane burst into giggles. The esthetician stood up and shook her head in disbelief. "In all my years of giving pedicures," she exclaimed, "no one has ever asked to keep the calluses."

There was no one more ladylike in the neighbourhood, though, than Gundy Goutouski, a regal German beauty with shimmering blue eyes and the lithe physique and grace of a dancer. Nichola had never known anyone quite like Gundy, whose backyard was across the alley from hers. In her fur stoles and glittering costume jewelry, the middle-aged spouse of a former reservist was a rose among much younger thorns. About the only thing she and Nichola had in common was the coincidence of sharing the same birthday, May 2. But from the moment Nichola first called out, "Hello, neighbour!" over the fence the day after she moved in, Gundy was hooked. She and husband Bryan, a gregarious former orchard owner from southern Ontario who was a personnel selection officer at Shilo, were older than Nichola's parents. But they were brought into the social circle, invited to Nichola and Jay's regular barbecues, or to the pubs in Brandon on weekends. "I think she picked us," Gundy told Bryan. "Meeting Nichola is the best thing to happen to me here at Shilo." Gundy's day didn't get off to a good start unless she saw Nichola, usually up before the sun rose, skipping down the street at 6:00 a.m., her two dogs at her side. She is so patient with animals, she thought, but when it comes to humans, she doesn't suffer fools gladly. Auntie Gundy, as Sam and Bill's regular dog sitter came to be known, loved that about her. She also loved the Nicholaisms: she was "torqued" when angry, said "cool" when she liked something; she called people "dude" and responded, "Sounds like a plan," to just about every idea, no matter how half-baked. Gundy and Bryan howled with laughter when Nichola told tales of her and Jay's misadventures, like innocently buying a carp for their aquarium that ate all the other fish, or how she'd yell at Jay, "Get up, you lazy fuck," after he hit the snooze button on his alarm clock one too many times. Although she told Gundy that she might return to RMC for a master's degree in English, her real dream was to one day open a kennel with Jay. Then, she and her husband could spend the rest of their days surrounded by animals.

In turn, Gundy opened her home, and her closet, to her much younger friend. Before events at the base mess hall where civilian dress-up was allowed, Nichola came knocking. "Auntie Gundy, I need help!" she cried. "What, Nichola?" Gundy replied. "Jewelry, shoes!" It didn't matter that Nichola's feet were a full size smaller; she'd simply stuff some tissue into the toes and run off in a pair of pumps. Gundy loved to spiff her up and send her on her way; no one she had ever met before showed such a child-like thrill in response to her generosity. One evening, Nichola had picked out a long gown for a formal mess dinner. It was the middle of winter, and she had no coat. The hall was a good kilometre away. "Don't worry, Auntie Gundy, I'll run fast," Nichola assured her. Gundy pictured the young woman in high heels and a gown, dashing like mad across the base, dodging snowdrifts, and wouldn't hear of it. She pulled out a stole from the back of her closet. "How do you feel about wearing fur?" she asked. "I'm okay with it." Nichola put on the mink stole, admiring her elegant silhouette in the mirror. "That looks perfect on you. I want you to keep it," said Gundy. "Cool!" exclaimed Nichola as she kissed Gundy's cheek before tearing out the door.

Throughout that first year, the bond between the two couples grew ever stronger. Bryan joined Nichola and Jay on canoe trips up the Assiniboine River, while Gundy made sure there was a pot of tea ready at the end of each workday. Nichola, thought Gundy of the young woman who brought her to tears of laughter with her daily stories and mishaps, "is the daughter I never had."

Julianne, a stunning blond with a love of fashion, was another help when Nichola needed to look good for special events. She'd do the hair and makeup before sending her over to Gundy's for the finishing wardrobe touches. When Julianne, known by her friends as Jules, was seriously injured in a car crash in 2004 just weeks before her wedding, the two traded places. "Nich would come over and do my hair for me," says Julianne. "She always put it in braids, but she drew the line at attempting anything fancy." With her artillery-officer fiancé, Andrew, away for months on a training course, Julianne, who suffered a broken neck and had to wear a halo and neck brace for several months, needed her Packway buddies more than ever. They didn't disappoint: Nichola, Chantal and Liane took turns doing everything, from making sure Howitzer, Julianne's pocket-sized Yorkshire terrier, got his daily walk, to cleaning her house and bringing over meals. When Jay came home on the weekends he mowed her lawn and performed whatever Mr. Fix-It chores needed doing around the house.

By summer of 2003, Jay and Nichola were finally living together as husband and wife. After waiting several months for his air traffic control course, he was told that in fact he'd still have to pass a physical. I guess you've got to be able to run for your cup of coffee between flights, he thought grumpily. Jay's boss in Winnipeg came to the rescue once more, pulling strings to get him a posting at Shilo in its communications area, doing computer work. He was thrilled to finally be with Nichola, but heartbroken to realize that all his years of training to be a soldier had come down to a desk job. Nichola assured him that in time they'd come up with another plan for his future, and encouraged him to enroll in a long-distance master's program in computer science. She was simply ecstatic to have her big rock at her side. "Hello, husband!" she cried out when she got home from work. "How is my wife today?" he'd respond. Nichola was thrilled when she arrived home to find supper on the table. "I could get used to this," she told Liane with a laugh. "He'll do everything but the dishes—he even makes my lunches."

Nichola had no doubts by now about where her career was going, or at least where it could take her if she made the right moves. She was growing ever more confident that she not only had what it took to become a commanding officer one day, but also that it was what she truly wanted. She was also becoming increasingly aware that how she was perceived would play a major role in her ascension through the ranks. She had joined a knitting group so she could learn to knit a baby blanket for Liane, the first of the gang to get pregnant. One night, a lower-ranked soldier came by the house looking for Nichola; Jay told him she was at her knitting group. As the words left his mouth, he knew he'd made a mistake: the soldier would no doubt share that little bit of gossip with the other boys. When she came home, Nichola was forgiving, and the two made a pact to keep the details of their personal life for only a select few. It was understood that Nichola had a tough job to do, and the less the others viewed her as a "girl," let alone one sitting around with a pair of knitting needles in hand, the better. She understood that in the coming months and years, her job was going to get a whole lot tougher.

■ ■ ■

On June 6, 2003, less than a year after those 800 Canadian troops began returning home from assisting the Americans in Operation Enduring Freedom, Minister of National Defence John McCallum announced that Jean Chrétien's Liberal government was sending troops back to Afghanistan with Operation Athena, named for the Greek warrior goddess. "When our soldiers patrol the streets of Kabul, they are also helping keep the streets of Calgary safe," said McCallum in an address at the Calgary Chamber of Commerce.

Not long after invading Afghanistan, the United States had diverted its energies to Iraq, in a war that would come to be seen by many as not much more than the execution of a vendetta on the part of President George Bush, whose father, George H. W. Bush, led the country into the Gulf War in 1990. In February 2003, U.S. secretary of state Colin Powell made a convincing argument for invading that country due to its stockpiling of weapons of mass destruction (WMDS), a claim that would later prove to be unfounded. But the die was cast. The hot potato of Afghanistan was handed to NATO and its twenty-eight member countries, which assumed control of the International Security Assistance Force (ISAF). As part of its NATO commitment,

Canada would reduce naval operations in the Arabian Gulf and increase its assistance to the ISAF in Kabul, led by General Rick Hillier, the new head of the Canadian Forces. The commitment would mean the deployment of 1,800 troops: out of 7,500 soldiers in the combat trades, more than 3,000 would now be committed to operations overseas in what were still being called "peacekeeping" operations.

SEVEN

The Conductor

IN LATE SPRING OF 2005, the prairie crocus, the floral emblem of Manitoba, was already in full bloom in the fields surrounding CFB Shilo, its brilliant lavender petals peeking out from the drab quilt of brown grasses and white snow. Inside one of the nondescript buildings dotting the base, Nich Goddard was performing her own rite of spring before an appreciative audience. A rookie soldier stood over her wielding a pair of scissors in one hand, a fistful of her hair in the other. As large clumps of silky brown tresses fell to the ground, the room erupted in hoots, whistles and applause. Scores of soldiers gathered on the gun floor to watch the shenanigans, but only one lucky guy, a corporal, known in the artillery unit as a bombardier, got to do the deed. As he lopped off the last remaining chunks and took an electric razor to the head of his superior, the laughter and cheers became deafening. The twenty-five-year-old officer alternated between grins and grimaces as she said goodbye to the longest, most glorious mane she had ever known.

The newly minted captain had just a couple of years earlier walked down the aisle as a princess-style bride in cascading ringlets. Now doing her best G.I. Jane impersonation, Nich more closely resembled a peach. From a distance it would have been hard to pick her out as one of the few females in the sea of buzz cuts and camouflage. But apart from the fact she'd collected hundreds of dollars for a cancer fundraiser by raffling off the barber's job, Nich harboured a deeper motivation for her public shearing. Privately, she wanted to test her conviction in surrendering this one permitted expression of her femininity as she mentally prepared for her first overseas tour as a Canadian peacekeeper, which, rumour had it, was in the pipeline for her and several of her fellow soldiers at Shilo. After all, with nearly three of her five years of mandatory military service under her belt, she hardly ever answered to the name Nichola anymore. While soldiers of lower rank called her "Ma'am," her friends on the base knew her as Nich. Some of her comrades might not even have known that Captain Nich Goddard's full name was such a pretty and romantic-sounding one, inspired by Russian royalty.

The head shaving was the kind of spectacle that made Nich's boss cringe, but Major Anne Reiffenstein had come to expect the unexpected from this soldier she was grooming to be a leader on the battlefield. Since she'd begun mentoring Nich not long after meeting her in the fall of 2002, Reiffenstein, the commander of A Battery, had witnessed the young woman's stubborn streak on many an occasion: Nich readily expressed her outrage over big and small injustices, and fumed when she encountered even the most minor procedure or policy that didn't seem fair. Reiffenstein soon got to calling her telltale expression—lips pressed tightly together, chin scrunched up and brows furrowed—"Nich's war face." It wasn't that Nich was the insubordinate type; she always called Reiffenstein "Ma'am," as per military dictates, and she never outright disobeyed an order. But the senior officer had long ago discovered that her protégée couldn't pull a poker face if her life depended on it. "You need to smile less," she told Nich on one of her first weeks on the job. "You shouldn't look so happy, or else people aren't going to take you seriously." Nich smiled tersely and said, "Okay, Ma'am," then turned on her heels and left. "Of course, she didn't listen," says Reiffenstein. "She was smarter than I was, and she was comfortable in her own skin."

No one would ever accuse Major Anne Reiffenstein of being anything less than smart—especially not to her face. The self-described embodiment of Liane Nicholson's "tough as nails" female soldier, Reiffenstein was the first to admit that her shoulders had long borne a chip the size of the Rock of Gibraltar. But one could hardly fault her. Her first eighteen months of regimental life had been nothing short of hellish. Growing an armour of granite had been an expedient coping mechanism. She'd entered the military in 1989, on the heels of Canada's Human Rights Tribunal ruling allowing women into the combat arms, a move that made Canada a pioneer in the developed world. In the United States, which even today does not officially allow women to fight in direct ground combat, the *Washington Post* declared it a "radical political, military and social leap." But the reactions back home ranged from apathy to outright antagonism.

Reiffenstein naively thought that "there would be tons of girls saying, 'Yeah, all right, what an adventure.'" To her surprise, few of her countrywomen were waiting anxiously on the sidelines for the call to arms. Those first years attracted only a trickle of women to the traditionally all-male domain. This was a trend that would endure: in 2002, women accounted for 3.9 per cent of personnel in Canada's army combat jobs, and only a small fraction of those held leadership positions. But the former Anne Proctor already had a track record when it came to breaking with convention. The daughter of conservative-minded British immigrants who came to Canada in the 1950s "with no money in their pockets" joined the army cadets as a teenager. She worked in construction after high school, preferring to be doing something physical in the great outdoors and "making way better money" than in stereotypical pink ghetto jobs, chained to a desk typing, filing and answering phones all day. Afflicted with a mixture of "blind confidence and complete ignorance," the native of Thunder Bay, Ontario, also admired her brother, David Proctor, a soldier ten years her senior who was a tanker with the armoured regiment Lord Strathcona's Horse. Reiffenstein knew there was no way she'd survive the physical demands of infantry. Artillery, the combat arm that dealt with indirect fire support—howitzers, mortars and other varieties of artillery are known as indirect fire, while bullets shot from machine guns and rifles are direct—appealed to her science and technical side. "Hey, they're doing math in their heads," she thought of the artillery officers. "That works for me."

Though she shuddered at words like "pioneer," Reiffenstein made it into the history books as one of three who, in 1991, became the first female officers in Canada's combat arms. Then, in 2003, she became the first female to command a combat arms sub-unit. Proving her mettle in overseas deployments in Cyprus, Uganda and Rwanda, she led hundreds of soldiers in domestic operations responding to floods, ice storms and forest fires.

The road to recognition was nevertheless filled with potholes and cultural landmines. Not everyone at CFB Shilo was excited to see the tough blond breaking through gender barriers when she arrived in 1991. "All of a sudden a fundamental shift was imposed on the military by a bunch of loony activists," she says of the prevailing sentiment. She learned a popular saying among the men that illuminated the challenges ahead: "We uphold democracy, we don't actually practise it." Faced with daily grief that included everything from shunning to verbal abuse, Reiffenstein decided to "just assume you hate me unless you prove otherwise." She dug in her heels, deciding she "wouldn't give the bastards the satisfaction" of seeing her scurry off with her tail between her legs. "If my being here makes you miserable," she imagined herself saying to her detractors, "then here is where I'll stay." Her appearance on a Canadian Forces recruiting poster, though, wasn't an act of defiance but obedience: when she resisted those fifteen minutes of fame, her commanding officer informed her it was an order.

By the time that next female artillery officer—the one who smiled far too much for Reiffenstein's tastes—arrived at Shilo in late summer of 2002, the world was a very different place. Women in the regiment weren't a big issue. This was no longer the Canadian army of the Cold War. "It's so hard to describe how much had changed in that ten years, in the social dynamic of the organization," says Reiffenstein. "We lost some lovely stuff, but also gained some great stuff." That new officer was a flesh-and-blood reflection of changing times. But meeting Nich Goddard didn't fill Reiffenstein with envy or resentment towards the young woman whose own shoulders were chip free; in fact, Nich's presence made her feel validated, that "all the crap" she went through earlier "was worth it." She was happy she was around to see this next generation in action, to witness Nich having the army experience she'd expected when she graduated from artillery school a decade earlier. She admired Nich's leadership ability, and wasn't surprised to see the higher-ups in

Ottawa green-lighting her promotions, her first year from second lieutenant to lieutenant, and then, in the spring of 2005, to captain. Reiffenstein was certain if Nich decided to stay in the military, the ranks of major, lieutenant-colonel and even higher were within the capable junior officer's grasp. Nich was also adeptly navigating her way through all the hoops of artillery, first as a recce (reconnaissance) officer doing such things as collecting the survey data needed to fire the guns, and next as a gun position officer, and now as a forward observation officer, or FOO. Mostly, though, Reiffenstein marvelled at how other soldiers increasingly looked to the young officer for guidance and friendship.

Sonny Hatton, the battery captain and husband of Nich's friend Chantal, was at first a bit wary of having a female officer on the team, "but the second you got to know Captain Goddard, you'd follow her to the ends of the earth." Sonny knew that others saw Nich in much the same way. "When someone would get posted out of Shilo, Nich was the only one they'd ever email," he says. "They'd all talk to her—her smile, her laughter, her ability to laugh at herself, disarmed people."

Bombardier Jeff Fehr was only the third young man from his hometown of Gladstone, a farming community about an hour's drive north of Shilo, to join the Canadian military since the Korean War. He was a no-nonsense soldier who, like the major, knew he'd never want a desk job but "something that got the adrenaline pumping," and signed on right out of high school. The non-commissioned member (NCM)—officers are university-educated soldiers, while NCMs and non-commissioned officers (NCOs) are considered career soldiers on a separate rank hierarchy—was apprehensive about RMC graduates. Most of them, he felt, came in with the attitude, "I studied at university for four years, so I know what I'm doing." By February 2003, the twenty-year-old had already been in the regular forces for three years. He and Nich went out together to the Rogers Pass, British Columbia, stretch of the Trans-Canada Highway as part of a team of soldiers with AVCON, or avalanche control. The plum assignment involved shooting 105-mm howitzers into the mountain hillsides in order to trigger controlled avalanches before they became larger and endangered the public. In other words, "It can be a lot of fun, if you're with the right officer and sergeant." Jeff discovered Nich was that most rare of RMC grads, one who took the approach "'I learned everything I could in school, so now I'm with guys who've been doing this for years and I'm going to be like a sponge and absorb stuff'—those are the officers that the boys respect," he says, "and that described Captain Goddard."

Nich's sense of humour even managed to melt the professional armour of fellow officer Bob Meade, an earnest type whose father had been in the air force, and whose grandfather was a gunner in World War II. "We were all talking one day, trying to figure out who was the tallest. I was, at only five-foot-eight," says Bob, who in time would form a strong friendship with Nich's husband. "So I said, 'How much do we weigh?' Nich said with a laugh, 'Shut up, Bob.' We'd all be out in the field, cold and wet and miserable, and she'd be the only one smiling and laughing." Reiffenstein often found herself shaking her head over Nich's incredible people skills. "The senior NCOs weren't freaked out by her, and the soldiers weren't freaked out by her."

Like everyone else who encountered the five-foot-five powerhouse, Reiffenstein immediately took a liking to Nich. Her passionate nature, whether expressing joy over a job well done, or seething with anger when disappointed in herself or others, never failed to bring a smile to the major's face. One day, Nich came to her office and closed the door behind her. Another officer was bending some rules and she didn't like it one bit. "This is not fair. I've researched it, I've got the regulations right here, and I'm going to intervene," she said, almost stomping her feet with each syllable. Reiffenstein looked over the evidence, and seeing that it was a relatively minor infraction from a soldier about to be posted elsewhere, advised Nich to back down. "You're right, it's not fair. But you know what? Life's not fair," she told her. "You have to pick your battles." Nich's flair for the English language was another sticking point. When she dropped off a beautifully written, three-page report on the major's desk, Reiffenstein burst her literary bubble. "Number one, no one in the army reads past the first page," she told Nich. "You're using too many big words—it's an exercise instruction, not Hemingway."

She rode Nich hard, not because she was female but because she was so darned good at her job. And that job was one of the toughest in the military. An artillery officer requires a quick mind and virtuoso multi-tasking abilities, in order to coordinate everything from Apache helicopters and missile-laden Predator drones (unmanned aerial vehicles), to B-52s carrying up to 2,000-pound bombs, to primary gun support as far away as twenty kilometres. "You're telling them what targets to shoot at," says Reiffenstein. "There are two different divides within the tactical artillery; one is getting bullets where they need to be, and that's the gun line. So you have your guns all laid out, you calculate all the data, get your radio calls from the guys up front, you do your calculations; you get them to the guys who shoot and fire, and boom." Then there is the forward observation officer party, the soldiers that spend much of their time in a LAV, directing the bigger picture of the battlefield. What makes the FOO's job even more complicated is coordinating all these assets—the planes carrying bombs, the "big gun" lines often several kilometres from the battlefield—into the manoeuvre plan of the Company Commander (CC), ensuring there are no "friendly fire" casualties, a task that requires knowing where the troops are at all times. The LAV—the 7-metre-long, 17-tonne, eight-wheeled troop carrier able to travel at speeds up to 100 kilometres an hour—provides protected transport for the infantry to get as close as possible to a battle, and then provides fire and other mounted support.

Like Nich, Andrew Nicholson was another rising star in the ranks who caught Reiffenstein's eye. One year behind his friend, he too had that rare combination of charisma and talent. It was only natural that Reiffenstein's FOO-in-training and her new gun position officer (Andrew) would become trusted allies, especially since Andrew's wife, Liane, was already a part of Nich's closest circle outside of work. Nich felt comfortable talking with the thirty-year-old native of Dartmouth, Nova Scotia, about her private fears. Behind her constant grin, she was concerned about keeping up with the men, about how she was perceived by the troops. Though he felt Reiffenstein sometimes singled out Nich for extra tasks and duties, Andrew didn't think it was because of her gender. "She knew Nich was special, and she wanted to set her down the right path—she gave her opportunities to shine and show leadership."

It's not surprising that artillery appealed to Nich's creative side, especially once Reiffenstein had compared the fire plan to a musical score, and the artillery officer in command as the conductor of an orchestra. "You need musical intelligence," she told her. "There are times when you're firing and rests in between. The person who writes the music is the FOO. He writes that music in support of what the infantry or the armoured commander in front wants you to do. And that relationship kind of goes up every level you go." Nich's job as a gun position officer was "to get the guns in position, get the rounds, while I was the one yelling at her. It was something she really enjoyed and I understood that—there are a lot of moving parts, a lot of things going on, so you never get bored."

The problem in the military is that once a soldier is adept at a certain task, he or she is moved up to the next one. In Nichola's case, her ascension to FOO meant she was no longer overseeing more than a hundred soldiers, but instead was the leader of a small team who works directly with the guns and is embedded into the infantry companies. Sophisticated computers and targeting systems in the turret of the LAV allow the FOO to call down fire missions, and direct that fire with pinpoint accuracy onto a specific building, vehicle or group of enemy soldiers.

Not only are FOOS communicating by radio with several contact people; along with all the other tasks, they must also frequently poke their heads out of the top of the LAV to make a quick visual survey of the surroundings. This fact usually stuns those in the civilian world. The LAV III, in many ways, is an almost impenetrable fortress—its body and bolt-on amour plates can withstand enemy fire both far and near, and it is armed with a large, turret-mounted 25-mm cannon, a coaxial 7.62-mm machine gun and grenade launchers. Yet the irony of the LAV III is that despite all the high-tech bells and whistles, the

commander and gunner must often be exposed from the armpits up as they pop out of the top of the turret hatch in order to
do their jobs.

Because of this requirement and the FOO's need to be always
at the front of the battlefield, it's long been considered one of
the most dangerous jobs in one of the most dangerous units of
the military. The job itself, however, often consists of long
stretches of waiting punctuated by short bursts of activity. It's
not about constantly moving parts, like the gun position officer's
job, but about monitoring. "You're painting the military picture,
so people can really see what it is," says Reiffenstein. "You have
to be very careful in your words."

"This is boring," Nich told her boss. "The shooting's fun,
but when you're not actually shooting, it's really boring."
Reiffenstein—who cautioned that "it won't be boring when
people are shooting at you for real"—suggested Nich come up
with word games to play with her FOO team, which usually consisted of five soldiers in total, or find topics of interest to discuss.
But she added a caution: "When you're not actually firing, you're
painting, working out scenarios. So when and if you do see it,
you can clearly explain it."

Despite her disappointment with some aspects of the FOO's
duties, Nich found the military life rewarding. She didn't mind
filling out paperwork, and quickly became known for her organ-
izational abilities. As to be expected, her favourite part of the job
involved going out in the field for training exercises, doing drills
and exercises outdoors, which sometimes included camping
with her fellow soldiers in the middle of winter. When she first
arrived at the regiment, she confided to Bryan Goutouski that
she wasn't sure. "I know I have a contractual agreement," she

told Bryan, a captain. "But how do I know this is the thing for me?" After her first year at CFB Shilo, something clicked. She reported back to Bryan that she loved working in the artillery unit, its intricacies challenging her mind; even the administration duties, which sometimes included the unenviable task of conducting disciplinary investigations, suited her strong personality and desire to lead. All her doubts, she said, had evaporated: "I'm totally committed." It was a sentiment many of her fellow artillery officers shared. Her friend Andrew Charchuk thought it was "the best job in the army, the epitome of what combat arms are all about."

Soldiers of all ranks were steadfast in their loyalty to Nich: sometimes, as the saying goes, loyal to a fault. Reiffenstein found this out after giving her extra duties following an assignment that had not been performed to her tough standards. A procession of soldiers that included Sonny Hatton, who with his wife went camping with Nich and Jay on weekends, publicly protested. "It was like I'd taken the stuffing out of her teddy bear," says Reiffenstein. "You'd think I was the Queen of Mean." She didn't want to go soft on Nich, for fear of raising the gender issue. Reiffenstein knew well that even though times were changing, gender was still the elephant in the Canadian military room.

Nich found this out for herself. At one after-work social gathering, a private walked up behind her and, as she later angrily described to Jay, "gave me a big slap on the ass." She turned around and jacked him up, military slang for verbal discipline. "She tore him a new one, yelled at him in front of everyone," says Jay. Other women in her unit experienced worse. "When I first arrived, the infantry company sergeant major wouldn't even speak to me," says fellow officer Lisa Haveman, who came to Shilo a year after Nich. On one occasion, during a pep talk in front of hundreds of soldiers, a master warrant officer used a pejorative term for a delicate part of the female anatomy to refer to the enemy. "Oops, guess I can't say that, we have one here," he said, looking at Lisa, the lone female in the crowd. Her second-in-command moved to stand beside her as a show of support. "No one else said anything," she says. "I've had lots of warrant officers try to bully me. I've thought, Is this what they do to all new officers, or is it because I'm female?"

Nich learned quickly her gender was a Catch-22: if you want to be one of the guys, you'd better keep up. But if you screw up, the boom will come down harder on a female officer. Reiffenstein had assigned her a quick action, which means pretty much what it sounds like. "You go to a certain spot, have to spin the guns up, weigh the compass, get them all oriented," says Reiffenstein. "It should take fifteen minutes; she comes up two hours later, having a hell of a time." The day had been a comedy of errors; various equipment failed at inopportune moments. On top of that, Nich had taken bad advice from another soldier, and her guns weren't in proper position. "She comes and says, 'We're ready to fire, Ma'am, we're good to go.' I say 'Hey, Nich, turn around. Look at your guns, three are pointing this way, three are pointing another way.'" The task, to put it in military slang, went for an extraordinary dump—a fact that spread like wildfire around the base. "There were guys who did things much more egregious than that and you might hear a bit of 'hmm' and that's it," says Reiffenstein. "I bought her a drink at the end of that day. That was when I told her to stop smiling so much."

At other times, being female singled her out for preferential treatment, which Nich disliked even more. On one exercise out in the field that required overnighting under the stars, she was horrified to discover her men had set up a private area for her, and even unrolled her sleeping bag, or fart sack, as it's known by the soldiers. "I can roll my own sleeping bag, and sleep under the LAV just like the rest of you," she said calmly but firmly. It didn't matter that she could march for hours with 100 pounds of kit on her back, that she was a highly competent officer; no matter that the unsentimental Major Anne Reiffenstein told her she'd never get a better gun position officer. These soldiers still felt they had to look after her, which caused Nich grave concern. She was supposed to be a leader, damn it, not some Cleopatra type that needed to be transported on a litter hoisted by the men she outranked.

While, for the most part, Nich managed to fit in with her fellow soldiers, it was always clear where her true loyalties lay. On the occasion of her twenty-third birthday, she went straight to the mess after a day in the field and put two hundred dollars down at the bar to buy drinks for her crew. She waited for Jay to join the party, but he was nowhere to be found. That morning, he'd gone to the doctor's in Winnipeg after "feeling sick as a dog" the night before. He had been diagnosed with appendicitis, and was admitted immediatley to St. Boniface General Hospital. No one had thought to inform Nich. "She spent her birthday calling all the hospitals trying to find me," says Jay. Once she found him, another officer lent her his car, and she sped to the city. When Jay came out of the anaesthesia later that night, his worried wife was at his side. "She ended up missing the celebrations at the mess, and didn't even get to enjoy any of the money she put down on the bar."

Seeing a bit of herself in Nich, Reiffenstein occasionally

allowed the younger officer a glimpse past the granite wall behind which she concealed her private self. It was only natural, after all the coffee breaks they had spent around a bowl filled with Gummi Bears and Nich's favourite, licorice, when she would regale the gathered officers with Jay's antics and those of their dogs Bill and Sam. "Nichola was such an expressive person, you'd have tears running down your eyes by the time she was finished telling her stories," says Reiffenstein.

One summer, she and Nich sat beside one another on a flight to the interior of British Columbia, where they'd been dispatched to fight forest fires. Reiffenstein's soldier husband John was on a tour in Bosnia, and she'd left her two young daughters in the care of relatives. She'd had only about thirty-six hours to mobilize herself and 135 other Shilo soldiers, and she slumped into her airplane seat feeling physically and emotionally spent. She confided that she felt like a lousy mother to just up and leave her two children like that. Nich told her about her parents' travels, and how they were often away on missions to help others. "I was fine with it until I was about twelve," she told Reiffenstein. "In my younger years I hardly even noticed." Nich confessed to her boss that she was excited about the firefighting, but upset it meant not being able to fill in for Andrew Nicholson, who was away on phase training, at Liane's prenatal classes. Reiffenstein looked at the bright, funny and articulate officer who'd pulled off the miraculous feat of winning the hearts of both the military wives and the crustiest of soldiers. God, she's well adjusted, she thought to herself.

While his wife's military career was just revving up, Jay's was in the process of winding down. He'd come to the gradual acceptance that his inability to fulfil the Canadian Forces' universality of service, or "Soldier First" requirement, meant the career he'd begun planning as a twelve-year-old cadet was not to be. In November, he received his medical release from the Canadian Forces. While the pair discussed the possibility of a lifetime military career for Nich—which might still include a stint back at RMC to pursue a master's in English—she also told him they'd be fine until he figured out his next step. They'd survive quite nicely on her paycheque, Nich assured him, while he continued his schooling in computer science. "I was going to be an army wife," says Jay. "And we were both okay with it. I was even starting to come around to us having kids down the road, especially seeing all our friends starting to have families. But there was still so much we wanted to do together." Though he had yet to commit to being a stay-at-home dad, the good-humoured husband even dropped by the wives' crafts nights, while Nich attended officers' nights.

Not long after that conversation, on a beautiful spring day in 2005, Jay Beam's confident wife strode into a building at CFB Shilo and plunked herself down in a chair before her peers. As each piece of long brown hair fell to the floor, the crowd roared its approval. The young woman who, only three short years earlier, had cowered in her PMQ duplex on her first day, was now sitting at the top of this male-dominated world. She had won respect and admiration for being just as good, and often better, than her male counterparts. After she happily surrendered her vanity to the cutting-room floor, Nich showed up that night at a party, dressed in a black halter dress and wearing big hoop earrings. She flashed her unforgettable wide-mouthed grin as she told partygoers how much easier it would be getting ready for work in the morning. "No more buns or hair clips for the next while," she said as she sipped on her favourite gin and tonic and was treated to a line-up of friends wanting to rub her down-to-the-wood cranium.

A few days later, Sergeant Dave Redford was walking across one of the hangars when he noticed a petite bald woman walking towards him. "Who in the hell is that?" he said to the soldier next to him. "Let's not go that way, it looks like she's sick or something." Despite living and working on the same base the past couple of years, Dave and Nich had barely crossed paths. The thirty-eight-year-old hulk of a career soldier who didn't have much use for officers "and their fancy three-dollar words" couldn't have known that he'd just walked by the very officer who would soon make him eat his words—and become his most trusted ally and friend in the sweltering heat of a desolate place on the other side of the planet.

EIGHT

"We're Going to Kandahar!"

"The Coalition may have all the watches, but we have all the time."

— *well-known Taliban saying*

WHEN SHE LANDED IN WAINWRIGHT, ALBERTA, for war training in the fall of 2005, Captain Nich Goddard was ready and raring to go. She was in the best physical shape of her life and, thanks to the tutelage of Major Anne Reiffenstein, confident in her officer abilities. Like the other soldiers, she was looking forward to putting her skills to the test. Along with her fellow artillery officers, she was excited about the arrival of the M777 155-mm howitzers, the ultra-lightweight gun the Canadian Forces had just purchased from the U.S. Marine Corps, said to be capable of delivering up to five rounds a minute during intense firing.

Her new boss wasn't quite prepared for the sight of the diminutive young woman in a buzz cut, and her second-in-command (21C), a hulking bear of a sergeant more than a decade her senior. "This is an odd pairing," Major Bill Fletcher chuckled to himself as the two strode into his office at the Canadian Manoeuvre Training Centre—despite no official announcement, everyone understood that the site was to be the training ground for an upcoming deployment to Afghanistan—and introduced themselves. The major, though, was the last man to judge a book by its cover, especially when it came to assessing a soldier's worth.

He himself had been picked by Lieutenant-Colonel Ian Hope over officers of higher seniority. Fletcher, a thirty-four-year-old graduate of RMC, wasn't considered a "fast mover," but Hope, like other senior officers in the Canadian Forces, saw something special in Fletcher. He had that rare combination of book smarts, street smarts and warrior aggression. His soldiers respected his mettle when he personally led his company on attacks during training exercises, rather than command from the sidelines. The self-described "army brat" son of a logistics officer in the Canadian Airborne Regiment had earned the respect of Hope, the commanding officer of the Edmonton-based 1st Battalion of Princess Patricia's Canadian Light Infantry, after working the previous year as his adjutant, or right-hand man. Though he couldn't officially confirm it then to his soldiers, Hope knew the unit was up next for an overseas deployment, involving a new mission to Kandahar, Afghanistan. He chose the whip-smart athlete to be Officer Commanding (OC) of Charlie Company, one of three infantry companies within Task Force Orion—Hope's name for the amalgam of soldiers heading out on the upcoming tour. Orion was named for the constellation representing the mythical Greek hunter of mountain beasts. By choosing the name, the lieutenant-colonel hoped to kick-start the bonding process among the soldiers before their boots hit the ground in Afghanistan. Hope also chose it, he would later tell his soldiers, so that when they looked up into the sky and saw that constellation, they might "feel part of a larger entity, enduring and meaningful." By the year's end, Hope and Fletcher would be two of the key leaders in charge of more than 1,000 soldiers in the combined team of infantry, artillery, armoured troops and combat engineers that made up Task Force Orion.

For any soldier still unsure of the reason for the gathering of this particular battalion in Wainwright, the country's Chief of Defence Staff General Rick Hillier offered up more than a few hints. Days after terrorists targeted Britain's public-transit system, Hillier announced the deployment of 2,000 troops to Afghanistan over the coming year. For months, there had been talk within the forces about a beefed-up presence in the turbulent southern region of the country, and Hillier's hard-hitting announcement confirmed as much, and then some. In a speech that called up memories of the Allied forces' fight against Nazi Germany sixty years earlier, he referred to the Taliban regime and the supporters of al Qaeda as "detestable murderers and scumbags," who "detest our freedoms, they detest our society, they detest our liberties." And, to ensure the entire country was fully aware that this faraway conflict required something more than Canada's blue-beret-wearing peacekeeping role, he added: "We're not the public service of Canada, we're not just another department. We are the Canadian Forces, and our job is to be able to kill people." The general's tough talk was met with praise by the editorial boards of the country's two national newspapers, *The National Post* and the *Globe and Mail*, although some were clearly alarmed, including Maude Barlow of the Council of Canadians, who decried the comments as "very aggressive." Even those with an insider's knowledge of the country's military were surprised by the rhetoric. Lieutenant-General Richard Evraire (ret'd), chairman of the Conference of Defence Associations, told the *Globe and Mail*: "I don't remember anyone else speaking like that. I think it's time to say things like they are."

Canada had been directed by NATO to take immediate command of a multinational brigade that also included American, Dutch and British coalition forces. They were to replace an all-American brigade in southern Afghanistan, as the United States looked to reduce its 19,000 troops in the country by as much as 20 per cent. This would be more than just a case of good guys with guns battling the bad guys. The Canadians would also run the Kandahar Provincial Reconstruction Team (PRT), from August 2005 to August 2006. Task Force Orion would be a part of this multinational brigade, its mission to set the conditions that would facilitate the transition from American to NATO control of southern Afghanistan.

The PRT base was a half-hour down the road from the massive coalition base that would come to be known as KAF—Kandahar Airfield. It comprised a mix of military and civilian representatives with a mandate to combine military security with civilian development and governmental aid provided by the Department of Foreign Affairs and International Trade (DFAIT), the CIDA, the Royal Canadian Mounted Police (RCMP) and the U.S. Agency for International Development (USAID). The initiative would come to be known as Canada's 3D approach to Afghanistan—defence, development and diplomacy.

Between August 2005 and February 2006, three distinct deployments of Canadians would head to Kandahar, Afghanistan's second-largest urban centre, strategically situated on major South and Central Asian trade routes. The first was the PRT, established in August 2005; the second was Hope's Task Force Orion, which would begin arriving in January 2006; the third was the Canadian-led multinational brigade headquarters. At the time, it was believed that approximately 200 Taliban insurgents were operating in the remote rural areas in Kandahar Province, with a very small number in areas surrounding the city. All intelligence was telling them that the "dushman"—the Pashto word for enemy—would repeat their habit of massing forces in the mountains of Shawali-Kot, and attempt ambush and improvised explosive devices (IED) attacks towards Kandahar City. In fact, they were already beginning to mass in the central part of the province, in the Panjwayi and Southern Zhari districts.

What Canadian intelligence officers didn't know was that before the troops' arrival, a commander by the name of Mullah Dadullah Akhund had convened a meeting of Taliban leaders in neighbouring Pakistan. In his book *Contact Charlie: The Canadian Army, the Taliban, and the Battle for Afghanistan*, author Chris Wattie detailed Dadullah's meeting, which centred around those thousand Canadians about to arrive in Kandahar Province. The Taliban commander was a close associate of Mullah Omar, and was infamous for overseeing a beheading binge of mostly women and children while fighting Hazaras in Bamiyan Province. Dadullah, having lost his left leg to a landmine during the Soviet pullout more than a decade earlier, wore his war wounds with pride. In 2005, the attention-loving fighter—known for offering videos of beheadings to major news agencies and conducting media interviews without concealing his identity—proposed a major surge of guerrilla warfare that included suicide bombers, IEDs and ambushes around Kandahar City. His proposal aimed at nothing less than capturing Kandahar, along with another goal: to inflict devastation on the soldiers of a country he knew was divided about its involvement in Afghanistan, and whose "fighters are good but politicians are weak." Dadullah wanted to create an uproar on the other side of the world. At the meeting's end, wrote Wattie, "Dadullah was sent to begin raising a small army in the Madrassas (Islamic religious schools) along the Pakistan-Afghan border."

Back home in Canada, with the mixture of optimism and wariness befitting his rank, Hope was busy putting together the team that would lead Task Force Orion. In his quarter century of military service, the forty-three-year-old son of an artillery NCO had spent time in both the infantry and airborne battalions of the Canadian and British armies, and had served overseas in Western Europe, the Balkans and Africa. He held two master's degrees in the areas of military and strategic studies, was plowing through a PhD in history and had spent time working as a strategic planner for the United States European Command in Stuttgart, Germany. Already making a name for himself in NATO circles as a leading military intellectual, Hope was familiar with Afghanistan, having worked there as a strategic planner in co-operation with Ashraf Ghani, the country's minister of finance. Hope's philosophy was that his large combat unit would be a powerful extension of the PRT, patrolling across all of Kandahar Province, and into adjacent provinces, in order to help PRT personnel connect with villages across the south. But he also knew that the men and women of Task Force Orion would be doing a whole lot more than patrolling crowded streets in LAVs and G-Wagons (light utility vehicles), and searching suspicious civilians for weapons. It was his strong conviction that their job was also to hunt down and kill or capture Taliban fighters, and there was no telling how heated that task might become. He planned for the worst case.

Still, Hope felt good about the skills and expertise of the more than 1,000 soldiers converging at CFB Wainwright, the base that was once home to a thousand interred Germans during World War II. He was also glad to have on hand the LAV III, the vehicle tailor-made for Afghanistan's rough terrain, with an imposing presence that would give his soldiers a psychological edge over the enemy.

By the time training was in full swing, Major Steve Gallagher had joined Fletcher as one of the sub-unit commanders reporting to Hope. Gallagher had recently taken over from Major Anne Reiffenstein as battery commander of Shilo's A Battery. Battery Sergeant Major Paul Parsons, considered "irreplaceable" by his superiors, assisted Gallagher in his command. The Battery comprised over 100 gunners, some of whom served the Battery's four new M777 155-mm artillery howitzers, and others who were allocated to serve as forward observation parties with each of Task Force Orion's infantry companies. One of these infantry companies was the Shilo-based B Company of the 2nd Battalion of the Patricias, requested by Hope to augment his 1st Battalion in order to help make up a shortfall. The Edmonton-based battalion had one of its three rifle companies already on tour in Afghanistan, and wouldn't be available to redeploy into Afghanistan in 2006. Gallagher knew the B Company soldiers well. His main task now was to prepare his battery to work with the Edmonton-based soldiers, with whom he was not so familiar. It was especially important for the forward observation officers— Captain Nich Goddard among them—to learn to work with the Edmonton soldiers. Nich had trained with Hope's 1st Battalion the year before when they came to Shilo for exercises, and was known by them. Nich's FOO party, Gallagher's Battery, B Company 2 PPCLI and soldiers from a platoon of military police and members of the 12ss Régiment blindé du Canada based out of Valcartier, Quebec, would all join the Edmonton soldiers in training, and later, in Afghanistan.

Like Fletcher, Gallagher wasn't the most obvious choice to those senior officers who looked upon the mission as a way of helping people's careers, but Hope believed otherwise. He had respected Gallagher from the first moment they met, sensing him to be an officer who encouraged initiative among his troops, telling them, "I'm not going to make you run ten miles for the heck of it—let's train the way we're going to fight." This was the kind of enlightened man needed to fight in this new, uncharted battle, thought Hope. The fact that Gallagher had already worked closely with many of the artillery soldiers was another big selling point. Gallagher pulled no punches when it came to his frustration over the limitations imposed on his team by those at much higher levels in the Canadian Forces. "I was only permitted to take four howitzers overseas," he says. "We were capped at a hundred people, which had no bearing on the operation and what we were expected to do . . . it didn't make a whole lot of sense." Understanding that his job was to make do with what he was given, he created three FOO parties—Nich Goddard led one, while her friends Bob Meade and Mike Smith headed up the other two—naming them Golf 11, Golf 12 and Golf 13—"Golf" being a standard radio indicator or call sign, with the G signifying "guns," or artillery arm. They were then parcelled out to the companies in the battalion. Nich's FOO team was assigned to C, or Charlie, Company, with the call sign Golf 13 (pronounced Golf One Three).

Hope knew that throwing together troops who were strangers to one another could breed dissent and disorganization. His number-one goal, then, was to get the various components interacting with one another as much as possible. He wanted to see strenuous, large-scale, live-fire exercises that forced all ranks and trades to support one another in high-pressure situations. Unfortunately, the way the training events were set up by the higher echelons in the Canadian Forces led to what Hope called "a bunch of coincidental incidents that denied us from having the training venue" required for combined testing. This meant that the Edmonton-based soldiers didn't have the opportunity to acclimatize to direct firing of artillery close to them: a dangerous, sophisticated cooperation between infantry and artillery that, when done right, is highly effective on the battlefield. It was a skill they'd need in the unique Afghan terrain, where the land and village structure often meant the enemy would fire at Canadians from very close range, yet would not always be visible. This in turn placed a premium upon skills that would have infantry soldiers stay within 100 metres of the enemy while artillery forward observation parties would "walk" Canadian artillery fire onto the enemy only a short distance from the infantry. In these conditions, dropping artillery shells on the enemy without hitting your own soldiers takes practice. Yet at no time during the pre-deployment training was live artillery allowed to fire in direct support of infantry soldiers, even at safe distances of 1,000 metres. Hope, Fletcher and Gallagher became increasingly frustrated over not being able to validate this essential skill and raise mutual confidence between infantry and artillery soldiers. This also meant that during the training phase, Hope didn't get a chance to see Nich Goddard or the other FOO team members in action. With frustration still evident in his voice, he confesses, "I did not know her technical competencies, or [that of] any of the other artillery officers. I did not know what this battery could do."

The soldiers under Steve Gallagher's command were put through their paces in exercises both familiar and novel. Shooting on rifle ranges was combined with training in blocking intersections with a vehicle convoy; they were instructed in how to search someone for weapons. "Who has the gun pointed, who does the searching? These are things artillery soldiers don't normally do, but we had to know these things," says Gallagher, who couldn't help being unnerved over the fact that the first chance his soldiers would get to handle the M777 howitzers would be when they landed at KAF. Reflecting on the bad timing, Gallagher thought that "we're going to have a significant learning curve when we get to Afghanistan"; he was also worried about not being able to send Nich or Dave Redford to Gagetown for the ten-week Forward Air Control Course, which would have certified them to be forward air controllers (FACS), capable of calling in aircraft fire. Once in Afghanistan, all they would be able to do was radio someone higher up in the chain of command and relay the grid coordinates. His only consolation was, having seen them in action in training exercises at CFB Shilo, he knew that "Nich and the other observers were good at it."

It was important to Gallagher that he equip his soldiers with not only technical expertise, but also psychological know-how. Earlier that year, another battalion at Shilo had paid for David Grossman, a retired U.S. Army lieutenant colonel whose books

On Combat and *On Killing* are two military must-reads, to come to the base and share his knowledge. Gallagher pulled some last-minute strings so the men and women preparing to leave for the next Afghanistan deployment could sit in. Nich was in the crowd that day, listening intently to Grossman's advice on training for war like an athlete, through constant repetition and a mastery of basic skills. Grossman reassured the soldiers that not wanting to kill was normal, not cowardly. He instructed them in the surprising effects of "combat high," which can lead a soldier to burst into laughter in the midst of battle, a strangely euphoric experience that is "very intense, if you live to tell about it." He warned them about experiencing tunnel vision on the battlefield and described how, during combat, soldiers often lose control of a host of bodily functions, including their bowels. He walked them through the after-effects of killing an enemy combatant, which paralleled the stages of grief made famous by Swiss psychiatrist Elisabeth Kübler-Ross. After the lecture, Bob Meade and Nich talked about how glad they were to get some tips on how to stay calm in a combat situation, even if Grossman tended to be a bit dramatic. "It seemed there were times he would wait for us to say 'hoo-ah,'" said Nich. "But we're Canadians," replied Bob with a smile, "so of course we don't do that."

During that training phase, Bill Fletcher started to get to know the FOOS who'd be supporting his infantry, and Nich Goddard quickly caught his attention. On the battlefield, the FOO, commanding his or her own LAV, would move in close proximity to the OC, waiting for the OC's go-ahead to let them move into a position of observation. Fletcher, who quickly became familiar with Nich's proactive, gutsy and independent style, realized the conventional war scenario left Nich's talents "being wasted with this approach." Since it was "physically impossible to tell Nich to stay anywhere near the rear," he let her move forward with his advance elements whenever possible, assisting in finding the enemy, then coordinating the artillery to fix them in place—providing Fletcher the ability to manoeuvre his forces to, as he described, "destroy the enemy."

"She loves to range out on her own, push forward to get her eyes on the bad guys," Fletcher told Hope, who agreed such initiative bode well for the upcoming tour. "She's incredibly effective at finding them and keeping them in sight." Working with Fletcher, Nich would come up with a plan to bring down indirect fire to support his infantry; while he too was concerned that she didn't have her FAC training, Fletcher felt assured of Nich's abilities to protect the soldiers' flanks and support whatever plan he came up with. During one training exercise that was observed by a group of generals, Fletcher called in Canadian fighters in CF-18s to do a bombing run at a distance. As he watched Nich bring in live fire in front of the whole company—"real bullets at a minimum safe distance"—Fletcher was impressed. She was coordinating the artillery, and she controlled the planes and suppressed the attack by talking through an actual forward air controller. For the first time, Fletcher thought, Maybe I don't need a FAC after all. When the company simulated a big-battalion-level attack, Nich volunteered her crew to go forward very close to the enemy positions to set up an all-night watch, rotating between them to keep eyes on the enemy. She was, he noted appreciatively, "always the first to volunteer."

Knowing that their training hadn't provided enough opportunities to foster a feeling of team spirit among these soldiers from dozens of different trades and units, Hope resorted to the old tried-and-true method of throwing a party. The pinnacle social event was the smoker, a big bash held in a field near the Wainwright training area the night after the soldiers' last day of training exercises. They were given two beers each and all the barbecued meat they could stuff down their gullets. At one point in the party, Hope climbed up on a stack of wood and, to a chorus of cheers, yelled out the official confirmation of what everyone had already taken as a given: "We're going to Kandahar!" He acknowledged that there were still training shortfalls, but promised to make them up. The next day, Hope and his commanders left for a recce mission to Kandahar.

The late 2005 visit to Afghanistan convinced Hope, Fletcher and Gallagher that further training was required in both the battery and the combined arms, the coordination between infantry and artillery. Hope decided that the "few questions still in my head" might be answered by an earlier deployment for what he called "on-the-job" training. When he received formal permission for this plan, the troops were informed that they'd be heading out in batches sooner than scheduled. Nich and the 100 soldiers of Shilo had their leave dates pushed up from mid-February to late January. Their next training ground would be in the dusty fields of Afghanistan, a country that was accustomed to foreigners—"ferrenghi" in Pashto—wearing camouflage and carrying high-tech guns.

NINE

"Until Our Paths Cross Again"

AT THE SAME TIME his daughter was preparing for war and being briefed in how she might feel in the likely event she killed some-one, Tim Goddard was learning his own lessons about warrior culture. For the past five years, the Kosovo project had taken him numerous times to the once-war-torn territory. He was now well versed in just how time consuming the simple act of meeting a new teacher could be. The introductions usually began with such statements as, "We are the Illyria, we were here before the Romans," before the teller proceeded to offer a detailed history of their country up to the present day. Meanwhile, the work of his team and its focus on empowering educators in their country's rebuilding had caught the attention of others. The University of Calgary was invited to form a partnership with Collège Boréal (Sudbury) and TEAM International (Beirut) to bid on a World Bank project to design and deliver an educational-leadership program in Lebanon. The bid was successful, and in 2005 Tim went to Beirut. Here, in the aftermath of another conflict, he worked to establish a leadership training program, which even-tually reached 450 principals. Of these, forty were designated as "master trainers" who could then deliver the program to other principals. His experiences there and in Kosovo made Tim feel passionate about the need for security to "come from within, from the people themselves," a sentiment he shared with Nich whenever they engaged in their regular debates.

A month before Christmas of 2005, Nich returned from her war training in Wainwright and sat down for a new military photo. It was purportedly for the euphemistic "official purposes," but the soldiers knew it would be given to the media in the event of their death. Seven Canadian soldiers had died in Afghanistan since 2002, a number not out of sync with recent peacekeeping missions—in the Balkans alone, during the 1990s, Canada suffered 11 fatalities and 102 wounded. Speaking before the Canadian Club in Ottawa two months earlier, federal defence minister Bill Graham had pledged that the country's soldiers would soon win over Afghan citizens and bring stability to the region as "warrior diplomats." They would become the "face of Canada for the people of Kandahar," and "the positive image of our country that they will generate will contribute to the great reputation that we Canadians benefit from around the world."

Nich put the finishing touches on her will, and made sure her military life insurance was up to date. Then she picked up the telephone for the last of her "in-case-I-don't-come-back" calls. She'd been making her way through her list since the summer, doing them only when she felt up to the task. One of her most difficult had been to Krista in Antigonish a few months earlier. She let her best friend know she was making the call as per military protocol. It wasn't the tear-filled conversation Nich was expecting. "That seems almost callous of them to make you do that," said Krista. "I'm sorry, there's not a chance anything will happen to you." Nich was adamant. "No, we need to talk about this, because it's something that could happen." Krista, who was back home for the funeral of her uncle, was in no mood to entertain such a possibility. "I can't even believe you'd think that; it's not going to happen and that's it."

After everyone's name on her call list had finally been checked off, Nich phoned Liane Nicholson. Andrew and Liane had recently moved off the Packway and into nearby Brandon when their daughter, Emma, the first baby from their Packway gang, was born. "It's now or never," she told Liane, who knew exactly what she meant. The day had come to realize the pair's long-standing plan to get tattoos. Liane wasn't sure she herself could go through with it, but she accompanied Andrew and Nich, hoping to screw up her courage on the two-hour drive to Winnipeg. Nich had refused to go to nearby Brandon for the tattoo. "If I chicken out," she explained to Liane, "everybody will know."

Fat Phil welcomed the trio into his tattoo parlour. Andrew went first, getting a maple leaf on his chest, to wear over his heart while in Afghanistan. Nich handed the tattoo artist an image of a dove holding an olive branch with a maple leaf, and told him she wanted it on her left shoulder. When she returned from Afghanistan, she said, she'd come back so he could put a heart on her hip. Liane didn't chicken out, either. She chose a treble clef on the small of her back, a nod to her university degree in music education.

Nich also fired off an email to Michael Hurley, her former English professor at Royal Military College. "I need wolf's eyes like Atwood," she wrote, reminding him of their animated conversations four years earlier. "How do the Afghans see their land?" Michael suggested she read *The Swallows of Kabul*, a novel by Yasmina Khadra that follows the lives of four Afghans as they struggle to live under Taliban rule while still keeping true to their own beliefs; *A Bed of Red Flowers* by Nelofer Pazira, the true story of a young Afghan girl who joins the resistance movement, distributes contraband books and studies guerrilla warfare; and *An Unexpected Light*, a non-fiction account by Jason Elliot of one British man's experience of fighting side by side with the mujahideen against the Soviets and his later explorations through the countryside.

Nich didn't need to offer any formal farewells to Major Anne Reiffenstein; as a fellow soldier, she would likely have recoiled at anything that smacked of being touchy-feely. Besides, Nich had already covered that off when her boss left Shilo in the summer of 2005 for a new posting, feeling "ripped off" that she wasn't going to Afghanistan. Nich dropped by as she was packing and handed her a copy of *Anne of Green Gables*, which had a long inscription in the front. "Don't read it right now," Nich cautioned her. "It's got the 'Ya Ya Sisterhood' stuff in there." When she settled back in Ontario, Reiffenstein finally opened the book.

> *Ma'am,*
>
> *As one can never have too many books, I wanted to share Anne Shirley's story with you. Anne Shirley is an orphan who spends the majority of her life being moved between foster homes and generally trying to fit in. She is constantly accused of "not being a boy!" Anne makes no apologies about her behaviour and mixes tomboy stunts with purely feminine concerns about her hair (red!) and nose (long!). Throughout the whole story, Anne only once regrets that she was not a boy. At that time, Matthew says, "I'd rather have you than a dozen boys" (page 282). Anne has earned her place and proven her worth to all she has met.*

I wanted to give you this story to thank you for all the guidance and professional development that you have given me. You have allowed me to develop my leadership abilities while being proud of my gender. You have caused me to view being a woman as an asset — not a detriment to the team or to my profession.

I can only hope to inspire other women to persevere and take pride in their accomplishments as you have for me. Thank you.

Nichola

A week before Christmas, Nich and Jay flew to grandmother Betty's home in the charming seaside village of Llangwnnadl, Wales, where they met up with Sally, Tim, Victoria and Kate, along with Tim's brothers and their families. Betty had retired there in 1990 with her husband, and had stayed on in the tranquil place after Tony's death in 1996. She was thrilled to have her family together once more even if it was a tense time, with her granddaughter just about to head off to Afghanistan. But Nich wasn't going to let a war spoil the fun. She hauled across the Atlantic a giant, 40-pound inflatable snowman, proudly plunking it down on her grandmother's front yard. She talked about what she and Jay would be doing several months down the line, when she'd be safely back on Canadian soil. She's trying her best not to panic us, thought Victoria, who asked her sister to bring her back "a really great rock" from Afghanistan. "You know what I'm really scared of, Tory?" she told Victoria with a laugh. "Spiders and scorpions." On Boxing Day, Jay and Nich participated in a polar bear swim for charity, dipping their bodies into the frozen waters off Aberdaron beach not far from Betty's home. It was the first time Nich had revealed to her family her new tattoo, perched on her left shoulder. At first, her dad thought it was only temporary: she had got one of those back in high school, pretending to pass it off as permanent, Sally remembered, "just to wind Tim up."

Nich reserved her last evening in Wales to finally address the one thing on everyone's mind. Pulling out an atlas and opening it on Betty's dining table after dinner, she explained to her relatives the mission she was about to embark on. It made Sally more nervous than ever. This sounds more like a briefing, she thought. With the map spread out before them, Tim compared her mission to the work he was doing in Kosovo and Lebanon. In typically passionate Goddard style, Nichola insisted to her father that civil society often needed military force in order to rebuild. Tim disagreed, arguing that education was the key to development for the marginalized, the poor and the oppressed; that it was by supporting teachers and other community workers that people like him could help them achieve their own emancipation. "You can't do that when the bad guys run things, Dad," Nich said calmly but firmly. "They just shoot you. You have to have peace and good government in order for the rest to happen. I do what I do, so you can do what you do." For once, her father was rendered speechless. Nichola won the argument, at least this time.

■ ■ ■

Upon her return to Canada, Nich continued her "See you later" rounds, refusing to shed tears or indulge in any similarly maudlin show of emotion. She was pumped about the prospect of putting all her years of training to work. On New Year's Eve, she and the two Andrews—Nicholson was off to Afghanistan the next week as a gunner, while Charchuk was the designated replacement FOO for the tour—talked with excitement while their concerned spouses tried to change the subject. A week later, Nich was on a plane to Sault Ste. Marie, to spend a weekend with her maternal grandparents. Michael West sat her down in his living room and told her a story he hadn't repeated in sixty years. He shared with his first grandchild some of the horrors he had experienced firsthand as an army medic during the Battle of Monte Cassino, a series of World War II battles in 1944 described by historians as the "Italian Bloodbath." The town's 1,400-year-old Benedictine monastery had been blown up, and a quarter of a million soldiers—Allied forces from America, England, Canada and New Zealand, along with the German Wehrmacht— perished. Of all the atrocities Michael witnessed, one stood out in his mind. As locals feted the victorious Allies, a girl of no more than twelve ran to the nearest pump to get water for the soldiers. "It blew her arm right off," Michael told Nich. "The damn Germans, they left booby traps everywhere." He wasn't trying to terrify his granddaughter. He wanted her to head to Afghanistan aware of what she would likely encounter.

When Nich arrived home from Ontario, she and Jay jumped in their brand-new copper-coloured Nissan Murano and headed west for one final family farewell. Before they left, she called the Goutouski house. "What are you doing on the eleventh of January?" she asked. Bryan, who with wife Gundy had moved earlier that year to CFB Cold Lake, told her they didn't have anything on the go. "Okay, we're coming over," she cheerily reported. "She's calling us from Shilo, and we're in this place three hours north of Edmonton," Gundy told Bryan with a laugh. "She's acting like she's a half hour down the road."

Nich and Jay arrived at Bryan and Gundy's in a celebratory mood. The four friends sat around a raclette of Swiss cheese and potatoes, talking animatedly about life after Afghanistan and Nich's upcoming post at the Canadian Manoeuvre Training Centre in Wainwright, where, once she returned from Afghanistan, she would be posted as an operations officer. They were going to stop in on their way to Calgary and case out some neighbourhoods where they might purchase their first home next summer. Gundy was thrilled that her young friend would be less than four hours' drive away, a distance Nich considered a stone's throw. "We hope you'll invite us to your changes of command," said Bryan, referring to the official ceremonies when an officer moves up to a higher rank. He was certain, as was Nich, that a promotion to major was in her imminent future. "Oh yeah, I'll get them. And you'll be invited." The next morning, Nich and Bryan rose early to go for a swim at a nearby recreation centre. She gave Bryan a kiss on the cheek. That's pretty unusual for Nich, Bryan thought. She isn't the mushy type. After she left, Gundy found a note that read simply: "Until Our Paths Cross Again."

The last stop on the whirlwind western tour would be Calgary, where Nich insisted on a happy family visit devoid of war discussion and filled with the revelry of her mother's fifty-fourth birthday. That night, Sally prepared her eldest daughter's favourite roast beef and Yorkshire pudding; afterwards they played the family's infamous Bucket Game, where names of famous people are thrown into a bucket and players offer their teams clues as to their identity. "You're not coming to the Crying

Room," she told her parents, referring to the big send-off at Shilo that would be attended by media and hundreds of others. "Take care, and stay safe," Sally said as she embraced Nich and inhaled her familiar scent. It always reminded Sally of the outdoors, "like clean sheets drying on a clothes line." As they parted, Nich looked at her mother one last time and said, "Don't worry about me." After they left to head back to Shilo, Sally noticed her usually fastidious daughter hadn't stripped her bed and thrown the sheets in the washer. She later found a handful of Nich's personal possessions strewn absent-mindedly in the bathroom, bedroom and hallway—the only hints that her tidy and conscientious daughter's mind was elsewhere.

Back home at Shilo, Nich spent the last week occupied with such military preparations as arranging her overseas kit. But she also made time for some pampering. She and Julianne booked afternoon appointments at Escape day spa in Brandon. Both had their eyebrows waxed; Julianne had a massage, while Nich chose the jet spa, where clients could dial up bubble speeds on a scale from thirty to sixty. Julianne emerged relaxed from her room to find Nich so doubled over in laughter she could barely speak. "I went for forty-eight," she told her. "When the jets came on, they shot me to the end of the pool."

Afterwards, the two friends went to a local mall. They picked out a cartful of items for Jay: sudoku and crossword-puzzle books, novels, miniature stuffed toys and several bags of candy. At Julianne's, they put the treats, along with hand-written love notes from Nich, in a dozen separate paper bags, with the understanding that Julianne would drop one off at Jay's for every week Nich was away in Afghanistan. Julianne read a couple of the notes, and was struck by how Nich was more worried about her husband suffering from loneliness than her own well-being. Her only concern about going to Afghanistan is leaving Jay, Julianne thought. And her biggest fear is making a wrong decision that would hurt someone.

The day before she left, Nich and Jay went for their daily walk in the field with the dogs. For the first time, she broached the subject of "what if." She told her husband she wanted to be cremated; she didn't want "a little shrine" somewhere. She also expressed that should anything happen to her, she wished only love and happiness for Jay. He should buy a nice little house with the life insurance, and think about one day having a family. "I want you to be sad, but not for long," she said matter-of-factly. "Then, you'll have to get over it and find someone else." Jay thought such talk was nothing more than abstract, but it still rattled him. Sensing his distress, Nich broke the tension with humour. She told him that of course he could remarry, as long as it wasn't to one particular woman she didn't like. The two burst out laughing, gave one another a big hug, then headed home.

On January 29, 2006, Jay drove Nich to the door of the base gymnasium where her fellow soldiers were saying goodbye to loved ones before they climbed aboard a plane that would take them to CFB Trenton, Ontario, the first leg of their long journey to Afghanistan. Jay stopped the car, but didn't turn off the engine. "Have fun. See you later," he said. She smiled and said, "Thanks. See you later." They didn't kiss or hug, and neither said, "I love you." It was what they'd agreed to the night before as she lay in her husband's arms one last time. Nich didn't want the men she led to see her becoming emotional; she wanted them to look to her for strength, as they would to a male officer. It was in keeping with all she had learned over those three and a half years at

Shilo, from the moment she first cowered in her empty house, to the day she boldly went bald in front of an audience. On that day, her performance entertained and impressed the boys. She hoped with every ounce of her being that she could be as confident when they entered a theatre of a wholly different kind.

PART III

BOOTS ON THE GROUND

TEN

Kandahar Honeymoon

"It's as if I have been studying for an exam for the last eight years. Finally, I get to write the test . . . some questions, I know the answers cold. Other questions, I will be the first one ever to answer."

— Nich to sister Victoria, March 9, 2006

FROM 30,000 FEET ABOVE THE GROUND, much of Afghanistan resembles the moon's lunar surface: a seemingly endless horizon of dull greys and browns, a desolate place that couldn't possibly be inhabitable. From lower altitudes, as one approaches Kandahar City, this country that is smaller than the state of Texas begins to reveal its stark beauty and natural diversity. A 20-kilometre belt of black volcanic rock to the north of Afghanistan's second-largest urban centre offers the first hint of the Hindu Kush mountain range in the distance; the Reg Desert and its scarlet sand dunes that blanket the compacted sand and rock dominate the south; dusty brown valleys, wadis (dried-out riverbeds) and mountains populate the east; and the relatively lush orchard-dotted terrain of the Panjwayi lies to the west, its irrigation districts fed by the Arghandab River winding along grape, wheat, opium-poppy and marijuana fields growing high enough to resemble a jungle forest.

As her plane dipped towards Kandahar Airfield just south of the city, Nich didn't get so much as a glimpse of the varied terrain below. The three-hour flight from the United Arab Emirates—the location of the base known as Camp Mirage, used as a pit stop for coalition forces both entering and leaving Afghanistan—only offered views of the soldiers sitting across from her, their legs almost intertwined in the cramped space allotted for passengers on the Hercules military aircraft. The bulk of the giant, well-worn transport plane was devoted to equipment both big and small; the human cargo, Nich discovered firsthand, was an afterthought. She knew their plane would be coming in tactical—a low-level form of flying that makes it harder for enemy fire to hit its target—and she knew it would feel much like a roller coaster. Her 21C, Sergeant Dave Redford, had one of the few views through a small porthole. His coveted spot turned out to be more a curse than a blessing. As the pilot dipped the plane's wings, Dave saw a blur of trees and camels whiz by. It's bad, but not as bad as what the Vomit Comet is supposed to be like, he thought, recalling what he'd heard of the famed ride into Kabul from Kandahar, while Nich thought of her childhood days flying into Pangnirtung in a propeller plane: "The Pang Screamer prepared me well." After four days of travel to arrive at their final destination, complete with a thirty-six-hour layover in Prestwick, Scotland, to repair the plane's fuel tank, Nich's biggest worry on the morning of February 1, 2006, was that one of the soldiers in her vicinity—some of whom had partied it up during the Scottish pit stop and were now nursing hangovers—might throw up on her. "You know how I've always had an issue with sympathetic vomiting," she'd later tell her mother on her first phone call home as the pair laughed over the scenario.

Focusing on everyone around her and working hard to stay awake after a few sleepless nights served to distract Nich from her bigger worries. After all of her studying and training, poring over books on artillery and honing her skills in the field, she had confessed in a letter to her mother her reservations during deployment training. Though she didn't like to use words like "killing," when talking to people like Sally or Krista it was clear she wasn't kidding herself as to the true nature of her role in Canada's first combat mission since the Korean War: "I am still wrestling with my conscience about doing this for real," she said in the letter. She was also terrified that a mistake on her part could mean injury or death for her men, a fear she frequently communicated to those closest to her.

On the flight to Scotland, she sat beside Dave and talked about wanting to see the countryside and how the people lived, and peppered him with questions about what to expect when out on patrols. "This isn't going to be a 'rub your shoulders with the natives' kind of tour," he reminded her, knowing they'd both heard time and again about the "new rules of engagement" reality on the ground. As she and Dave enjoyed the first long leg of their trip, Nich was excited and upbeat; she had faith in her country's promise to create the conditions needed to help Afghans get on their feet. It was a promise that Chief of Defence Staff Rick Hillier had done a good job of promoting to the public back home for this latest mission to Afghanistan, which the army had named Operation Archer. "At least as part of the Provincial Reconstruction Team," she wrote to her parents, "we will be enforcing the attempts on positive change and supporting the Afghan army . . ."

She agreed to a certain extent with the popular soldier's assertion that her primary task was not to be an expert in international relations; that was the job of her government. Hers was to be trained to the best of her ability as a soldier, to ably carry out the will of her country. But like her friend and fellow artillery officer Andrew Nicholson, with whom she discussed required reading like *The Bear Went Over the Mountain*, an examination of Soviet tactics in Afghanistan during its invasion in the 1980s, she approached everything in her life with a scholarly eye.

In those weeks leading up to her departure, her dad had made sure that Nich had done her homework, and that she kept thinking about her reasons for continuing to don the soldier's uniform. On several occasions, the pair had long phone chats, filled with academic debate on the merits of Canada's involvement in Afghanistan. Tim argued for the need to see democracy and civil society through Paulo Friere's notions of a pedagogy of the oppressed, through which people are helped to develop and experience a new awareness of self. Such an awareness, the South American educator argued, provides dignity and a sense of agency, the realization that "we were blind, now our eyes have been opened." People are empowered to make decisions that enrich their own lives, rather than simply be objects responding to events that occur around them. In response, Nich would quote scholar and historian Michael Ignatieff's book *Empire Lite*, and its contentions that "humanitarian action is only possible, in many instances, if imperial armies have first cleared the ground and made it safe for humanitarians to act"; and, "The Afghan people will never overcome the rule of the warlords and consolidate their own form of peaceful self-rule without a preliminary military occupation by foreign powers." She believed firmly in Ignatieff's assertion that the terrorism of 9/11 had "collapsed the saving distances" between the developed world and places like Afghanistan, and it was the West's obligation to help bring order to these once-remote nations. Tim, who often ended his letters with "Take care my girl" and "I'm so proud of you," wasn't trying to shake Nich's conviction in the task that lay ahead; constantly challenging his daughters' motivation and understanding of life's big picture came as naturally as reading to them from *The Hobbit*. This, Nich implicitly understood. In two separate notes over those first weeks, she encouraged her dad to "please continue to challenge me," and thanked him "for being on my side for twenty-five years or more!"

■ ■ ■

If there was ever a place in need of rebuilding, it was Afghanistan. The country of more than twenty-three million souls ranked a dismal 174th out of 178 countries on the United Nation's Human Development Index, which combines life expectancy, standard of living and education. Life here was brutal and short: 50 per cent of the population subsisted on less than two dollars a day, while 70 per cent lived in poverty and substandard conditions; 25 per cent of the population didn't have enough food to meet minimum daily needs. Life expectancy was around forty-two years, while 142 of every 1,000 babies born died before their first birthday. While the male literacy rate was a shocking 43 per cent, nearly 90 per cent of females couldn't write their own name. This, along with such infamous Taliban tactics as burning down schools and attacking female students and teachers, was an effective way of virtually obliterating half the country's population. It wasn't surprising to see why the opium trade, worth more than three billion dollars a year and Afghanistan's largest export, proved to be such a stumbling block for those trying to help Afghans help themselves. It was all too tempting for a farmer to grow these crops—the financial fuel of the Taliban—rather than take his chances on something far less profitable.

Once their plane touched down at KAF, Nich and her fellow soldiers—citizens of a country with a 99 per cent literacy rate and a life expectancy nearly double that of Afghans—would spend those first few days of February getting their footing on the rough soil of this unforgiving land. While they acclimatized themselves within the relatively safe confines of the base, the very foundation of their government's enlightened approach to Afghanistan was crumbling underneath them. Two weeks earlier, a roadside bomb had been detonated not far from the PRT's home—also known as Camp Nathan Smith—in a former factory on the outskirts of Kandahar City. The blast killed Canadian diplomat Glyn Berry and seriously injured three soldiers as they patrolled the area in a G-Wagon. The death of Berry, a man determined to undermine the opium drug-trafficking industry, along with the insurgents, as part of rebuilding the area, elicited near panic in the Department of Foreign Affairs and International Trade and the Canadian International Development Agency; both halted funding of the PRT for six months while it underwent a review. In his 2009 book, *A Soldier First: Bullets, Bureaucrats and the Politics of War*, General Rick Hillier wrote that the decision virtually eliminated the two latter elements of Canada's 3D approach—defence, diplomacy and development—and "set our operation in Kandahar back a minimum of two years." Hillier told the Privy Council Office, DFAIT and CIDA that "it was pointless for the military to be doing our mission unless they were holding up their end by helping to rebuild Afghan society." The 3D approach was now, wrote Hillier, "a farce, and we were on our own."

But on those four days of air travel from Canada to Afghanistan, the morale among the soldiers was at an all-time high. Many had spent several years training to fight; some had even been able to practise their skills in places like Bosnia. But this was a test like no other, and they all knew it. As they made their way from Winnipeg to Trenton, Ontario, to Scotland, Croatia and then the United Arab Emirates, they spoke animatedly to one another of the adventure ahead. Some even placed bets on which lucky FOO team, as Master Bombardier Jeff Fehr remembers, "would get the first bullet—call in the first artillery fire on enemy troops." It was exciting, this realization they were embarking on a mission so different from that of the past several decades. The last time Canadian troops had called fire in an offensive, rather than defensive, stance, had been in that country known to its inhabitants as "The Land of the Morning Calm." As part of the newly formed NATO, with its mandate to promote global peace and security, more than 26,000 Canadians began making their way to Korea in 1950, 7,000 of them serving in theatre—the military term for the geographical area in which armed combat takes place. Over the next three years, 1,558 Canadian soldiers joined the 490,000 NATO fatal and non-fatal battle casualties; 516 Canadian war dead were later inscribed in the Korean Book of Remembrance. They likely weren't much different from Nich and her fellow troops in at least one important aspect: they were young, fit and brimming with optimism.

The soldiers of Roto 1 of TF Orion, the name given to this first seven-month tour into Kandahar Province of 2006, had no idea just how heated it was going to become. Yet it was already considered a given that they were on the cusp of something new: Commanding Officer Ian Hope, who reported to Brigadier-General David Fraser, the commander of the multinational brigade in Afghanistan (south), had already made them aware, through his own words and those of the commanders below him, that they would be fighting a counter-insurgency war, something generations of Canadian Forces personnel had never experienced. In a counter-insurgency, he cautioned, there was no purely military victory, because it wasn't a conventional war against an enemy army. The best they could hope for was to keep the enemy off balance long enough for the Afghan National Security Forces (which includes the Afghan army, the army air corps and the Afghan National Police) to get on its feet, and for government and reconstruction reforms to be established.

Since Nich had yet to hear that Canada's much-touted integrated rebuilding effort was now on ice, there was little to dampen her enthusiasm as she stepped off the Herc just after 8:30 on the morning of February 1, 2006. She looked forward to settling in at KAF, a 16-kilometre-long camp housing 1,000 Canadians out of 7,000 troops from several nationalities, along with more than 5,000 civilians, many of them local Afghans getting paid US$1 a day to do such menial tasks as cleaning toilets and washing dishes. While Nich was initially shocked at the paltry pay, she soon discovered it was for a good reason: when the workers were paid three dollars a day, they'd be shot and killed after work by other unemployed Afghans, who would then come in and ask about the new "job opening."

That very first day at KAF—a place described by some new arrivals as resembling a small Alberta frontier town that had just struck oil, thanks to its sea of mobile trailers, gravel and dirt roads—Nich began chronicling her experiences and observations on her laptop, that high-tech North American necessity that represented more than the annual salary of an average Afghan. The exercise would become a daily ritual when she wasn't "outside the wire"—the term for leaving the relatively safe confines of KAF and entering the dangerous and unpredictable world outside its gates—and in time, her updates would be distributed to and read by family, friends and supporters across the country and around the world. In typical upbeat Nich fashion, over those first two weeks she painted a colourful, engaging and often amusing portrait of life inside the wire.

The spartan amenities didn't bother her—KAF, which now boasted a Pizza Hut, a Burger King, a Subway, and by midsummer, a much-anticipated Tim Hortons, had improved tenfold since it was taken over by the U.S. Air Force in 2001. Still, her new home left a lot to be desired. "There are two cesspools in the camp where all the raw sewage is dumped and purified," she wrote. "We are about 300 metres from the closest bathrooms. You walk into a room and there are ten toilets, each surrounded by a curtain that never shuts the whole way." The gravel surfaces of the camp made "the danger of rolling an ankle ever imminent. I imagine it is like walking on the beach—I will get used to it." It was a far cry from the luxurious Camp Mirage, which boasted air conditioning, minibars and a putting range. "I can't wait to stop over there when we fly back."

The honours English graduate described with good humour the small tent she shared with nine other officers, before the massive structures quickly coined the Big Ass Tents, or "BATS," were erected to house 200 soldiers at a time. "There is a foot between our cots, so it is pretty tight. This morning, I put my lock inside my combat boot. Then, I picked up my boots and yelled 'Scorpion check!' as I tipped my boot upside down. There was a big 'thump' as the lock fell out. My buddy, Howard Han for those Shilo folk, shot out of bed like he'd been shot. It was pretty good. The good news is that I no longer need to worry about being the first one to scream like a little girl."

Life wasn't much cushier in the BAT, despite the much-appreciated addition of electrical power. "I got a top bunk so I'm happy," she wrote. "Sgt. Redford is six-foot-four and has to sleep diagonally. Jay would hate it! They are also quite flimsy. I almost knocked mine over climbing and without the Sgt down below to anchor me. We have a standard operating procedure (SOP) established now, so there haven't been any other incidents. My crew all gets to sleep right beside one another, which I really like."

She waxed comical about the dangers of being in such close proximity to her fellow soldiers day and night. "Two hundred men in one tent after a busy day rivals the cesspool outside. I don't think my nose hairs will ever be the same again :-)." Seeing that she was still in the "honeymoon" stage of a long deployment, Dave cautioned her: "First you're going to be really excited; then you're going to settle into a routine; then, you're going to get really bored."

When they arrived at KAF, Nich and her crew were far from being combat ready. As Dave described it, the situation was "kind of a gong show." Some of the equipment hadn't shown up yet, and Dave was quick to point out, "You can't go outside the wire with pieces of your gun missing." Once that was cleared up, they were out within the week, accompanying another coalition force from Romania, whom they nicknamed the Romulans.

Though much of Canada's military equipment was in need of upgrading, it was still a step up from that of other coalition troops, some of whom didn't even have thermal imagery—which would have enabled them to "see" objects in the dark—in their vehicles. When Nich's crew turned off their headlights at night, the Romanians screamed that they couldn't see them. "Hey, fellas," Dave called out to his FOO team's amusement, "we've got twenty-first-century stuff here."

They all took well to the "beat cop" method of patrolling that Ian Hope advocated in a counter-insurgency: getting up close to the inhabitants, in order to become "aware of the environment and able to sense measures of local confidence and the swing of operational momentum." The gregarious captain described those early experiences with her usual joyful exuberance: "It is an amazing feeling to get out and actually do our job. I knew that we were well trained, but I didn't realize quite how well until we started actually doing road moves and patrols. I am very confident in my crew and in our equipment. Don't worry, Dad, confidence does not equal carelessness. We are very careful."

Also armed with her camera on these trips, Nich began snapping the first of hundreds of photographs to burn onto CDs and ship home to Jay. Sights like the Reg Desert literally took her breath away. "It was amazing. I don't think any description or photo could do it justice. It was silhouetted on both sides by the mountains to the east, and the plains to the west. It stretched south for as far as we could see. It wasn't flat like the deserts in the movies. Instead it was rolling and a blood red colour." Every time they saw a beautiful vista or stunning landscape, she and Dave would cry out in unison, "*National Geographic* moment!"

forgetting briefly about the thirty-five-degree-Celsius heat and the nearly one hundred pounds of kit they hauled around.

In keeping with her nature, Nich demonstrated a healthy sense of humour when observing the absurdity that can result when hundreds of young soldiers are thrust into one place, such as toilet paper raids on other countries' supplies and ear-splitting karaoke nights. But she also understood that, amidst the picture-postcard beauty of the landscape she was becoming acquainted with in the countryside and mountains north of Kandahar, and funny stories about life at KAF, there were constant reminders of the country's desperate poverty, as she noted in one mass letter:

Leaving KAF is like moving to another world. First, we cross about 2 kilometres of garbage. The field of garbage always has people shopping, as Mum would say. It is quite sad. There are a couple of apartment buildings that have collapsed. When you get to the other side, you see that they don't have a back at all. Apparently, they were hit by 500-pound bombs some time ago. They are filled with people. The kids all run out to watch us drive by. Sometimes they wave and smile, but other times they swear at us and throw rocks. I still find it pretty shocking to see young children so full of hate at us being here. But others wave and smile and seem to want us around. It is hard to know who is right. I just have to believe that we are doing a good thing, especially when I hear our intelligence updates about the widespread violence and I see the terrible poverty. It actually makes me sick to my stomach to see how little these people have. In the countryside there are lean-tos made out of old tarp and almost see-through cloth. It seems like dozens of people fit into them. We went to practice shooting our weapons and the locals all got around to watch. That was fine, but as soon as we were done, they came to scavenge the area. They collected all of the used casings from our weapons. They were actually pushing and shoving each other to get at it. I have also never seen so many people maimed and wounded. People with crutches and people without who should have them.

In those first days, Nich spent her time alternating between sporadic day-long stints outside the wire and interminable waiting at KAF. To keep herself and her crew busy, they took hour-long ruck marches around the base, and created make-work projects like cleaning and checking their equipment several times over. It was a quiet time for a soldier trained for combat; the local Taliban, their numbers in Kandahar Province estimated by military intelligence to be around two-hundred-strong, had yet to show up in any substantive form, which gave Nich and her FOO team an opportunity to train together, get to know one another and forge a strong bond. By the time they arrived in Afghanistan, she'd already become familiar with her right-hand man, Dave, better known to the team as "Sergeant Red." She'd even go as far as calling him a friend, although as a non-commissioned officer not on equal footing, he never called her Nich. It was "Ma'am," or more often, "Boss." While she occasionally fell back on nicknames for her men, she never addressed them by their first names. She was always the boss, and if other soldiers were nearby, her men knew to revert to the even more formal "Captain Goddard."

At thirty-eight years of age, Dave was the oldest of his FOO team, not to mention one of the oldest in the entire battalion that had just arrived for duty. During their training phase back home, the native of Mississauga, Ontario, and Nich got on like they'd always known one another: she liked his dry sense of humour and straightforward, shoot-from-the-hip style; he appreciated her ability to adeptly handle being a woman in one of the last bastions of macho-male culture. Having completed only high school, he also admired her smarts, which included recognizing him as an invaluable mentor. He'd never met a woman quite like Nich, and told her as much. "You're rather unique," he said with a smile after one casual, non-military conversation about life, making it clear he'd just paid her the ultimate compliment. Their mutual admiration served both well, since the FOO and her gunner had been attached at the hip since Wainwright, and would continue to be during their time in Afghanistan. With more than a decade of experience gleaned in war-torn places like Croatia and Bosnia, as well as working as a driver for a top general, Dave knew a lot of things his boss didn't. He got Nich up to speed on everything from how to form a leaguer (a square, circle-the-wagons formation of vehicles, with the fighting ones on the outside), to what to expect on a day-to-day basis as part of a large battle group.

By the time the pair landed in Afghanistan, they were almost able to finish one another's sentences. "We kind of know exactly what the other is thinking," said Dave. "She counts on me for certain things, and I count on her for others." Nich acknowledged his street smarts. She always let him "have my two cents," and amused him with stories of her dogs while he talked about his wife, Barb, and his love of motorcycle riding. "You sure come from a smart family," he told her. "They're always travelling to Europe, going to this or that school."

Master Bombardier Jeff Fehr got to know Nich during their time at Shilo while training under Major Anne Reiffenstein. She was happy to have the hard-working, reliable soldier as part of her crew and let him know as much. Jeff realized at a young age he had the right temperament for the army. "It's just something that needs to be done," he'd often say about his career choice. "The world needs everything from doctors to burger flippers. I'm just suited for doing stuff like this." While still in high school, he was a volunteer firefighter in his rural Manitoba hometown of Gladstone; he knew that unlike his older brother, Rod, who became a lawyer, he wasn't cut out for a desk job. "I don't like the idea of knowing what I'm doing day in and day out," he was fond of saying. "I like the heart pumping once in a while." Like Dave, Jeff loved motorcycles, along with late 1960s muscle cars. Even though he was two years younger than Nich, back at Shilo he occasionally referred to her as "Little Sister," a nickname Dave came up with and that "Nich hated." Bombardier Clint Gingrich, their driver, was the quintessential strong-and-silent type. A bodybuilder since his early teens, Clint took up the sport at a young age when his father, who had entered a couple of body-building competitions, took him along to his workouts.

Bombardier Chris Gauthier, the fourth member of the FOO team, teasingly called Clint "Lou Ferrigno," after the star of the 1980s *Incredible Hulk* television series. But Nich called him "Newt," after the conservative pundit Newt Gingrich, and that was the moniker that stuck. She could have called the soft-spoken muscleman anything and he wouldn't have minded. He knew that officers were trained to tend to the physical and emotional well-being of their soldiers, to look out for them on the battlefield, but also to know and read them on a personal level. The twenty-five-year-old native of Kitchener, Ontario, felt that Nich "isn't just going through the motions—she asks how you are, and it's genuine."

The only wild card in the bunch was Bombardier Chris Gauthier. He wore his reputation as an opinionated rabble-rouser like a badge of honour. "You know that Denis Leary song, 'I'm an Asshole'?" Chris would say by way of introduction. "That pretty well describes me." The newly married soldier had been at Shilo since 1995 and knew the other men. He had rarely crossed paths with Nich; he only knew that she was well liked and respected by her men. The thirty-three-year-old native Montrealer—who signed up at age twenty-one because "I figured I'd go through life using my brawn instead of my brain, then found out that in the army you had to use both"—quickly got on with his new boss. Though she described his attitude towards life as "it's too good to last, something will happen tomorrow," she appreciated that, like Dave, Chris had spent time in Bosnia, a place he'd later describe as a "cakewalk" compared to Afghanistan. Chris had joined Nich's FOO team only a month before deployment, replacing a member who had failed to gel with the other four during training back home.

Also like Dave, Chris was an old-school soldier who had little time for officers. He found the bulk of them too haughty and rule-bound for his tastes. But Nich broke the mould. She had taken to heart Ian Hope's philosophy that rules among soldiers in this environment had to be adapted to the circumstances. "The Canadian soldier is a combat soldier and requires from our NCOs and officers combat leadership, not garrison management techniques," Hope taught his officers, whom he described as "the centre point of moral well-being in a unit." Neither Nich

wo-year-old Nichola standing on a canoe, Losuia, Trobriand Islands, 1982.

LEFT: Tim and Sally's wedding, Alotau, Milne Bay Province, Papua New Guinea, July 9, 1977.

RIGHT: Tim and Sally at Nichola's christening, Passam, East Sepik Province, May 1980

Nichola with Kiriwina High School students, September 1981.

TOP: Nichola and Sally on Kiriwina Island, 1981.

RIGHT: Nichola with Susie, daughter of Ernest Goweli, September 1981.

TOP: Nichola and Sally at Kiriwina High School, September 1982.

LEFT: Nichola and Victoria with Bala, a student at Aiyura National High School, East Sepik Province, July 1983.

Victoria and Nichola leaning against their dad's snowmobile, Black Lake, Saskatchewan, December 1984.

Tim, Nichola, Sally and Victoria, Basswood Lake, near Thessalon, Ontario, at their grandparents' fortieth wedding anniversary, August 1987.

TOP: Seventeen-year-old best friends
Nichola and Krista, Maryvale,
Antigonish County, summer 1997.

RIGHT: Nichola and Zeph Williams,
grade-twelve graduation, June 1998.

Nichola, Victoria and Kate, Livingstone Cove, Antigonish County, Christmas 1998.

Nichola completing
the Obstacle Course,
Recruit term, Royal
Military College,
September 1998.

Nichola and her grandfather, Dr. Michael West, at the Royal Military College Graduation Ball, May 2002. He is wearing his campaign medals from World War II.

Nichola and Jay, Basic Officer Training Course Graduation Day, July 1998.

Tim, Kate, Nichola, Victoria and Sally at Royal Military College Graduation, May 2002.

Jay and Nichola's wedding, December 28, 2002, at St. Barnabas Church, Calgary, with Reverend Grant Rogers presiding.

ay, Nichola, and Chantal and Sonny Hatton, Riding Mountain National Park, Manitoba, October 2003. PHOTO COURTESY OF CHANTAL HATTON

ay, Nichola, Kate, Tim, Victoria and Sally, Sault Ste. Marie, Christmas 2004.

TOP: Nichola and Sam in Sonny Hatton's backyard on the Packway, 2003.

PHOTO COURTESY OF CHANTAL HATTON

RIGHT: Bombardier Jason Kirk shaves Nichola's head for charity at CFB Shilo, spring 2005.

Master Bombardier Jeff Fehr and Nichola repair an irrigation ditch after accidentally destroying it with their LAV, April 2006.

A Canadian soldier speaks to villagers in the morning of May 17, 2006, as the troops get organized in Bazaar-e-Panjwayi.

PHOTO COURTESY OF JASON ADAIR

The FOO Team: (left to right) Bombardier Chris Gauthier, Sergeant Dave Redford, Nich, Bombardier Clint Gingrich and Master Bombardier Jeff Fehr, stand before their LAV and the Reg Desert.

Nichola at the beginning of the tour, near the Shawali-Kot District.

Jeff Fehr holding the fire mission on the afternoon of May 17, 2006—the data for the first high-explosive and illuminated fire mission on enemy troops by Canadian soldiers since the Korean War.

Nichola's ramp ceremony at Kandahar Airfield, the morning of May 19, 2006.
PHOTO COURTESY OF COMBAT CAMERA

Nichola's coffin in the Hercules transport plane, preparing for the long journey home,
May 19, 2006. PHOTO COURTESY OF COMBAT CAMERA

nor Dave harped on about proper military attire and hygiene when they were outside the wire. Chris appreciated that "as long as you do your job right, and aren't a bag of shit, they're pretty well good to go—it's more about the big picture." But what impressed him most about Nich was her unflappably sunny disposition. At first Chris couldn't believe she was for real. On one particularly arduous patrol in the searing afternoon heat, he stopped and marvelled at how Nich was "humping her ass up a mountain and smiling." Although he joked with her that he didn't enjoy being made to feel like a grump in comparison, he knew it was part of what made her a good leader. Her attitude began to rub off on him. I don't know what the hell she's smiling about, but she's smiling, he thought to himself. I guess it can't be all that bad, then. Jeff also took note of how he could always rely on Nich to stand up for her team. "If someone else hassled us and told us to be more professional, like shave every day, she'd tell them to go fly a kite," he says. "As long as we did our jobs, she couldn't have cared less."

During those half-dozen forays outside the wire the first couple of weeks, Nich always worried about her men; scanning the new and unknown landscape, she found the burden of leadership at times "mentally exhausting." But it was a relatively calm time. Nich and her FOO team spent every waking moment together; when they later stayed outside the wire for a few days, they'd all lie on the ground under the stars at night, under the protection of their vehicles formed into a leaguer. On a few rare evenings, they watched movies on Nich's laptop together inside the LAV. Clint got creative with his workouts and made a gym out of the light armoured vehicle, using various parts as resistance for bodybuilding. Nich shared with them her ever-growing supply of candy and other assorted treats sent to her from Canada: Clint's weakness was Gummi Bears, Chris loved Pringles potato chips, Jeff was a pistachio-nut eater and Dave got first crack at the licorice allsorts. Nich always made sure Jay would include her favourite, big white mints, in his regular care packages.

When Major Bill Fletcher's Charlie Company crew first arrived in Afghanistan, the plan was to immediately mobilize to Spin Boldak, a small town on the Pakistan border long known as an important trucking and fuelling stop. A few years earlier, it had been seized by the Taliban from Kandahar warlords. American-led coalition forces under Operation Enduring Freedom had wrestled it back, and it was currently being pa-trolled by French troops. The plan was for Fletcher's crew to relieve them but the French forces weren't prepared to hand over the job to the Canadians just then. So while Alpha Company and Bravo Company, the other two of TF Orion's three infantry companies, deployed to other regions, Charlie Company was left back at KAF. Fletcher sensed "a palpable frustration amongst the company," and did his best to keep up the spirits of the group that would come to be known as "Contact Charlie" for the dis-proportionate number of times they'd soon tangle with the Taliban. "Be careful what you wish for" was the phrase he'd use a few months later when reflecting on those quiet early days.

Charlie Company caught up on their training at KAF, and started doing low-level operations around Kandahar City. Every time a platoon (a military division of about thirty soldiers) went outside the wire, Nich's FOO team followed. Over the coming weeks, they'd venture a little farther out and into the mountains, introducing themselves to the locals, attending shuras—sit-down meetings with the village elders—and just letting people know, as Fletcher instructed them, "there's a new player in town here, we're Canadians—not better than the Americans, but different." Their attending the meetings was a way to show the Afghan civilian population they were interested in their concerns, but also a way, thought Fletcher, of "throwing down the gauntlet. If the bad guys are here, we're ready to take them on." But they didn't find any. The constant deployment of the FOO team meant Fletcher quickly got to know Nich and her crew. And what he saw, he liked. Nearly every night, Nich would volunteer for overnight surveillance, prompting Fletcher to tell her, "I have to have some of my guys take a turn so you and your crew can take a break from all-nighters."

Nich continued her regular mass-email updates, which stayed for the most part intentionally "cheerful," as Nich put it to her crew. She was well aware that her growing email distribution list, partly spurred on by her mother and other friends back home, had now expanded to everyone from family friends and fellow soldiers to schools and St. Barnabas Anglican Church in Calgary, where she had said her marriage vows three years earlier. She wrote even more prolifically to her husband on those interminably long days at KAF waiting for orders, sometimes emailing him up to three times a day as well as penning more personal letters to send by snail mail, which weren't subject to self-censorship, something that soldiers had been instructed on prior to deployment. That correspondence had a decidedly different tone. While her mass letters sometimes read like a recruiting campaign for the Canadian Forces, she knew that to Jay she could unleash her deepest fears and dark moments; she could express the emotions she kept from everyone else. While things had yet to heat up in the countryside, Nich was on a roller coaster internally, alternating between infectious enthusiasm—on her first time outside the wire on February 6, she confessed she was "so happy . . . to do my job"—and frustration, fatigue and self-doubt. To Jay, she was able to freely vent about things she wouldn't dare mention around the troops. "If we can go this whole tour without shooting anyone, I will be so happy," she wrote him that first month. "I don't know if that makes me a weak soldier or not." In another, she joked that "someone forgot to tell me that I'm not supposed to be nervous anymore. I'm a Captain—Captains have all of the answers . . ."

Most of all, she missed Jay's physical presence, which she had anticipated when she sent a brief email from CFB Trenton, just before boarding the flight to Scotland on January 29. It was the first of many reminders that her biggest sacrifice on this tour of duty was being half a world away from her husband of three short years:

> *Thank you for a wonderful couple of weeks. Actually, thank you for a wonderful couple of years — like, eight. I love you more and more each day. I know that I am going to miss you like crazy, but I also know that it will be so much fun to share my stories with you. Thank you for keeping the home fires burning and for encouraging me every step of the way. I wouldn't enjoy it nearly as much without you. I love you, with all of my heart. I will be thinking of you all of the time. All of my love, always and forever, Nich*

ELEVEN
Tightwire

"I care so much about these guys — I hate the thought of causing them harm by my being female and attracting trouble."
— Nich to Jay, early April 2006

WHILE HER OLDER SISTER was finding her footing in Afghanistan, Victoria Goddard's life was in a state of flux. The twenty-three-year old excelled in the sciences, but she was happiest with her nose buried deep in literary, fantasy and historical tomes. Most of her relatives had chosen careers in helping professions: both Tim's and Sally's families were filled with doctors, nurses, therapists, educators and police officers. Tory, as her family called her, felt selfish and impractical for wanting to pursue a master's degree in medieval studies. A phone call from Kandahar in early February set her mind at ease. Victoria knew that Nich's choice of a military career was "problematic in our family"—while her parents had accepted her desire to be a peacekeeper when she applied to RMC in 1998, they were still grappling with her new role as a fighting soldier. Victoria admired her older sister's tenacity in the face of opposition, that she stood her ground and passionately defended her decisions. In that phone call, Nich gave her the answer she was hoping for: "It's important to feed the soul as well." She insisted her brilliant sister embrace that which called out to her. As thanks for the pep talk, Victoria mailed her a copy of Rudyard Kipling's poem "If," which Nich proudly showed to Sergeant Dave Redford. Nich had highlighted the lines "If you can keep your head when all about you/Are losing theirs and blaming it on you" and "If you can meet with Triumph and Disaster/And treat those two imposters just the same . . ." Those words, Dave understood, "had a lot of meaning for her as a soldier."

In choosing the path of the warrior, Nich would soon, as Lieutenant-Colonel Ian Hope put it, be permitted to "throw off the trappings of civilization and temporarily submit to primeval instincts." Yet right from those early days when she smiled too much for the liking of her boss, Major Anne Reiffenstein, Nich forged her own path; with few female role models on the front lines, it was a strategy borne of necessity. She rejected the old-school notion that a serving soldier—referred to by some writers on military history as *homo furens*, or "fighting man"— should rein in emotions when corresponding with loved ones back home. But she also knew well to keep such sentiments close to her chest while in view of her fellow soldiers. She'd long ago learned that on an overseas mission, this stiff-upper-lip rule applied even more to a female than a male officer. She had, she felt, "as much of a 'Soldier First' mentality as anyone," and was able to go most days without showing any chinks in the armour. Though none of her foo team knew for sure, they could have guessed that Canada House, where ten computers and ten phones sufficed for the 1,200 Canadians at KAF, was Nich's sanctuary for venting her frustrations, fears and passions.

While her carefully edited mass letters were winding their way around the world, Nich shared her secret moments of doubt with her family. Two weeks after arriving, she confessed to her parents moments of soul-searching, as she and her fellow soldiers "risk our lives every time we head out of the wire, and I'm not completely sure why." She knew there were "bad guys out there," but having to wade through crowds of frightened young children, checking to see if they were carrying hidden weapons, and encountering angry villagers who stared with hatred in their eyes—the Taliban had abandoned their custom of wearing long beards and large turbans when coalition troops moved in, so it was near-impossible to distinguish civilians from insurgents—gave her pause. "Our government decided who was right and who was wrong," she wrote, well aware that Canada's decision to send troops to Afghanistan was partly a compromise to appease the Americans for not following them into Iraq three years earlier. "No one wants us in Iraq but we need to be somewhere . . . and let me tell you, this is better than Iraq . . ." Tim didn't hide from her his own growing unease with the underlying, often backroom, politics that had put his child in harm's way: hearing Canada was considering a decade-long involvement in Afghanistan, he told her he was concerned this was being done "without a full and vigorous national debate . . . you were sent there by a prime minister that did not seek a mandate for this action."

Nich knew that Sally was growing increasingly anxious. An Onion Lake medicine healer, from the northern Alberta First Nations where Sally had been regularly flying in as a curriculum consultant the past two years, had blessed five assorted-colour ribbons for her and her family. Sally's Onion Lake friend and colleague Irene Carter told her the ribbons would keep Nich safe. Kate took hers to Poitiers, France, where she had headed in early January for a grade 11 school exchange, while Victoria kept hers in her notebook. Sally hung hers over her car's rear-view mirror, while Tim carried his in his wallet, the ribbon always with him whether he was in Lebanon, Montenegro or his office at the University of Calgary. Nich pinned hers to the inside of her uniform, "close to the heart," she told her mother.

Not wanting to unnecessarily alarm her parents, the protective Nich saved the worst for Jay. On a daily basis, he coached her on how to handle the challenges she faced, and always reminded her to "keep smiling." She shared with everyone the sadness of attending, not long after her arrival, a ramp ceremony, the pomp-and-pageantry-filled sendoff at KAF, for four Americans killed by an IED. But it was only to Jay that she wrote of an incident later the same day that disturbed her almost as much: an infantry soldier she knew from Shilo joked that he looked forward to writing her "Dear Jay Letter," sent in the event of her death. "I didn't find it very funny," she wrote. "Most of us who have actually gone 'out of the wire' find it really inappropriate." When Jeff Fehr later handed her his real just-in-case letter for safekeeping, it was even more upsetting. "The fact that he trusted me with it and that he had to write one almost unglued me . . . my love, I wonder how I can possibly keep smiling sometimes." When she was part of a convoy that "roared through the backyards" of a village in the middle of the night, she lamented how "real people's lives get fucked up when we ram into a wall; real kids and women get scared when they see us coming." Two weeks later, when a LAV collided with a civilian taxi, killing one Canadian soldier and wounding six others—a convoy Nich and her crew were initially scheduled to be on—she told him about the rising tension at KAF while the names of those injured or killed were being held, pending notification of next of kin. "It is horrible to sit and wait. I love you."

Nich made sure she frequently and effusively rewarded Jay for playing the vital role of unfiltered sounding board: "I wonder sometimes if you are a dream that I made up. I read your letters and cards that you sent me, and I have to ask myself how you can be so amazing. Your letters make me laugh and they make me feel less far away—oh love. I would love to see you for just a minute—love to hold your hand, see your smile, feel your kiss. How did I luck out and find you? You are so wonderful to me and you mean everything." She signed off most correspondence with AMLAAF, the acronym for "All my love, always and forever," the letters that were inscribed inside each of their wedding bands.

While Nich was becoming acclimatized to the violence all around, her life back home in Canada was constantly on her mind. She and Jay debated about various houses for sale in Wainwright, her next posting; Nich asked him to book a romantic weekend at the Fort Garry Hotel in Winnipeg, "with a king sized bed and a fireplace," when she came home on leave in April; and she shared a dream she had one night outside the wire, in which she was pregnant. The dream prompted her to bring up the backburner issue: "on the kids thing—your call. I'm officially handing the decision over to you. With the caveat that if we have them, we have to have at least two."

Though she wasn't shy about her status as a happily married woman, the four men who were with Nich twenty-four hours a day couldn't have known they were in the presence of a great romantic. Throughout her military career, Nich had endeavoured to make those around her gender blind so they would judge her on her merits as a soldier and nothing else. She was, as much as any woman can be, one of the boys. It had been an ongoing struggle, but she was always up to the challenge. Five years after Canadian newsmagazine *Maclean's* scandalized the Canadian Forces with an exposé on sexual harassment and assault on female soldiers throughout the 1990s, Nich had been having a different experience altogether. Although some of her male colleagues were being dragged kicking and screaming into the twenty-first century, she'd learned the ropes from one of the best female officers around, and had earned the respect and loyalty of her fellow soldiers at Shilo.

But Afghanistan was a different playing field. She knew that walking through a village not concealed by a burkha—the head-to-toe garment, complete with face veil, that the Taliban imposed as appropriate female dress—would draw a crowd. Her FOO team and Major Bill Fletcher had already discussed backup plans while training at Wainwright, what to do in the event of locals getting hostile at the startling sight of a western woman in combat fatigues. Yet from the moment she landed at KAF, being a woman in a sea of mostly men—soldiers from several differ-ent countries, Afghan locals working on the base in positions both important and menial—took on far greater gravity than she had anticipated inside the wire. In her first twenty-four hours, she discovered the heavily fortified base, which had mark-ings near the runway denoting the presence of mines still buried in the ground, couldn't shield her from some ugly realities. The constant stares and leering by the Afghan civilians working on the base made her feel like "a piece of meat." When they whistled and made "pretty rude gestures" in Nich's direction, she tried not to let anyone see the distress it was causing her.

The threat went far deeper: "There were six rapes in the camp last week, so we have to work out an escort at night," she wrote to Jay. "I also had a freaky dream last night that I went to the bathroom and got jumped. I couldn't get it out of my head; I kept on shouting for help but no one heard." Even packing a loaded pistol for the journey, she still wasn't assured of safety. Dave told her that any time she needed to go somewhere after dark, she should let him or one of the other members of her FOO crew know. "Some countries don't have a lot of standards for signing up soldiers," says Dave, his subtle way of indicating that it wasn't only the Afghans they needed to worry about, although he won't name the countries he is referring to. "They base it on quantity, not quality. Because of that, it wasn't good for women to walk alone at night." It drove Nich up the wall to be a boss with a constant "two-person shadow wherever I go," in essence "trapped." Hoping to buy an Afghan rug at a base store run by locals, she got a small taste of what it felt like to be a female in a country where women are considered the subhuman property of their husbands, fathers and brothers. The vendor talked to Dave, not once acknowledging Nich's presence. "It was as if I was invisible," she wrote. "I didn't get mad, but it made me feel very insignificant. . . . I just have to pretend to be confident and okay with everything."

Nich tried to shake off the tension of living in a fortress where men outnumbered women ten to one, in a country where rape within marriage was considered acceptable among a good number of its citizens. She had more pressing concerns, she told Jay, like "not getting shot at." But at times her nerves got the better of her. Even during the day at KAF, she found herself adapting her behaviour in ways she would never consider at

Shilo. The elite athlete began to avoid certain parts of the fitness complex on the base. "I miss doing weights, but not quite enough to force myself in among the testosterone-driven men in there."

■ ■ ■

As he cast a wary eye on the new BATS in mid-February, Lieutenant-Colonel Hope couldn't help thinking of the challenges inherent in leading one of Canada's first deployments of male and female combat soldiers in a war zone. Surveying the massive marquees with more than a hundred bunk beds lined up in rows, he realized he had a potentially dangerous situation on his hands. There are absolutely no walls, no privacy, he thought. He knew soldiers well enough to be certain that "if they have enough time on their hands, they can get into trouble. And if we mix genders in there, we could have some trouble about privacy issues." Like the Americans who had hastily arrived a few years earlier and first lumped all the soldiers together, he was confronted with the fact that his country hadn't addressed the specific needs of women in a war zone.

Hope had enough to contend with outside the wire, and he settled this relatively minor hiccup quickly: a swath of tarp demarcated a "women only" zone so the half-dozen or so females in each BAT could change and get ready for showers away from the eyes of close to two hundred men. Nich was now the only officer separated from the men who served under her. She had quickly learned to sleep through the constant nighttime roar of planes landing on and taking off from the nearby airstrip; she'd laughed off the air-hockey table that had been set up five feet from her bed. But she was livid about this new development.

"We've taken a benign situation and created a fantasy," she told anyone who would listen, including Dave Redford, Jeff Fehr and Bill Fletcher. She wrote a memorandum to Hope protesting the move, and showed it to her Shilo friend Andrew Nicholson. "This is ballsy, but it's within your right," he told her from his bed just on the other side of the tarp from hers. "You're speaking your mind, and taking it right to the top. But understand, Nich, the likelihood of you changing this is limited."

As he read over the eloquent letter stating her argument for why she shouldn't be separated from her fellow soldiers with whom she'd been "living in the field, living in the tents and trenches," Hope couldn't help chuckling. The commander who considered himself an enlightened military man thought about Nich's impassioned assertion that the days of "objecting to mixing genders in combat are over." He realized he might have been "a little old in my thinking about the maturity levels of men and women in the Canadian Forces." He also admired Nich's daring for going straight to the top: a junior officer writing directly to a commanding officer wasn't a practice that was encouraged. But Hope understood such defiance had a noble motivation: loyalty to her troops. He pulled Nich aside and explained his decision to stand firm, which came down to a matter of common sense and expediency. "I hope I didn't offend you, sir," she responded. "No, I needed this," he told her. "I don't have any female advisers who I can talk to about things like this, and if you think I need one, feel free to step in," he said. "Thank you, Nicky."

Hope walked away thinking, "This is an officer with guts, a good, clear head and obviously a good leader." Nich walked away fantasizing about the day when she'd be of an equal rank to the commander and could tell him, "It's not Nicky, it's Nich or Nichola." Her final comment on the issue came a few days later, when she paraded out in front of her fellow soldiers in fleece pajamas and a pair of fluffy pink slippers at 6:00 a.m. and chirped, "Good morning, boys!" to a startled crew of air force personnel returning home after the night shift. Andrew Nicholson laughed at how Nich had defused her earlier outrage with subversive humour. "It's my way of saying, 'Fine, if you think I'm a girl,'" she told him, "'here's some girlie stuff.'"

The four members of Nich's foo team took on the role of protectors both inside and outside the wire. Dave and Jeff were the first to jump up whenever Nich needed to go somewhere at KAF after sunset. Jeff respected her as the boss, "but at the same time you always have an eye on her." When the team ended up spending several days in April at Forward Operating Base (FOB) Robinson, located in Helmand Province west of Kandahar, Dave didn't like the interest the Afghan National Army (ANA) soldiers showed in his leader. It was harmless enough at first—on Nich's day of arrival, they excitedly lined up to get their picture taken with her—but in time the constant attention grew menacing. As fascinated as the ANA troops are, thought Dave, there's always the underlying smirk.

The local soldiers and police Nich was supposed to be working with now followed her around far too closely. After watching for a week as an assortment of them went out of their way to stroll past the LAV, Dave found himself "getting pissed right off." A few nights later, an ANA soldier, "stoned out of his mind," raced towards the LAV, where inside Nich and the boys were watching a Vin Diesel movie on her laptop. The men had him on the ground in no time, and then handed the strung-out

Afghan back to his fellow soldiers. As Nich watched in horror while the Afghans beat the trespasser, an interpreter explained with a shrug, "He's had too much hash." Feeling certain the soldier had targeted their group because of its lone female member, Dave approached a higher-ranked non-commissioned officer and asked him for permission to place concertina wire, superior to barbed wire for deterring intruders, around the section of land where they were parked. "They're just ogling, wanting to see what Captain Goddard is doing," he told the sergeant major, who granted him permission. "I feel like I'm a burden to you guys," Nich told Dave despondently. "It's no big deal," he responded, trying his best to wave off her worries.

When it came to the deplorable conditions of the FOB, though, Nich hardly flinched. Casting her eyes on the communal toilets—two toilets for 150 soldiers—she joked that the sight, and the stench in the fifty-seven-degree-Celsius heat, was "something right out of *Jarhead*," referring to the 2005 black comedy about the conditions experienced by American troops during the 1990 Gulf War in Iraq. After a few days of hard living, she got her hands on an old scrub board. Together with Jeff and Clint, Nich went to a big pump and, to everyone's delight, used old pioneer-style scrubbing to wash their clothes. "This makes you appreciate the little things," said Jeff with a laugh as the trio scrubbed away days of dirt and grime. "Like showers, and cold drinks. All the little things KAF has to offer."

While Nich grew increasingly concerned that she was a liability to her men, Hope was starting to see her as anything but. He knew the tales of Malali of Maiwand, the mythical nineteenth-century Afghan female warrior who was said to have turned her headscarf into a banner and led her countrymen to victory against the British army in the Panjwayi District. In a place where modern-day female heroism was embodied in the simple act of walking down a dirt road to study or teach in a school, Hope saw Nich as a key asset in the winning of hearts and minds. He watched her at a shura and witnessed the awe with which the village elders welcomed this flesh-and-blood woman warrior. Future success in Afghanistan, Hope was convinced, would start with a shift in gender power at the grassroots level. Nich's presence at such meetings, he felt, "could educate them on the need to change their thinking on these issues." The more women in authority they could show to Afghan villagers, Hope felt, "the more progress we can make slowly in allowing some rethinking to go on."

Seeing local life up close was at times almost too much for Nich to bear. Children played atop blown-up rockets, and looked quizzically at her and her fellow soldiers when they offered them crayons and construction paper: "How could we possibly begin to explain what crayons are?" Nich later wrote. When they first ventured outside the wire, she and Dave would toss water bottles to young children. They quickly dispensed with the practice after seeing older children wrestling the kids to the ground for the bottle, and then those children being beaten by even older children for the coveted trophy.

That was matched by the absence of any women in public: Nich's only opportunity for a sighting came when, from the top of the LAV, she could see over the village compound walls burkha-clad figures scurrying in the shadows. "The guys don't realize quite how horrible it is to me to contemplate the lives of women here," she told Jay. It would be weeks before she saw her first burkha-clad woman in public, on a day when the temperature surpassed the thirty-five-degree-Celsius mark. "I can't imagine never feeling the sun in my face," she wrote later that day. "Not really being able to see where I'm going." The only thing that buoyed her in these darker moments was her trust that "the government and NGOs will be able to do their thing because of what we are doing."

The shuras were quickly becoming the high point of what was so far a relatively uneventful overseas tour. Nich's job was mostly to watch over the soldiers and higher-ranked officers as they sat with the village elders and keep an eye out for any suspicious activity on the periphery. But once she was spotted, she became the main attraction. "Woman! Woman!" cried villagers of all ages as they pointed in her direction. Youngsters took turns running up and poking her. Watching this, Dave thought the skittish children behaved as though Nich might bite them if they touched her. While they found it amusing initially, in time Dave would yell, "Knock it off, kids," and shoo them away from his boss. The elders and village men were just as fascinated. "Where is your husband?" they asked her through an interpreter. Nich and her FOO team burst out laughing when one of the elders expressed shock that Jay had only one wife. "My husband would definitely say one wife is enough," she responded to gales of laughter. Commander Hope was impressed to hear Major Fletcher's report of Nich sitting down with the elders to a celebratory meal of roast goat, served up in a pocket of naan bread, and digging into the strange cuisine as though it were her favourite roast beef and Yorkshire pudding. Thrilled that she could charm the locals in this manner, Hope couldn't have known then that after a childhood of dining on everything from moose and caribou to decomposed seal, goat was far from exotic cuisine for Nich's well-travelled palate.

On a few occasions, Nich even managed the miracle of temporarily transcending the gender divide between her and the paltry-paid Afghan soldiers. Many of them, she discovered, were competent professionals determined to "work towards peace." The compliment was later returned when, after witnessing her hike 10 kilometres up a mountain with a 2,000-foot altitude gain, an interpreter approached her and said, "They want me to tell you that all of the ANA are talking about you because you have done this march with us." Nich replied that she was impressed with their ability to run up and down mountains, seemingly effortlessly. An ANA soldier came over to Nich, and in broken English, said, "I fight Taliban. I fight al Qaeda. You fight also. Dersi [very good]. Mananna [thank you]."

Nich held dearly to those rare breakthroughs, which buoyed her when she suffered the occasional setback in mood and resolve. Although at times she felt "I am earning every $ of this friggin' tour," she too remained professional and committed.

She'd fully expected to encounter sexism and harassment in one of the world's most repressive, anti-female regimes, even amongst some of the coalition soldiers of other countries. What caused her true despair was when such treatment came courtesy of her fellow Canadians, supposedly enlightened men from a country that walked the talk of equality. "Word on the street is you and me are having an affair," Dave blurted out one day, knowing full well "she'd lose her mind over this one." Nich's face instantly went red with rage. "Who the hell is saying this?" she cried out. He wouldn't tell her, knowing such information would only throw fuel on a fire he thought better to ignore. "Don't worry, I pointed out to them the fact that we're never alone together, so it's impossible. We get along, and we're two different sexes. People are gonna talk."

Nich had done everything she could not to give malicious gossip the slightest traction. But common sense did nothing to quell whisperings about the captain and her men: a few weeks later, Jeff reluctantly came forward with tales he'd heard about how she and he were supposedly sneaking off to the Green Bean coffee shop at KAF for romantic tête-à-têtes. Nich knew that such innuendo, however baseless, could hamper an officer on the way up. But her main concern was Jay. "I don't want you to hear something and be upset," she wrote. "I know that you trust me, but I need to hear you say it, I don't want to upset you, ever." He responded within hours: "I don't think you need to be worried about how others are perceiving you and your crew," Jay wrote, then quickly moved on to an amusing story about their dog Bill.

Despite the regular trials and tribulations, Nich kept her sense of humour, and was rarely seen without that by-now-famous grin. Standing in the searing Afghan heat as they chugged down bottles of hot water, she and the guys joked, "We're here for a long time, not a good time." She laughed over the bizarre situations that were part and parcel of being female in a man's world. One day Dave pulled her aside for yet another "serious talk." He thought that if they ended up outside the wire for a stint lasting weeks, and if she needed "some girlie stuff"— guy code for feminine hygiene—they should brainstorm ahead of time for emergency preparedness. "You mean, like, we should develop a standard operating procedure for this?" Nich asked him before bursting into laughter. "Thanks, but I've been managing this on my own pretty well. I should be fine."

She was in near hysterics when one of her many care packages from Canada (in addition to the ones from friends and relatives, Sally had gathered a "coalition of women" from across the country to send gifts and newspaper articles) was filled with dozens of Harlequin novels, Danielle Steel novels and Canadian women's magazines. She and Jeff shared a laugh later when he told her, "Some of the boys have started reading them." Her growing fame back home meant the arrival of scores of packages every week, many of them containing gifts that weren't all that useful in this inhospitable environment. To entertain the boys, a laughing Nich put on a couple of hats, a purple scarf and some gloves while Jeff took pictures. "They're going to have to charter a plane just for your deliveries," Chris joked.

When she went to the Unit Medical Station (UMS) to deal with a sprained wrist she had sustained outside the wire, she did her best to talk the doctor out of giving her a medical chit, which would likely have kept her KAF-bound for a week or two. "Take it easy typing for a while," the doctor told her. Nich smiled, happy to be given the all-clear and amused at the doctor's assumption.

Over those first few weeks in Afghanistan, the pressure outside the wire was ramping up: the start of March brought with it the death of Shilo friend Corporal Paul Davis in a LAV collision with a civilian vehicle, several IED strikes against coalition forces and confirmed rocket attacks against coalition convoys. At the same time, Nich's FOO team was growing increasingly confident in their boss. They admired her ability to roll with the punches: after a mortar attack near the end of March narrowly missed KAF, she laughed with them while thousands of others screamed in panic. "It's hard enough to hit things with artillery when you can see what you're aiming for," she later told Jay. "To just lob it over is going to be pretty, touch wood, random." They were all thrilled they were getting outside the wire so often, and Chris said that even though they had yet to engage in direct combat, he'd fired more with Nich's party than he had in eight years of going on operations. She beamed when Dave told her he couldn't have picked a better officer to team up with. She felt the same, and despite her longing to see Jay, switched her leave-departure date from April to June 14; word was, a big operation was coming up, and she didn't want to leave her crew without their FOO. If something bad happened and she wasn't around to help, she'd never forgive herself.

As she was gaining the confidence of her team, Nich was also developing confidence in herself as she caught the eye of her superiors. On an operation in Shawali-Kot north of Kandahar City, Bill Fletcher watched as Nich called in rounds up a mountainside as a show of force; in that moment, she became the first Canadian to direct 155-mm HE (high explosives) outside the wire. "Are you the first person ever to call in high-explosive rounds on an actual operation?" he asked her with a smile. "Yes, I am," she responded, flashing Fletcher the biggest gap-toothed grin he'd ever seen.

Hope had finally been able to watch Nich in an operation, and he liked what he saw. During combined training with American soldiers and the Afghan National Army in northern Kandahar Province, he too was impressed with how Nich handled that climb up a mountain, saddled down with about 100 pounds of kit. He marvelled at how she "did this without even thinking about it." This officer was strong, she was tough and she was good at calling in artillery fire. He knew that a female officer had to be able to pull her weight. His initial questions about Nich—whether she was strong enough, and could his soldiers put their lives in her hands—had been answered. She's proving it in spades, thought Hope.

TWELVE

"A Lifer Now"

"This whole tour reminds me of being sixteen and going on benders. You know, the way you have to get yourself all pumped up to go out and stay up all night and party hard? Then, you crash, eat, and do it all over again."

— letter to Jay, March 5, 2006

WHEN SHE FIRST HEARD the name Nich being bandied about by the soldiers of Charlie Company, Lisa LaFlamme naturally assumed, in this male-dominated world of combat arms, they were talking about a man. It was only when TF Orion commander Ian Hope—whom Lisa nicknamed "Errol Flynn" after seeing the blue-eyed colonel ride into KAF atop his command LAV, chomping down on a cigar, the scarf around his neck flapping in the wind in true swashbuckler style—raved to her about his rising-star junior officer that she realized the FOO everyone wanted her to meet was female. Like any good journalist, Lisa was intrigued with the woman who held a powerful position on the front lines and was well regarded as highly competent and professional.

Nich was less than thrilled to hear that the CTV reporter was looking for her. It wasn't that she didn't have a healthy respect for the embedded media (the term for journalists attached to military units involved in armed conflicts) who regularly rotated through KAF. "I agree that soldiers are often misrepresented, and the only way to fix that is to get media onside and to give them honest stories," she wrote in one of her mass-email updates. That is, as long as it wasn't her doing the talking. "But you must appreciate that your being female makes you unique," Lisa told Nich after the pair was introduced the second week of March. They were the very words she didn't want to hear. "I got snappy and backed away," Nich wrote to her sister Victoria. She was also a little edgier than usual when reciting to the new visitor the "Nichola, or Nich, but never Nicky" rule. Lisa, who'd spent time covering the war in Iraq in 2003, quickly surmised that if she wanted to interview this soldier, she'd have to "tread carefully," knowing words like "female" and "woman" were hot buttons. She's going to shut me down if I go down that road, she thought.

Dave Redford sat his friend down for a tough-love pep talk. He knew that Nich was a feminist, but "not the kind who would ram it down your throat." She had shared with him her conviction that having people see competent women in positions of power was the most effective way to promote equality. "Why don't you go up there and say, 'Listen, I'm female and I do just as good, if not better, a job, than any of the men out there,'" he told her. "I can't understand why you wouldn't brag about it—and if you don't sell the fact that you can do it, more women won't join up." Nich was pleased. He really doesn't see my being female as an issue, she thought happily. Later that day, she emailed Jay about the opportunity for "my fifteen seconds" of fame. "That is neat that you are going to be on TV," he immediately replied.

Buoyed by the positive reaction of two of the most influential men in her life, Nich relented. Besides, Lisa and her cameraman were following them the next day to Operation Sola Kowel (Pashto for peacemaker), Nich and her team's fourteenth trip outside the wire. They would be deployed for two weeks near the village of Gumbad, about 100 kilometres northwest of Kandahar City and located near the famed Belly Button, a bowl-like valley surrounded by jagged mountains forming part of the Hindu Kush. Hope's plan involved seven platoons, including three from Charlie Company, working in the area to "introduce the idea of enhanced governance and reconstruction while at the same time demonstrating our strength." Attending shuras and conducting reconnaissance of the mountain terrain would form a big part of the infantry element's daily activities, along with encircling and searching nearby villages and doing "soft knock" methods—politely knocking on doors and asking questions—in an attempt to weed out Taliban fighters hiding in the local population. Several multiple artillery "show of force" missions would be conducted over the two weeks, and on at least one occasion Nich's LAV would fire several rounds from its 25-mm cannon up the mountainsides, its 4-kilometre trajectory ending in a burst of fire against a mountain peak. The impressive show of force that also included dismounted patrols, LAV manoeuvres, artillery fire and helicopters, would prove effective in making the Taliban nervous, generating panicked radio messages between Taliban commanders, which would be intercepted by the Canadians—a method for getting intelligence about the enemy that Hope would incorporate in operations over the coming months.

Their home was the area surrounding the Gumbad Platoon House, a mud-hut compound used as a patrol base for coalition forces. The compound was located near a series of villages known to have been used by the Taliban as transit areas. Over the first four days of the operation, Lisa and her cameraman tagged along, when they were allowed, while the soldiers conducted searches in the nearby mountains and patrols in the villages. At various points in the day Lisa would interview individual soldiers, including the FOO. Despite her initial misgivings, Nich quickly warmed up to the charismatic reporter. Like the soldiers, Lisa and her cameraman rolled out sleeping bags at night, bunking down in the middle of what Lisa called "a scorpion-infested gravel pit," while a few yards away, the ANA soldiers sat in their better-appointed, large tent watching porn videos smuggled in from India, on a DVD player powered by a portable battery. Nich liked that Lisa didn't complain about the lack of running water, the plywood outhouse or the bad taste their food rations, called individual meal packs (IMPS), left in one's mouth.

"Eight days without a shower or any plumbing whatsoever is a pretty big chunk of time for anybody, let alone one without any real 'hardship' training," Nich wrote of their encounter. "I was impressed." In their taped interviews over those four days, Lisa asked Nich about her fears and concerns outside the wire. Every time she said the words "fear" or "danger," Nich's brow furrowed as she carefully contemplated her answers. "It doesn't matter if you're going out for a couple of hours, or a couple of weeks," she told her in tough-soldier style, chewing down hard on her gum while her smiling FOO team stood in the background, glad that it was her on camera and not them. "You do all the same stuff, face the same stresses." At times she was almost curt when the camera was on, for the most part succeeding in keeping her brilliant white teeth from view. But her responses were genuine. "My big concern is my crew," she told Lisa. "The big pressure on me is if I make a call that's the wrong call." Watching Lisa's reaction to this last admission, Nich later told Jay, "I don't think that was really moving enough for her, which was kind of ironic because it is almost all consuming to me."

Only days after Captain Trevor Greene was attacked and nearly killed while attending a shura in the village of Gumbad, Nich, who had met the multilingual officer during predeployment training in Wainwright, clearly had on the war face Major Anne Reiffenstein had come to know so well back at Shilo. "I hope we get the guys . . . it's brutal," Nich said, shaking her head in disgust as she was reminded of the axe-wielding Afghan teen who had split open the skull of Greene, a Civil-Military Cooperation (cimic) Officer, whose specialty was to meet with local elders to hear about their concerns and help villages in the area access clean water, medical facilities and schools.

But any significant confrontation with the Taliban was not to be: over those two weeks in Gumbad, they'd exchange small amounts of fire with the enemy and capture a few, but nothing that came close to the earlier reports of massing of the enemy in the area. At one point, Nich and her men thought they had spied armed Taliban walking outside a village compound, only to find it was two civilians carrying umbrellas. "That was kind of disappointing," Nich told Lisa with a slightly embarrassed expression. At other times in her interviews, she visibly relaxed and let her guard down. When Lisa asked her if she knew what was she was getting into nearly a decade earlier when she'd decided on Royal Military College, Nich fell back on her charming ways. "I gotta say, I signed up to go to university, and that was it—I needed a job, I had no money. Somewhere along the way, I fell in love with it. And I'm probably a lifer now." Lisa laughed. "You got a university degree and an all-expenses-paid trip to Taliban country?" "Sunny Afghanistan," Nich quipped. Lisa replied with more laughter. "You have a very positive outlook, that's good. We'll need that."

Off camera, Nich grew increasingly candid. She told Lisa about her family, her husband and her dogs and cats. She regaled her with stories of growing up around the world: on separate pages of her reporter's pad, the native of Kitchener, Ontario, had written the words "Antigonish," "Baffin Island" and "Papua New Guinea." Where is this girl from? she later thought as she flipped through her interview notes. Nich also confided that she liked the fact that her ballistic eyewear, frag vest (the army's version of the bulletproof vest), helmet and baggy combat jacket made for great gender camouflage. She could freely walk around villages with the guys when she was outfitted in this way, she told Lisa, because "they don't always realize I'm a woman." Lisa couldn't help thinking how Nich's comments echoed that of an Afghan woman she had met earlier, who used similar words to describe how her burkha, which clearly marked her as a woman but hid any of her female qualities, gave her the freedom to move about in society.

■ ■ ■

A week after returning to KAF from Operation Sola Kowel, Hope gave the orders to Major Bill Fletcher to take a special team from Charlie Company out to Forward Operating Base (FOB)

Robinson, to come to the aid of U.S. Special Forces and the ANA, which had seen a few violent clashes with the Taliban. The biggest fight came on March 28, when an ANA convoy bringing supplies was ambushed a few kilometres from the FOB, killing eight ANA soldiers. As coalition troops were preparing to assist the stranded convoy, they too came under attack. Two U.S. Apache attack helicopters, along with two British Harrier fighter-bombers, were dispatched as air support. The massive air bombardment eventually forced the Taliban to retreat, but it also resulted in civilian casualties.

Private Robert Costall of 1st Battalion, PPCLI, and a soldier with Charlie Company's 7 Platoon, was part of the thirty-eight-member Canadian quick-reaction (QR) force that had been dispatched by U.S. helicopter earlier in the day to assist the convoy. After a firefight with insurgents later that night, Costall and an American soldier lay dead, and three other Canadians were injured. In his March 29 official statement announcing the death of Costall—the first combat death of a Canadian soldier in Afghanistan—federal defence minister Gordon O'Connor reiterated Canada's reason for being there: "The overarching goal is to help the Afghan people achieve peace by preventing their nation from relapsing into a failed state that gives terror- ists and terrorist organizations a safe haven."

It would take more than a year for a U.S. Army report to officially confirm what was suspected from the very start: the twenty-two-year-old native of Thunder Bay, Ontario, had been accidentally shot in the head and back by an American soldier who opened machine-gun fire on him during the insurgent attack. Two days after the firefight, Nich, who during training in Wainwright had met Costall, the father of a one-year-old boy, stood in the front rank beside the three injured soldiers. She joined them in the salute to a man whom she felt "epitomized everything that Canadians in Afghanistan represent." It was the most upsetting and moving ramp ceremony (the official sendoff for dead soldiers at KAF) she'd attended, leaving her hoping she could "only be half as brave" as Costall's closest friends and comrades within the company.

Forty-eight hours later, Nich and Charlie Company readied for Operation Ketara (Pashto for "dagger") to help reinforce the base in the heart of Sangin District, in Helmand Province, said to be the home of nearly half the world's opium production; its plethora of poppy fields explained the area's relative affluence, and also why many of the locals were said to be Taliban sympathizers. Parts of the district were uncharted territory since coalition forces had arrived in 2002: the citizenry had at first mistaken some of the earlier coalition soldiers for Soviets. On April 2, 2006, Canadian soldiers headed out for what was expected to be an operation lasting no longer than a week. The name of their new operation, suggesting an attitude so different from the forces' earlier peacemaker role, reflected the understood dangers. They were fuelled by adrenalin, knowing they'd be heading into the area where Costall had been killed in the deadliest battle involving Canadians since 1974, when two soldiers were killed in a firefight in Nicosia, Cyprus. It was a region that was also being compared to the fight for the Medak Pocket in the former Yugoslavia a decade earlier, which had also involved the soldiers of Charlie Company.

Thus began a complex day-and-night move consisting of a column of between fifty and sixty vehicles, in five packets of eight to ten vehicles each, and more than 200 troops and support people, into Helmand Province. The 150-kilometre trip west of Kandahar was estimated to be a three-hour drive; Fletcher thought it might take five or six, due to the large number of people and equipment involved. He entrusted Nich and her FOO team to be out front as a critical component of the lead reconnaissance element for Charlie Company, coordinating the movements of the vehicles on the ground, and the helicopters above, helping to lead the massive column to its destination.

The operation went south from the get-go: the plan to leave at first light from KAF was delayed, as interpreters, medics and other support personnel weren't quite ready. They arrived in chaotic Kandahar City just in time for the start of the Sunday-afternoon market. Nich's jaw dropped at the sight of scores of huge vehicles lurching their way "through a city teeming with people, kids, donkeys, dogs, carts, shops, and cars on streets that are designed for small cars." One of the vehicles hit and killed a donkey; another made a wrong turn and was now halfway up a one-way street going the wrong way and with hardly enough room for even a Smart Car to turn around in. Nich laughed when one of the gun troops came over the radio and said in a calm voice, "Um, we seem to be going the wrong way up a one-way street. We are trying to convince the traffic in front of us to turn around. Any security you could send us would be appreciated."

Moments later, reports came over the radio of a suicide car bomber in the vicinity. Every second car seemed to be a white Toyota Corolla, the vehicle of choice for suicide bombers. Nich and her crew pulled over to the side of the road, dispatching Chris and Jeff to help the infantry soldiers in an hour-long vehicle checkpoint. As the soldiers looked for bombs strapped to chests under clothing and suspicious packages in back seats and trunks, Nich's LAV sat parked in front of an orphanage where a group of boys were playing soccer. Curious about the soldiers, the boys kicked the ball over the fence several times, coming out en masse to retrieve it, smiling at Nich and the other soldiers as they sauntered past. "Boys will be boys," she said to Dave with a laugh.

Once the searches were completed, Nich got word that one of the column's vehicles couldn't go faster than 5 kilometres an hour. It took about an hour for a team to arrive from KAF to re-cover the disabled vehicle. But the worst came next: just a few kilometres outside of Kandahar City, one of the LAVs in another packet passed too close to a jingle truck—the ornately painted transport vehicles from Pakistan, their jingle sound coming from chains and chimes hanging off the front bumpers. The LAV hit the truck with its turret-mounted gun barrel, spinning the turret wildly. It struck two soldiers standing in the back of the LAV, and they had to wait for a medical team to come and evacuate them.

Just before sunset, they were ready to complete the last 30-kilometre cross-country leg of the journey, which would take them through a desert scattered with deep ditches holding burned-out vehicles, testament to the constant and continued threat of ambushes, IED strikes and landmines. These drives were always dangerous, as Lieutenant-Colonel Hope knew only too well: on March 4, just 7 kilometres out of KAF, his own vehicle had been hit by an IED. The blast had shattered much of the right arm of fellow passenger Master Corporal Mike Loewen. As they travelled without lights, using thermal and night-vision devices to guide them, Nich got word that a large truck in the convoy had vanished. She later learned that "when everyone else turned left, these guys turned right, and drove off a 10-foot drop, where they scared the crap out of themselves." Four hours later, they were found and ready to move forward.

They had just started going again when the vehicle in front of Nich's LAV hit a giant pothole, knocking out their communications and stunning the driver. Nich, knowing they were in the middle of nowhere in an area ripe for an ambush, finally lost her patience. She took off her headset, got out of the LAV and marched angrily over to the vehicle. At that very moment, Dave heard over the radio that someone had spotted tracer fire. As she yelled out, "Start your fucking vehicle!" to the crew commander, a frantic Dave yelled, "Get back in the fucking vehicle!" Settling back into her LAV, Nich couldn't help chuckling to herself, "If only Lisa LaFlamme were here for this one."

The entire trip was a classic example of a "clusterfuck," the crude military term for the Murphy's Law dictum that "if anything can go wrong, it will, and at the worst possible moment." The marathon of mishap and misadventure turned what should have been a three-hour trip into a more than twenty-four-hour ordeal. One of the few things that did go right, according to her superiors, was the performance of Captain Nich Goddard. Throughout the gruelling operation, in which she saw the first tracer fire of her tour and her first unmarked minefield, Nich kept her cool, and sense of humour. Listening to her on the radio, Fletcher couldn't believe how calm and collected she remained through it all, confirming his initial impression of Nich as someone who could go "a little above and beyond." Hope approached Fletcher the next day to talk about the FOO saddled with the road trip from hell. "Boy, did you listen to Nich last night on the radio, wasn't that a great psychological effect she had?" he said, shaking his head in wonder. "To know she was there and on top of everything, that was calming."

Aside from the constant attention of the Afghan soldiers, the disgusting communal toilets and a miserable Afghan dog the American soldiers kept on a chain, a feral animal that liked to "search out Afghans and then try to kill them," Nich found life at the dusty FOB Robinson preferable to the garrison mentality at KAF. An external fence of concertina wire, and internal ramparts of sandbags, protected the camp, located on a high plateau on the banks of the Helmand River. With no way to email, Nich scribbled notes to Jay about her experiences. The Americans were more than welcoming, relieved to see help come their way after losing three of their own in the last two months. They showed their appreciation one evening by sharing steaks they'd brought from KAF. Steak, thought Nich, never tasted so good.

She far preferred sleeping in the four-man tent with her crew to the BATs, even though her air mattress had a leak that would ensure she woke up each morning on a sheet of flattened plastic. "It is different than being in the field in Canada—here, I am rarely cold," she wrote of the way the nighttime temperature plunge was a welcome respite from the day's oppressive heat, joking, "I sound like something out of Davy Crockett . . ." The soldiers had been told they'd be out no more than a week, but were well aware that plans for operations were constantly in flux. FOB Robinson was no different: the British and American forces they were there to help quickly saw the value in having the Canadian LAV/M777 mix, and kept extending their stay. While infantry platoons from Charlie Company would be on a rotation basis over the coming weeks, there was no one else available to replace the artillery troop and Nich's FOO party.

Nich wasn't in any hurry to get back to KAF, but she was elated when, two weeks into the operation, a four-stall shower booth was built. A fellow officer visiting from KAF, who had flown in by helicopter, was also dazzled by such luxury in the middle of nowhere. Deciding he could use some cooling off, he asked Nich if he could borrow her towel. "Buddy, I came out here with four sets of clothes. I have been here for twenty days, and I don't know when I'm going back to KAF," she told him, surprising even herself with such bluntness. "Even if I had a towel, I wouldn't let you use it."

There was one thing about FOB Robinson that Nich couldn't easily shake, though. One morning as she and Dave headed to orders groups, the two came upon about a half-dozen detained Afghans, captured after the March 28 IED attack on the ANA convoy. They were kneeling on the ground in an area cordoned off by concertina wire. Nich stopped and stared at the hooded figures with their hands zap-strapped—tied with thick plastic ties that served as handcuffs—behind their backs, waiting their turn inside the sea container, normally used for transporting military kit but here doubling as a questioning room. As a specialized asset attached to a company, Nich and her crew hadn't been directly involved in the capture and detention of suspected Taliban. She felt confident the Canadians were handling them in accordance with the Geneva Convention, which ensured basic humane treatment for all persons in enemy hands, despite U.S. president George W. Bush's insistence not long after the 9/11 terrorist attacks that suspected al Qaeda members were not entitled to the international treaty's protections. Still, the reality of it stopped her in her tracks. "One of my worst fears is being taken captive," she wrote both Jay and her parents after the encounter. "Seeing these guys was pretty sobering . . . when it got dark, a glow stick was put around their necks. None of it was abusive—but it sucked pretty bad."

In the spring of 2006, Canada, like most other NATO countries involved in Afghanistan, didn't have a policy for the handling of prisoners; in the early days of the mission, most were handed over to the Americans. By early 2006, they were regularly being handed over to the Afghans and the Afghan judicial system, despite the fledgling nature of those entities. Canada's Department of Foreign Affairs and International Trade had drawn up a memorandum of agreement with the Afghan government in late 2005 making the practice official. "After all," wrote former Chief of Defence Staff Rick Hillier in his 2009 book *A Soldier First*, "Afghanistan is a sovereign country and, almost without exception, it was Afghans that we were detaining."

■ ■ ■

Only days after settling into the base named after American soldier Christopher Robinson, Nich got another chance to impress her superiors. A known Taliban commander, called a high value target, was said to be hiding in a nearby compound in Sangin District, just a few kilometres from the base. It was the same compound where, in late March, U.S. Special Forces had endured a fierce battle with the enemy. Nich and Platoon 8 commander Jon Snyder were directed to lead the company on a 28-kilometre, mounted and dismounted night patrol, to advance upon the compound. But Hope kept getting conflicting intelligence about which compound the Taliban commander was in. Twice, new control measure and fire support information was issued; Nich, who had done a brief map reconnaissance in her LAV in the middle of the night, kept pace with the changes. "Nich, can you adjust all the fire planning?" asked Fletcher when informed of the first change. "Yes, sir," she responded with confidence. But just as the troops were closing in on the target area, Hope received intelligence that the Taliban commander was back in the original compound. Working in the middle of the night, Fletcher informed Nich and Jon they needed to reroute once more. He was once again impressed by the "absolute calm" in Nich's voice despite the changes.

Over the next few hours, Nich quietly talked to everyone on the radio, directing between thirty and thirty-five armed vehicles coming through the dark with their lights off, negotiating their movement into positions where the soldiers could then dismount and Fletcher could circle the compound. While Nich handled the coordination of all the various elements, Hope sat back and wondered, How is she doing all this? She's sitting in her LAV, in her turret. She's got three radios, and she's working off a map with a little flashlight on it, with a little piece of paper to write notes on. And she's processing it through like a computer would. While the others dismounted, Nich stayed in her vehicle and oversaw Fletcher as he went in close to the target area. But there was no Taliban commander to be found: they had missed him by mere minutes.

The American soldiers who had been in the village earlier had suffered multiple casualties after coming into contact with up to sixty Taliban fighters. Fletcher and his crew were given American intelligence assets, along with close air support in the form of B-1 bombers with their precision guided bombs, un-manned aerial vehicles (UAVs) and attack helicopters. Hope, who was back at FOB Robinson directing the operation from his 9er Tac (the call sign of his mobile command centre, pronounced "Niner Tac"), was positioned next to an American Special Forces operating centre. One of the American officers handed him intelligence that showed the fleeing Taliban were massing north of the coalition troops. Surprised that he suddenly had "a lot of information being passed to us that we never had before," Hope didn't have time to question this sudden change. Instead, he sent the information to Fletcher via his FOO and Company 21C. Although the soldiers knew where the Taliban were, they never got close or tried to engage them with fire; Hope determined his troops were too vulnerable to risk engaging such a large number of Taliban fighters. But he felt the mission was a success in its own right. Moving stealthily throughout the night, they had demonstrated to the locals how they could be covert with big armoured vehicles—the Taliban described the LAVs in a Pashto term that is loosely translated as "the dragons that shit out white men"—and had sent at least psychological shock waves through the area. At first light, close to two thousand civilians had emerged from their compounds and walked to the open desert to the east, convinced another bombing battle would occur because of the presence of the Canadian troops—and offering a sure sign that the Taliban were there, even if they had chosen on this day to stay out of the fight.

The operation gave Nich a chance to show her bosses what she was truly made of. Not only had she done a masterful job of coordination on operations, she also directed artillery fire near the compounds where Taliban commanders were thought to have been. The firing took place on the west bank of the Helmand River that flows through the mainly desert region, in an open area that wouldn't risk collateral damage but would have a deterrent effect on those using the ferries crossing the river as an escape. Hope thought to himself, These are good tactics, she's cut them off from their escape route. Although the Taliban had already disappeared into the complex terrain of compounds and serpentine pathways, Hope was glad to see Nich identify another strategy.

Over the next three weeks, Fletcher and his troops began operating in the area in daylight and at night, patrolling, attending shuras and conducting leader engagements, all the while reassuring the locals they could move about freely. They did their best to show the people that the Taliban were not their only option. Throughout most of the month of April, this is the way their days went, building relationships and doing very little real fighting other than dealing with the odd scrap in the desert.

Still, Hope was seeing firsthand the capabilities of Charlie Company. He had grown increasingly confident that through his leadership, they had shown flexibility and agility, were able to change plans with little warning and deal with complex, sophisticated manoeuvres. I've got a real fierce force here, thought Hope. If I'm really in trouble, this is the organization I can call upon.

A big factor for Hope was Captain Nich Goddard. He admired her combination of technical competence and innovation. Before heading back to KAF, he had a sit-down with Fletcher to discuss the promising young junior officer. "Look, my impression of Nich Goddard is this: she is the best artillery officer that I've ever seen." Her leadership skills, he told Fletcher, were second to none, and she possessed a quick mind mixed with courage. "This is a person, I think, a young officer to whom there is no limit to where they can go with a career in the Canadian Armed Forces. And in fact, should be pushed." Fletcher wholeheartedly agreed. "Okay, then be prepared some time in the next few months to help me write out sufficient reports for the rapid promotion of this individual, because the army needs her in higher responsibilities now." With that, Hope prepared for his imminent leave, certain that when he returned a couple of weeks later, he and Fletcher would pick up where their conversation had left off.

About the only person who gave the promising young officer a tough time was Nich Goddard. She nearly beat herself up following one nighttime show-of-force mission. After doing a thermal scan on a target—and ensuring no collateral damage was possible—Nich and Dave shot ten rounds into the area. Later, when the sunrise revealed a compound right in the middle of the target zone 5 kilometres away, Nich felt her stomach turn and nearly threw up at the sight. "Oh no," said Dave, looking at Nich with a horrified expression. She sent in a helicopter to investigate further. "Nope, that compound is abandoned," he radioed back to the two relieved soldiers. The operation had also involved a cordon and search "in force," which meant they used overwhelming firepower, aviation and presence to, as Nich later wrote to Jay, "scare the shit out of everyone." It was highly effective: women and children fled the village in terror. "I just wish there was a way to intimidate the bad guy," she wrote, "without scaring everyone else."

She saved her strongest self-censure for a night when she, her FOO team and just one G-Wagon separated from the rest of the platoon during a search in the Sangin District. Dave hadn't been paying attention to Nich's conversations with the platoon commander on the radio, so he didn't realize she'd agreed to take them in a different direction until it was too late. The enraged veteran dispensed with protocol and gave his boss a tongue-lashing. "What the fuck are we doing out here with no other LAVs?" he asked Nich, knowing both were well versed in the rule that nothing leaves the wire without three LAVs. "We're here with the CIMIC guys," she responded. "What are they gonna do, talk everybody to death?" he snapped back. In that moment, Nich "felt about two inches tall." She'd taken a risk, and for no good reason. They eventually made it back to link up with the rest of the platoon, and Nich and Dave made their peace. "We are just lucky that no one shot at us. I could've gotten us all killed . . . I am really disappointed in myself. It is hard to have made those mistakes," she wrote her husband, no doubt silently vowing to never put her men in harm's way again.

THIRTEEN

The Changing Tide

"This was a long haul. Good, but long. It is always so good to be back in here, and to know that my guys are all back safe and sound. Sigh."

— *email to Jay, April 30, 2006*

AS HER LAV ROLLED UP to the front gates of KAF on the last day of April, Nich Goddard reminded herself of all the good things about the place. By the next morning, she'd be waking up to day ninety of her first overseas tour, having the night before enjoyed a home-style cooked meal, a warm shower and an hour of reading thanks to electricity—luxuries unknown to most Afghans, and for the past month, to the Canadian soldiers working out of FOB Robinson. She'd even get to drink some cold water: she'd had her fill of drinking from hot-to-the-touch plastic water bottles, which kept her hydrated but provided little comfort throughout long days in the scorching fifty-plus-Celsius heat. Best of all, by the time her head hit the pillow, she'd have sent a few emails out, and heard the voices of her husband and parents for the first time in a month.

The unexpectedly long stay outside the wire had been a good one. The soldiers of Charlie Company took advantage of multiple opportunities to practise the skills they'd learned back home and, over time, the icy reserve of the villagers in the opium-rich Helmand Province had thawed considerably. Kids started to wave as they passed, old men would approach and try to talk to them. In combat terms, it had been a relatively uneventful month, aside from one roadside bomb detonated just outside the base on April 20, injuring two soldiers from the company when it struck their Bison, an older-model armoured vehicle used to ferry gear. Prior to their departure at the beginning of April, both Hope and Fletcher had warned the troops to prepare for the Taliban; to the commanders' surprise, the expected confrontation didn't materialize. The Canadians' month-long show of force, with dismounted infantry, armoured vehicles and U.S. aircraft roaring overhead, kept the insurgents in the shadows. The only scare for Nich came on an even longer trip back to KAF than the original plus-twenty-four-hour foray out, when a roadside bomb went off too early to come in contact with any of the convoy's vehicles. A week earlier, Dave had headed back to Manitoba for his leave and Jeff Fehr had stepped in as Nich's 2IC. In the area around FOB Robinson, a relatively affluent part of Afghanistan dotted with homes boasting electricity and water pumps—where some of the two-storey structures, she thought, "wouldn't look out of place in Brandon"—and where the white and pink opium poppies were blossoming in the spring heat, the enemy had remained a phantom. He rarely showed his face, preferring to fight in the form of IEDs in a region reputed to contain 150 hard-core Taliban, protected by the wealthy drug lords.

But all had not been quiet on the Afghan front. In mid-April a reported Taliban ambush of a prominent Afghan security commander triggered a protracted fight in the village of Sangesar, known as the birthplace of the Taliban. This resulted in several dead police, along with one dead civilian and a dozen injured. The poor coordination between Afghan and coalition forces became the focus of Canadian commanders, and reforms were initiated to ensure that it wouldn't happen again. The same day, three Canadian soldiers were injured in a vehicle accident in the Shawali-Kot District. The month also saw rocket attacks on KAF, along with a powerful roadside bomb detonating less than a kilometre from the PRT in Kandahar City.

For Task Force Orion, the month's most significant event occurred a week before Nich returned to KAF. On April 22, four soldiers from Alpha Company were killed when their vehicle hit an IED near Gumbad, the area where Charlie Company had spent two weeks in March. The four—Corporal Matthew Dinning, Bombardier Myles Mansell, Lieutenant William Turner and Corporal Randy Payne—were travelling back to KAF as part of a mixed-vehicle convoy in a G-Wagon. They died in an area the United Nations had kept staff members out of over the previous two years, and from which UN contractors had been withdrawn several months earlier, citing security concerns.

The four deaths marked the beginning of Canadians' growing divisions over the mission. Up until late April 2006, there was relatively little controversy brewing back home: polls were showing Canadians had at least moderate support for the mission; a Strategic Council poll revealed 55 per cent of Canadians supported sending troops to Afghanistan, while 78 per cent believed Canadian troops would have a positive impact on the life of the Afghans. But much of that could be attributed to the fact that the true nature of the mission still remained under the radar for most citizens: 70 per cent believed the major purpose of Canadian troops was peacekeeping, not combat. Their ignorance was not surprising: while Ian Hope was making it clear to his troops they were fighters in a counter-insurgency and were there to hunt down the Taliban, federal defence minister Gordon O'Connor continued to assure Canadians their soldiers were serving in a security role, that they weren't going to aggressively go after the insurgents, but would, if attacked, "attack back."

On April 11, the Conservative government finally relented to weeks of pressure and held a parliamentary debate on the mission in the House of Commons. It wasn't much of a debate—some political pundits even described it as a "sham"—with all sides unanimous when it came to the men and women serving in Afghanistan. "We support our troops," Opposition leader Bill Graham affirmed. "We are here to support our men and women in uniform," NDP leader Jack Layton insisted, a week after peppering the government with questions about Canada's role, the mandate and the rules of engagement, and in return, being blasted by O'Connor, a former brigadier-general in the Canadian Forces, for being anti-military. "Should we stay in Afghanistan or should we leave?" Claude Bachand, of the Bloc Québécois, asked, and answered: "We have to chase the Taliban. . . . Let's go on." Liberal leadership hopeful Michael Ignatieff, who in 2005 had traded his post as director of the Carr Center for Human Rights at Harvard University for a seat in the House of Commons as a Liberal member of Parliament—also spoke strongly in favour of the deployment. "I've been to Afghanistan twice," he said, "once under Taliban rule and once since then. What I've learned there is that you cannot do development in Afghanistan unless you control the security situation." Ignatieff, though, broke from the group by being the only opposition member to call on the Tories to renegotiate its agreement with Afghans on the issue of detainees. O'Connor wrapped up the debate by referring to recent terrorist attacks in Bali, Madrid and London. "Must we wait for terrorists to appear in Vancouver, Montreal or here in Ottawa before we recognize the very real threat that they present to our security?" Two weeks later, as the bodies of the four soldiers began making their way back to Canada, Brigadier-General David Fraser described the losses as the price of progress in a war-ravaged country slowly regaining peace: "The Taliban are starting to press their attacks right now, and they're not being as effective as they have been in the past, which is indicative of how well we're doing."

But the deaths of those four soldiers, and the government's response, foreshadowed a slow but sure change in the political and national climate on the issue. First, the Tories came under fire for the decision not to lower flags to half-staff at federal buildings in the wake of the deaths, a practice followed by the previous Liberal government when the first dead soldiers returned home. O'Connor defended the decision, saying that the Liberals "unfairly distinguished some of those who died in Afghanistan from those who have died in current and previous operations. Lowering the Peace Tower's flag on November 11 ensures that all of Canada's fallen heroes are justly honoured."

An even bigger furor erupted only days later, when, in a move disturbingly similar to the George Bush administration's decision to shield Americans from the sight of soldiers' coffins, the government changed its policy on repatriation of dead Canadian soldiers. Media, now banned from the solemn ceremony at CFB Trenton, were forced to use stepladders along a chain-link fence outside the base in order to capture images that weren't ringed with barbed wire. Everyone from politicians (some of them Harper's own MPS) to parents of the fallen blasted the move, accusing the government of deliberately trying to hide the reality of the mission from the public's view. People weren't buying O'Connor's assertion that it was in the best interests of the families of the fallen, and argued it should be the individual families' decision whether or not to have media present. "We need to have the Canadian people see the consequences and the cost of lives of our soldiers," said Richard Leger, father of Sergeant Marc Leger, killed in Afghanistan in 2002. "It's the ultimate sacrifice. They need to see it and they need to understand."

While Nich kept up with the goings-on back home thanks to the newspaper clippings Sally inserted in her packages, it did little to deter her from the ever-present desire to head outside the wire, to be doing the work for which she was trained. While she and her team had missed the ramp ceremony for the four in late April, previous ceremonies only firmed her resolve to keep going despite the dangers. She preferred what she called "the real deal"—soldiering in the villages and mountain areas, sleeping under the stars at night—to the predictable days at KAF. "I'm used to feeling the wind on my face," she told Jay. She also hated "listening to all the stupid rules and dumb gossip" while on the base, "and pretending that I care." Like her fellow soldiers who'd spent the bulk of their time outside the wire, Nich began to assess other soldiers, especially leaders, by the degree of personal risk they were willing to take on. She found herself bristling at superiors who'd never set foot into the volatile countryside; she grew distant from some Shilo friends whose entire tours consisted of staying within the safe confines of KAF, or the relative luxury of the PRT in Kandahar City. At one point, she and her fellow soldiers were cautioned against developing "snotty" attitudes. Hearing this general directive, Nich couldn't help suspecting "I am pretty much the target audience."

Once she received word that she and her crew might not be heading outside the wire for the next month, Nich did her best to settle into a routine at KAF. She tried to create make-work projects for her crew—she almost wept with frustration when emailing Jay to tell him "there is NOTHING for us to do"—taking them out on ruck marches in the fields on the base, getting them to clean equipment and conduct vehicle checks and do ammunition counts. "I don't want the guys to go crazy, and I don't want to go crazy," she told Jay. The only positive was that she and Jeff Fehr had settled into a good groove. She'd been despairing over the temporary absence of Dave, who wouldn't be back from leave until the third week of May. But her growing confidence in Jeff had eased some of her worries. He was earnest, professional and, just like Dave, would bring back coffee for her from the Green Bean coffee shop on base. "Can't you just call me Jeff?" he asked her at one point, a sign of their growing friendship, along with his tiring of Nich always using the drawn-out "Master Bombardier Fehr" when addressing him. But the whispers and gossip were never far from her mind. "When we get home, maybe," she told him. "But not when we're working like this."

With little soldiering work to do at KAF, Nich kept busy dealing with her growing mountain of care packages. Over the next two weeks, she'd receive more than a hundred parcels from all across Canada, a testament to both Sally's efforts and Nich's growing celebrity status back home. Despite the ribbing she received from other soldiers, no one turned down her offerings of surplus candy, coffee, books and magazines. Some people were telling Nich she should consider publishing her letters when she got home, a prospect she wasn't so sure was a good idea. "To me, they seem kind of personal," she told Jay.

With so much time on her hands, her preoccupations alternated between frustration with the long days at KAF, and her excitement about joining Jay back home and begining their plans for the Wainwright move. "Can you believe that we are really, honestly, truly going to buy our very own house? I am SO excited. I can't even really describe how excited," she wrote with a cheerfulness that leaped off the page. "I don't even care if it is a dive down by the river . . . just not a trailer. Please, my love, not a trailer." She couldn't wait to start the long trip home, which would possibly include a pit stop in Cyprus or Greece, where Nich was dying to go swimming. "I feel like I've been hot forever . . ." For his part, Jay was relieved that his outgoing wife would soon be at his side. "Everyone I meet wants to talk about how hard it must be to be apart from you and what we are going through," he wrote. "I'm just not sure what to tell them anymore . . . yes, it obviously sucks and no, I don't enjoy it."

On May 2, Nich turned twenty-six at KAF, and spent the day reading scores of birthday greetings sent by mail and email and writing back what would be, by day's end, more than fifty letters, to everyone from closest friends to a grade seven boy who volunteered to be her pen pal. "Happy, happy birthday," wrote Sally. "I hope you played limbo and wore 'Today's My Birthday' on your uniform. We have been thinking about you and where it all began, twenty-six years ago. It sometimes seems like yesterday."

As she tried to ignore the shirt-soaking heat of an Afghan spring day, Nich opened several presents, including a box of cookies from Jay, eating at least a half dozen in one sitting. She used her extra phone credits accumulated while at FOB Robinson to make several calls home, including a birthday call of her own, to the dear friend who shared the same birthday as her. When Gundy Goutouski picked up the phone at her home in Cold Lake, Alberta, all she heard at first was static. She thought it was family calling from Germany. Then, that familiar voice: "Happy birthday, Auntie Gundy!" Gundy nearly burst into tears of joy at the nickname she'd gone far too long since last hearing. For nearly an hour, Nich caught her up on her experiences outside the wire, and her happiness that they'd soon be living again in the same province. "We'll always get together," Nich said. "We know you'll be really busy on your leave, but Bryan and I would drive anywhere, no matter how far, to see you and Jay," Gundy told her, which reminded Nich why they were two of the best friends she'd ever have the good luck to find.

The only way Nich could get through so many letters was to use the old "copy and paste" function on her laptop. But she made sure that the ones to those closest to her included some personal touches. "I have to say—seeing you both so happy with her makes Jay and I (mostly me) think about the kids thing a lot," she wrote Liane Nicholson, whose toddler, Emma, had inspired Nich to try her hand at knitting. "The thought still terrifies me, but you guys make me feel that we (Jay and I) are really missing out." She encouraged Julianne Charchuk in her upcoming final exams for courses she was taking, and thanked her for organizing and delivering the care packages for Jay while she was in Afghanistan. "You rock!" she told Julianne. "I miss you, Jules." To sisters Victoria and Kate, she included one identical passage:

It was such an accident of birth that we ended up where we did when we did. That we are where we are now, with the choices that we have available to us. It seems to me that we have such a burden of responsibility to make the world a better place for those who were born into far worse circumstances. It is more than donating money to charities . . . it is taking action and trying to make things better. My current job and role in Afghanistan is part of that . . . but it is more the non-governmental organizations that come later. They are the ones that really make the difference. I like to think that my being here means that they will be able to come that much sooner, and operate more freely.

Though her FOO team had yet to see any real combat against the Taliban, other than what Nich dismissed as "a bit of spec firing," she was pleased with the first three months of the tour. She was doing a good job, her guys were doing a good job, and they got to spend more time outside the wire than most. To add to her happiness, she had received her performance review on the eve of her birthday. "I ranked 7/12 captains in the regiment, which surprised the hell out of me," she wrote to Jay. She had, the report said, "Mastered performance; above average potential; ready for promotion." It was beyond what Nich had hoped for. "That is a pretty kick-ass PER (review) for my first one as a captain."

But as one day began melding into the next, Nich found that even her prolific writing and other time-consumers—she was hitting the gym twice a day and had finally managed to buy an Afghan carpet with the help of Jeff Fehr—wasn't enough. So much time on her hands meant too much time to think about things both good and bad, often resulting in mood swings that threw her off balance. "Being in KAF is starting to kill me . . . I am obsessing. This is probably the fourth time today that I have logged on to the computers," she wrote. One evening, a conversation with Andrew Nicholson returned to the possibility of children for her and Jay. She knew it was something that would resolve itself in its own good time; but still, it left her flustered. "I said that I was okay with it in an abstract way, but that you were still pretty unsure. I also said that, basically, it was up to you. I hope that is okay," she wrote Jay.

She tried to keep her mind occupied by going on to the house listings website, checking out possible houses in and around Wainwright, and sending Jay her thoughts on the pros and cons of each. But it didn't prevent her from "feeling like a basket case," riding an emotional roller coaster of joy over the thought that she'd soon be home, and worrying that "something is going to happen to my guys" when she was away. "I just keep thinking of all the near misses we've had . . . and all the ones that are bound to be coming. Except now, I'll be the one gone for a month." She and Jeff headed back on a few occasions to the KAF bazaar, where she bought a bedspread and two scarves from a pair of "really cute and very convincing" children, a marble chess set for Victoria, two marble-camel bookends for Kate, and an Afghan hat for Tim. At one stop, an Afghan seller held up a bikini made from metal, telling Nich she could wear it while learning to be an Afghan dancer. "I thought Master Bombardier Fehr was going to swallow his tongue," she wrote to Jay. "I said, 'I don't think that it will fit,' and beat a quick retreat."

Over those two weeks, Nich went "out for coffee" on a couple of occasions, forays outside the wire lasting only a few hours at a time. Things changed on May 14: the rumour was that another operation might be in the offing, and she warned Jay that "we might decide to go out unexpectedly for coffee, so if I don't email for a while, that is why." Nich and her team had yet to be briefed on big changes both outside the wire and on Ian Hope's plan for his troops. Local Afghan intelligence was reporting a massing of Taliban in the area known as the Green Zone just west of Kandahar City, and in the Helmand River valley farther west. Some TF Orion commanders were becoming increasingly convinced that the previous estimate of 200 Taliban in Kandahar Province should likely be doubled, or even tripled. But military intelligence failed to read the enemy build-up. There was a lack of trust in TF Orion's estimates of the situation: higher head-quarters considered them too inexperienced, and given to see the situation as worse than it actually was.

Thanks to grape fields, high village compound walls and other hiding places, the two areas had been traditional havens for the mujahideen. Five Afghan National Police had just been involved in a TIC (troops in contact) with the Taliban in the Panjwayi area. Hope, just returned from his leave, began to sense "we were up against something very different than we had in January, February, March and April." He wasn't alone: there was a growing sense of urgency among the Kandaharis in general, and particularly the ANP, who were deployed in Zhari and Panjwayi. On April 29, one of the Canadian patrols in Panjwayi had come for the first time under sustained direct fire in daylight from the Taliban. Several vehicles got stuck in riverbed mud during the exchange, and the Canadian troops had to extract from the area rather than fight. When they returned, the Taliban had disappeared. For Hope, the incident provided further proof that there was a "more robust enemy presence." Knowing that the opium-poppy harvest, the lifeblood of drug lords and the insurgents, would soon be wrapped up, he was predicting an imminent surge in Taliban activity. Hope devised a plan—Operation Bravo Guardian—with the Afghan police to take a portion of the area and do a systematic clearance in cooperation with the locals. After an official request for assistance on May 15 from the Afghan National Security Forces, Hope set to work on what he expected would be some routine clearances.

The plan was to head out on May 16 to the PRT in Kandahar, then in the early-morning hours of May 17, go to a triangle-shaped area around the townships of Nalgham to clear out massing Taliban. The military's leave policy had taken away some of his key leaders, including Major Bill Fletcher and B Company commander Major Nick Grimshaw; in his absence, Hope assigned Grimshaw's 21C Captain Jay Adair to lead the three platoons of close to 200 troops, with Captain Nich Goddard as his FOO.

Back home in Canada, the stress of their daughter's tour was weighing on Tim and Sally more than ever. To try to keep their heads clear, they took regular hikes with their two dogs up to Nose Hill, an oasis of wild grassland in the heart of Calgary, not far from their university-area home. Each night before bed, their nervousness would grow as they began flipping between various news stations to make sure nothing big had happened in Afghanistan. By late morning each day, they'd start to relax for a few hours, knowing it was night in Afghanistan. When word came of another Canadian soldier's death—between the first of February and the end of April, it had happened seven times— Sally would heave a sigh of relief before castigating herself for being so selfish. But there was a chance Tim would soon be able to see his daughter: the United Nations Institute for Training and Research was planning workshops in Kabul, scheduled to run the last ten days of May, and had invited Tim to participate.

"It would be really neat if this did happen, and even better if—as a result—I was able to see you!" he wrote Nich, knowing the odds were slim that one of them could somehow find a way to bridge the 483-kilometre distance between the two cities.

One night, Nich watched the film *Pearl Harbor* on her laptop. Sitting alone on her bunk, the images flickering in the dark as she listened to the audio on her earphones, Nich quietly wept at the romantic story. It made her miss Jay, and prompted her to type out a long letter in the middle of the night. "I have been thinking a lot about death, lately. It is so horrible to me that one day, one of us will have to live without the other," she wrote. "I don't know if I'm strong enough to deal with that. I worry that, because of that, I will be tested." To make sure Jay understood the depth of her feelings, she told him a story she remembered from one of her literature classes at RMC:

> There is a beautiful Greek myth about a couple who be-friended a god who was down and out with his luck . . . they took him in and looked after him, not realizing that he was immortal. Once he was stronger, as a thank you, the god asked the couple what they would like as a reward. They did not want a reward but, when pressed, they asked that they be allowed to always be together. The god agrees and leaves. Many years later, the couple is standing outside of their house, watching the sunset. They are holding hands. Suddenly, they start to turn into trees. Their roots go into the ground and intertwine. Their hands become branches that intertwine. They live the rest of eternity as trees, together. That is what I want, my love.

FOURTEEN
Poise and Precision

Hi my love,
Things are going better here. We're heading out for coffee now. I
will call when I get back.
Love always and forever, Nich

— *email to Jay, May 16, 2006*

IN THE PREDAWN HOURS of May 17, 2006, Captain Nich Goddard woke feeling more worn out than refreshed. "I didn't get a wink of sleep," she told Jeff Fehr. "That's weird, neither did I," he said. They couldn't figure out why both had experienced such fitful nights: their accommodations—consisting of pillows on the floor of a conference room at the PRT—weren't any worse than the BATS at KAF, and a lot more comfortable than their gravel beds outside the wire. And the operation they were about to embark on that morning wasn't expected to be much different from what they'd already seen in the first three months of their tour. They'd come to know their enemy as elusive, preferring cat-and-mouse games to head-on confrontation. As its name implied, Operation Bravo Guardian would be focused on the 3D approach: they'd be on the lookout for Taliban, but the primary

objective was to gain the trust of the local population and establish a presence in the area.

The previous evening before dinner, Captain Jay Adair had
sat down with Nich and given her confirmatory orders on the
next day's plan. Charlie Company commander Major Bill
Fletcher was at the start of his leave and had flown out earlier
that day to Camp Mirage, and Ryan Jurkowski, his 2IC, had not
yet returned from his leave. For this operation, Adair would
report directly to Hope, who, not having control over the leave
process, found himself reorganizing commands and platoons·
on an almost daily basis. But Hope was confident in the young
officer he was putting in charge: like Nich, Adair, a native of
Barrie, Ontario, had graduated from Royal Military College
with an arts degree; also like Nich, the sharp and professional
thirty-year-old officer, back for his second tour in Afghanistan,
was on his way up in the Canadian Forces.

Adair would lead more than 200 troops drawn from his
Bravo Company, a platoon from Charlie Company and the FOO
team led by Nich Goddard. They would start out in the village
of Kadahal in the Green Zone in an effort to flush out Taliban.
An additional rifle platoon, a tactical psychological operations
team (PSYOPS) and an ANA company would round out the
force. While Nich and her FOO team often operated somewhat
independently, attaching themselves to platoons and companies as required, she'd spent the bulk of her Afghan tour with
the soldiers of Charlie Company. But in that second week of
May, battery commander Major Steve Gallagher didn't have
much of a choice when it came to which FOO would accompany
Adair: Captain Bob Meade, attached to Alpha Company, and

Captain Mike Smith, attached to Bravo, were both up in the mountains north of Kandahar City.

Although Adair knew of Nich from Shilo, he didn't know her well; the circumstances of the leave process made this their first time working together as leaders in an operation. But he had heard the raves from Fletcher and Hope, two officers for whom he had the utmost respect. Adair sat down with Nich to discuss the procedure involved in firing an artillery mission in the Arghandab River bed as a deterrent. Nich was already adept at such shows of force, having conducted them in the Sangin District near FOB Robinson, her home for most of the month of April. Based on their scheme of manoeuvre, they worked out where Nich would best be employed: Adair's 5 Platoon would lead, and depending on how the situation unfolded, Nich would stay close to either Adair and his group of command vehicles, or 5 Platoon.

Hope had taken Adair on a recce mission to the area days earlier, introducing him to Afghan officials and bringing him up to speed on the local intelligence that was pointing to a massing of Taliban. Hope was relying on the well-informed counsel of Captain Massoud, whom he had first met two years earlier while working as a development strategist under then lieutenant-general Rick Hillier.

Massoud was an officer with the Afghan National Police who, unlike many from its ranks, was literate and well respected. He was also renowned for his tireless fourteen-year mission to eradicate the Taliban from his country. Massoud had warned Hope of a rapid build-up of insurgents in the centre of the province, in Zhari and Panjwayi districts, and of their reputed plans to attempt a takeover of Kandahar City—a move that would probably be quickly quelled by the thousands of coalition troops in and around the city. Nevertheless, the Taliban would see the resulting casualties and carnage as a symbolic victory, a demonstration of their ability both to impress Afghan civilians and inflict terror on a Canadian public that had yet to fully wake up to the reality that their country was at war. Despite his trust in Massoud, Hope still believed the reported increase in fighting-age men in the area might be more connected to the poppy and hash harvest than to the Taliban's success at recruiting both locally and from neighbouring countries like Pakistan. Although he carefully considered the Afghan officer's warnings, Hope wasn't expecting much in the way of direct confrontation. He waved off Massoud's personal guarantee that they would see an exchange of fire within thirty minutes of the battle group's arrival into the area: an earlier sweep by a platoon of Charlie Company had resulted in only "soft contacts," the occasional potshot from a rifle or badly aimed rocket propelled grenade (RPG). Going in, the goals were mainly to disrupt and nip in the bud any possible increase of Taliban activity, gather on-the-ground intelligence and gain the confidence and trust of the locals.

No operation in this strategically important, yet mostly uncharted, territory for Canadian troops could be undertaken without an appreciation of its logistical challenges. The relatively lush terrain once known as Afghanistan's Fruit Basket offered up a treasure trove of hiding places: because farmers were too poor to use wooden frames in their vineyards, the grapevines were supported by deep furrows cut into the ground and overlaid with layers of vines, replicating the effect of row upon row of World War I trenches. When he first saw the scores of thick, mud-walled grape-drying huts with narrow ventilation slits, Adair couldn't help thinking how these structures, just wide enough to accommodate a rifle barrel, reminded him of "medieval fortresses, perfect for hiding in and shooting from." In time, the Canadians would discover the fields also served as a convenient storage place for everything from 82-mm, anti-tank Soviet recoilless rifles, rocket launchers and bomb-making supplies, to western-made medical products such as intravenous bags, dressings and surgical instruments.

Ample compensation for the otherwise flat landscape could also be found in the veritable jungles of tangled marijuana plants growing up to seven feet tall, and grass-covered ditches as deep as six feet, wide enough for two men to walk in side by side, and lined by trees with large overhanging branches that hid them from helicopters and planes flying above. Canals, clusters of compounds and networks of serpentine paths too narrow for much more than pedestrians and donkeys to squeeze through were hallmarks of village life; mud-brick walls framed the few routes wide enough to accommodate a motor vehicle. When skimmed by the turrets of passing LAVs, the thick overhanging branches of the mulberry trees dropped hundreds of berries on the passing soldiers and their equipment, staining everything a disturbing hue of brownish-red that mimicked the colour of dried blood. It took only a cursory glance at the landscape to understand why the Soviets had suffered so many casualties at the hands of the mujahideen a quarter of a century earlier. The jumble of civilians, Taliban in civilian clothes, and animals, buildings, walls, trenches and foliage made it confounding for a force with even the most sophisticated weaponry to rout out the enemy. The plethora of secret corridors and bunker-like structures, familiar to any Afghan child in a country where maps were almost non-existent, made the region the perfect base from which to stage the hide-and-seek tactics of guerilla warfare.

Hope joined Captain Massoud that morning in Zhari district, along with Major Steve Gallagher and an artillery troop of two M777 155-mm howitzers and several ANA soldiers. They would be observing and coordinating the operation from Hope's Niner Tac, located at a hilltop fort at Gundy Ghar, about 40 kilometres out of Kandahar City. Known as the "Nipple" to the troops because of its appearance—a flat-topped hill 400 metres across, jutting out 30 metres from an otherwise prairie-like landscape—the location, about 3 kilometres away from the area of operations, was ideal for spotting anyone moving in or out of the labyrinth of pathways and interconnected compounds. Once targets had been identified, the LAVs positioned with Hope's team could bring rapid fire from their cannons, and the artillery's M777 howitzers could drop their rounds wherever the attacking companies needed them. Hope marvelled at Gundy Ghar (Ghar means "hill" in Pashto). It was obviously an ancient fort, but after centuries—perhaps a millennium—the mud-brick walls had "melted" together with the internal structures to form this impressive mound. Very few discernible walls were evident, but on top of the mound were trenches and bunkers built by Soviet troops two decades earlier. War, Hope understood, was not new to Zhari and Panjwayi.

Under the cover of early-morning darkness, the massive convoy of more than thirty vehicles made its way through the streets of Kandahar City. The urban centre was deserted in comparison to its cluttered daytime frenzy; but still, people seemed to be everywhere. They wandered the streets, popped out of buildings and alleyways, witnessing the large movement of vehicles with a mix of fear and wariness. At the western edge of the city, the convoy made a left turn onto Route Fosters—earlier coalition troops had named it after the famed Australian lager—and headed for the objective area only a half hour west of the city limits. The highway started out paved, but like most major Afghan roads, quickly turned to dirt and gravel.

Sitting in the gunner's seat, Jeff Fehr felt the adrenaline pumping through his veins. His anticipation over moving into the 2IC position made him quickly forget the previous night's restive sleep, as did his discomfort over squeezing his six-foot frame into the cramped space of the seat to the left of the LAV commander. Besides, he was looking forward to showing his boss that he was more than worthy of her growing trust and confidence. With Clint Gingrich at the wheel and Chris Gauthier at the back controlling the radios, in what they referred to as the "trunk monkey" position, they had all set out on the operation in good spirits. They had a fifth person with them that morning, a CIMIC officer who'd hitched a ride from the PRT and would be charged with talking to the village elders once the area was cleared and secured. Jeff and his team didn't know the man, but such an occurrence wasn't unusual: CIMIC operators often worked in pairs or alone, attached to specific companies and platoons, and travelling with troops throughout operations.

On their way to Nalgham, the convoy made a pit stop in Bazaar-e-Panjwayi, a bustling district centre that by dawn's early light was already coming to life. The goal was to link up with a force of about 80 ANA soldiers, who would then carry on with them to the final destination a few more kilometres down the road. Adair, with his 200 soldiers and thirty vehicles, tried to round up the disorganized crowd of ANA men amidst a gathering throng of noisy villagers. He couldn't help thinking, This is a complete gong show, but they did manage to finally all fall into line and head out of the village, due west. By mid-morning, the columns of armoured assault vehicles, armoured jeeps and pickups filled with men providing the necessary "Afghan face" to the operation arrived at their chosen assembly area alongside the dried-out Arghandab River, which meandered through the area and was known as a convenient expressway for the Canadians' large vehicles and LAVs.

Only minutes after their arrival at the launching point, Adair received a call from Niner Tac with new orders. Massoud had informed Hope that a large number of Taliban were hiding in a mosque in Pashmul, a tiny cluster of villages about 9 kilometres away. Hope ordered Adair to "re-orient your compass" and head back to Bazaar-e-Panjwayi, the scene of the morning's frustrating exercise of rounding up the ANA troops. There they would regroup before heading northwest to Pashmul. All of the previous evening's planning was now out the window; there was no time to develop a battle procedure for this new location. Yet Adair was able to adapt instantly to the altered plan, as was Nich, who issued new artillery advice on the radio and assisted Adair with the movements.

As they made their way north and back across the Arghandab River bed, approaching Bayanzi village just after ten o'clock in the morning, more than a hundred women, children and elderly people were walking hurriedly along the roadside. In his three months in Afghanistan, Adair had seen nothing like it. Many of the soldiers felt the hairs on the back of their neck stand up at the eerie sight. This is unreal, Clint thought to himself, shaking his head in awe as he peered out of the small slit from his driver's seat position in Golf One Three's LAV.

The locals clearly knew the truth of what Massoud had tried to tell Hope: a battle was indeed imminent. Within minutes of their arrival, Jon Snyder's 8 Platoon from Charlie Company, on the south flank, received incoming small-arms fire and RPGs. Thus began a fierce, forty-five-minute-long firefight between the Canadians and the Taliban. When the attack first began, Hope looked at his watch in his Niner Tac, 6 kilometres away from Bayanzi, and realized that "Captain Massoud was off by only four minutes." He sat back from his radio headset for a brief moment to absorb the implications of this new development. "They're not running away," he said to himself. The Taliban didn't even budge when the Apache attack helicopters swarmed in, and in fact shot back. Okay, this enemy has got some gumption, Hope thought. But why? When this battle is over, I'm going to find out why they are staying and fighting here.

Hope was transfixed over the next two hours as he listened to Adair and Nich, the two most senior ranks on the battlefield, coordinate their efforts. Neither had trained as company or battery commanders; neither had gone through advanced courses to learn how to manoeuvre multiple platoons. No one in TF Orion had received training for what was required on this day. And yet there they were, two young junior officers, taking on their duties with remarkable skill. They were the front-line leaders in the first close-quarter combat experienced by Canadian soldiers in nearly half a century. They were using sophisticated artillery, attack helicopters, fighter-jet support and electronic-warfare assets. Hope couldn't help shaking his head in wonder.

How was he going to relate this back to his own superiors, he thought, "without sounding like I'm exaggerating everything?"

The morning proved to be as momentous for Nich and her FOO party as it was for Hope. As sporadic fire continued after the initial firefight, she juggled communications with the three platoons and Adair, coordinating their movements as they spread out in a nearly 2-kilometre firing line through the villages. Standing in the open hatch of her LAV, Nich calibrated the exact locations of the farms from which Taliban fire was coming, and radioed the targeting information back to the 155-mm cannon about 11 kilometres to the west of the battle group. High-explosive shells rained down on the precise location she had intended, while other LAVs pounded the targets with machine-gun fire. The significance of the act was not lost on all the members of her FOO party: they had just called in the first artillery fire against enemy combatants since the Korean War.

Observing his two leaders on the battlefield, Hope knew he had been right to entrust the operation to them. Adair was risking his life going back and forth between platoons, fighting with his men on the front lines, and doing it "as calm as could be." Nich's orchestration of artillery was sheer perfection. As he listened to her over the radio, Hope once again took comfort from her steadying presence. As she had done several times before, Nich served as the station taking the information, synthesizing it and passing it around, with her usual cool, calm-sounding voice. Thank God she's here, thought Hope. Over the course of nearly two hours of sporadic fighting, Nich had been given the go-ahead to control the attack helicopters that fired rockets in the enemy's direction, despite not having the FAC training that would certify her for the job. She accomplished the task, thought

Adair, "with poise and precision," giving him the confidence to direct his attention to manoeuvring the forces on the ground.

That morning, Nich's indispensable competence was dearly missed at one particular place in this extended battlefield. While she was with the platoon to the north-northeast of the Canadian line, another group of infantry vehicles called for artillery fire onto a target building that was pouring out Taliban machine-gun and RPG fire. The building was only 100 metres from the troops. Nich was unable to reach their location in adequate time, so the infantrymen—who are trained in the rudiments of calling in artillery fire—made their own request. But it was too complicated a mission. The artillery shell flew longer and went farther than calculated—a factor, Hope would later speculate, likely due to variables such as higher-altitude winds—dropping within 70 metres of Adair and Snyder's vehicles. Looking through his binoculars from the turret of his LAV, Adair said, "That's a little close. . . . Enough, don't fire that mission." Clearly, Golf One Three's expertise was vital in order to effectively conduct such missions.

During the fight, Nich and Jeff had given Chris control of two U.S. Apache attack helicopters. It was a move Jeff knew would be considered "crazy back home, to let a bombardier control aircraft." But Chris, who earlier in the tour had completed a brief course on controlling choppers, did an exceptional job with the firing helicopters as they performed runs upon the enemy. As they executed their various tasks calmly and with precision, the team could hear gunfire in the distance, but as Jeff would later remember, the mood in their LAV was "relaxed."

Under the blazing fifty-degree-Celsius heat of the midday sun, the Taliban finally retreated and—to the relief of the soldiers of Operation Bravo Guardian, scores of whom were suffering from the weakness, muscle cramping, nausea and confusion that accompanies heat exhaustion—a hush fell over the battlefield. Replenishing themselves by guzzling scalding water from plastic bottles, the infantry soldiers conducted searches for the next several hours, finding weapons in the fields, several bags of nitrate fertilizer (used in Afghanistan both for bomb-making and farming) in a compound, and fifteen fighters hiding in various compounds and in the surrounding grape fields. The captured fighters were taken to Bayanzi's White Schoolhouse to await their transfer to the ANA. The school, one of two in the area, had earned its nickname thanks to its exterior of whitewashed paint. One of many Afghan schools built with funds from foreign-aid agencies, it had since been taken over by insurgents who were using it to shelter fighters, care for their wounded and store weapons. They had painted Taliban slogans on its walls, and, through word of mouth, had warned locals to keep their children away or face death. Over the coming months, the structure would become not only a symbol of the fight between coalition troops and the Taliban, but also the physical epicentre of the insurgency.

Once it was apparent that the insurgents had pulled back, Nich gave her men the go-ahead to celebrate the morning's achievements. They got out of the LAV and while Chris and Clint exchanged high fives, Nich pulled out her camera. "Hold this up," she said to Jeff, handing him the mission coordinates he'd scribbled on a signal form—coordinates that had rained artillery fire on the farm from where the Taliban had been shooting. Jeff held the form in his hand as Nich's camera zeroed in on the image. As he took in the implications of the day, Jeff felt a twinge of regret that Sergeant Redford wasn't there to share it with them. But he realized "it was a sort of Catch-22": if Dave had been there, Jeff wouldn't have stepped into the 21C role and been able to shoot the mission. Later, Jeff, who as the FOO tech shot the mission and appreciated that his boss "didn't micromanage it," would remember Nich smiling ear to ear as she shared her joy with her team. Chris, who sent the mission over the radio, would recall them being "happier than pigs in shit." Nich suggested they do something formal back in Canada, to properly celebrate the milestone. "All the other guys are gonna be pissed off with us," Chris told them with a laugh. "We're gonna be the ones in the history books."

From his mobile post at Gundy Ghar, Hope was feeling equally proud. Adair, Nich and Jon Snyder, he felt, had been handed a highly sophisticated operation in a dangerous setting, and had done an incredible job. There's no limit to what this organization can do, he thought, provided I get it the support it needs. His job was to aggressively hunt down the Taliban, get his soldiers as close to them as possible "and let them go—let them do their job."

The next few hours were uneventful for Nich and her men. They waited and kept watch while the infantry conducted foot patrols and searches of compounds in the area, along with tracking the blood trails, drag marks, and, in some cases, body parts that pointed to four Taliban killed and numerous others injured. Since the insurgents had an uncanny ability to quickly round up their wounded and dead—an unnerving practice Hope suspected they had learned from studying Viet Cong tactics—such numbers were only estimates. Clint had been in his tiny driver's compartment for what seemed an eternity and was itching to stretch his legs. Knowing they weren't planning to go anywhere for the foreseeable future, he finally popped out to get some air, and reclined atop the hatch to play games on his hand-held game console. "Put your helmet on, Newt, it's important," Nich told the sweat-drenched soldier, who had attempted to shed some of his kit in order to survive the rising temperature. Chris, whom Nich cheerfully chided for being the resident pessimist, was growing wary of the constant flow of locals walking by and glaring in their direction. He was anxious to move and, as always, shared his sentiments with his boss. "We can't really stay here for twelve hours in the same location," he said of their place at the end of a 100-metre line of vehicles on a narrow road flanked by compound walls. "It's just not healthy."

But a plan was already in place: the fight would resume the next morning, and in the next couple of hours, they'd retreat towards the White Schoolhouse for the night, where they would form a leaguer with the rest of the battle group and sleep once again under the stars.

FIFTEEN
Last Light

AS THE EARLY-EVENING SUN began to set on the dusty landscape, it cast a hazy golden glow over the now-quiet fields and dusty compounds. Nich received orders from Adair to begin preparing to mobilize. Chris had signed off with the Apache helicopters, which then headed back to KAF to refuel. About ten minutes after the choppers departed, Clint was sitting in his driver's seat, waiting patiently for the go-ahead from his FOO boss. Nich and Jeff were standing up, armpits out of the turret, doing some final checks of the area with binoculars, and taking turns scanning with the guns. Before they headed back to link up with the rest of the battle group, Nich signalled to him to move his headset to the side, so they would be "off line" for a few seconds. Leaning across the 4-inch bar between the commander and gunner seat, she spoke in a voice barely above a whisper.

"I'm proud of you guys—you got to do it, and you did it very well," she told Jeff. Chris had just popped out of the LAV's back hatch to light a cigarette. As he stood there, one foot up on the ramp while he took his first drag, Chris watched carefully as two ANA soldiers marched an Afghan in a white turban past. He suspected the six-foot-tall man, unusually large for an Afghan, was working as a spotter for the insurgents. Just then, his left eye started to twitch uncontrollably. In that moment the superstitious soldier thought to himself, Uh-oh.

"Ka-boom!" is the next thing Chris heard, and the only thing Jeff later remembered as he and Nich were thrown into the bottom of the turret by a thunderous explosion. Chris looked up to see an RPG rip into the side of a mud wall, the explosion felling one of the two ANA soldiers and the tall Afghan man, who was "split right in half" in front of Chris's eyes. Seconds later, Jeff, who was briefly knocked out by the blast, regained consciousness. "What the hell was that?" he asked, shaking his head in confusion. At that moment, the LAV's fire-suppression system detonated, filling the inner compartments with a white cloud. In the midst of the melee, Jeff heard the sound of gunfire pummelling the armour-plated vehicle's exterior and RPGs whistling past. His soldiering instincts kicked in. He grabbed hold of his 25-mm stabilized chain gun, the main weaponry on the LAV, "and let it rip" in the direction of the enemy, firing off about fifteen rounds. "What are you guys shooting at?" Clint asked, not realizing the initial blast wasn't their own cannon firing, or that their radio communications had been knocked out from the force of the hit.

Later, Jeff would learn just how much had happened in that single moment: his LAV had been hit with three simultaneous RPGs and a barrage of bullets from Soviet-made AK-47 assault rifles. The incoming fire had damaged both their 25-mm mounted cannon and their coaxial machine gun. The radio sitting atop the LAV, which Chris had just used to sign off with the Apaches, had been ripped to shreds. In the same instant, all three of Adair's platoons had also come under heavy fire. Snyder's platoon and the two platoons from B Company were in their own separate scraps; two other platoons from Charlie Company, which were in outlying areas in cutoff positions, were also hit. The Taliban had implemented a highly coordinated attack, launching multiple RPGs at the two LAVs stationed at either end of the battle group's blocking force's position; by disabling those LAVs, they could effectively trap everyone in the ambush zone. At the same time, heavy machine-gun fire hammered away at the whole of the battle group, while the Canadians started a counterattack with thousands of rounds of gunfire. From Niner Tac, Hope started doing quick math: If all my organizations are being fired at, from five different locations, he thought, there is probably a hundred or more Taliban firing on us. No intelligence has told us that there were that many there.

After about thirty seconds, the radio communications came back on. "We've been hit," Jeff finally told Clint. "All right, guys, you're both okay, everybody's okay," Jeff called out as his driver watched tracer fire light up the blackening sky. "Clint, get the LAV going . . . Chris, get that ramp up in the back." Realizing he hadn't heard Nich's voice yet, Jeff went back into the bottom of the turret to check on her status. She was slumped over, her eyes closed as though, he thought, she was "knocked out, or sleeping." Then he saw the blood coming from the back of her head. Not wanting to remove Nich's helmet for fear of causing a neck injury, Jeff grabbed a scarf and stuffed it into the helmet to try to staunch the flow.

As the LAV continued to be battered with fire, Jeff clicked on the radio again, momentarily forgetting what frequency he was supposed to be tuning into. "My Sunray's down! My Sunray's down!" he cried into the receiver, using the generic military term for commander. He got back on the 25-mm chain gun and started shooting rounds until the cannon jammed. He switched to the coaxial machine gun, mounted just to the right of the now-disabled cannon. That, too, he cried out, "is pooched." Chris, having determined that he hadn't been hit and was "good to go," jumped into the LAV and grabbed hold of the C9 machine gun and pulled the trigger. Nothing happened. His worst fears realized, Chris began to laugh uncontrollably at the tragicomedy of errors as bullets whizzed by his head. He cocked the gun once more and pulled the trigger—nothing. This time he didn't laugh. He grabbed the machine gun and threw it, then reached for his own rifle. "Why isn't the machine gun going?" Jeff cried out. "Because it's fucked," Chris yelled as he began shooting. "Why aren't you getting the twenty-five going?" Jeff yelled back. "It's been hit, too," said Chris. Jeff, realizing "this is pretty much the worst-case scenario," grabbed his rifle from where it sat on the rack beside his hatch, and "started to let go . . . going to town."

A moment later, Jeff went back down a second time to check on Nich. From his driver's-seat position, Clint couldn't see what was happening, and alternated between fearing the worst and telling himself he was mistaken. He learned Nich had been hurt only when Jeff cried out, "Don't die on me, Boss!" Clint felt a bolt of fear run up his spine, convinced they were all going to die. Jeff finally told Chris what he'd suspected the moment he saw Nich slumped over. "The captain got hit! I don't know if she's dead—I think she's dead." While Chris covered the right and the rear of the LAV with his rifle, Jeff tried to compress the bleeding and checked Nich's breathing, still hoping against hope she could be saved. The Taliban continued the rain of fire on their LAV. "Where the hell are these people shooting from?" yelled Chris. Jeff, trying desperately to help his boss and keep the rest of them from being hit, stood up again in the turret to see what was going on. He spotted an infantry platoon helping them in the firefight, engaging the enemy with small arms and grenades, and went down to check on Nich a third time. Things had only got worse. "Field dressings! Bandages!" he yelled out. The ambush had lasted only a few minutes, but for Jeff, Chris and Clint, time seemed to stand still. Jeff, his head reeling from a concussion and the sight of blood everywhere, tried to take in his FOO team's new reality as the bullets continued to pound their LAV. He also tried to absorb the fact that, despite standing less than 4 inches away from Nich, he didn't have so much as a scratch on him.

"Well, there's three of us left in this crew, let's get the three of us out of here," he called to the others. All of them knew full well they had to find a way to extricate themselves from the kill zone. "Clint, let's go forward." At the same time, however, the infantry platoon was starting to back up on the alley-like narrow road where Golf One Three sat at the rear of the line. "Whoa, whoa, stop," Chris called out. "You guys gotta back me up," Clint said, "because everyone's in front of me—I'll have to go backwards." During the ambush, three ANA vehicles—a cluster of battered Ford Rangers and Toyota trucks—had pulled up behind them, essentially boxing in Jeff and his crew. We're like a bunch of fish in a barrel, Chris thought as he cried out to the ANA soldiers, "Back up, back up!" While still taking fire, the two men directed Clint to make the vehicle do a one-hundred-point turn in its tight spot, so he could face forward for the kilometre-long dash back to an area where support personnel were waiting. As he did so, he came into contact with a compound wall. "What the hell, smash it back through the wall," said Chris. "If we get stuck, and the guys in front get stuck, we're all screwed."

As soon as Clint had turned the vehicle around and had a straight line, he gunned it. "Slow down, Newt!" yelled Chris. Infantry soldiers were everywhere, and they drove right over the detainee who had been split in half by the first volleys of RPG blasts. "You're trying to figure out where the friendlies are, find out where the enemy is—it's chaos," is how Chris would later describe the experience of combat in close quarters. "You've almost got shutters on but you don't, because you can't afford to have shutters on." Clint slowed down so the rest of the column could catch up, and led it out to the area where the command vehicles and support units were gathered.

From his command post 6 kilometres away, Hope was trying unsuccessfully to contact Nich Goddard. He was growing alarmed over going so long without that now-familiar steady, smooth voice. He received news of a casualty, but no call sign was provided. Oh no, he thought, that's got to be Nich's vehicle. He knew he shouldn't jump to conclusions, and waited for the four-digit zap number—which identifies troops who have been injured or killed without providing names—to be delivered. Hope carried with him an eleven-page list of the names and zap numbers of everyone in Task Force Orion. He pulled it out and waited. The number that first came over the radio, though, didn't equate. He asked for confirmation: it was Nich's radio call sign. "Okay, that's Nich, she's only wounded," he reassured himself. The voice on the radio told Hope that the casualty was "Priority Four." In Canadian Army parlance this usually means not serious enough to require immediate evacuation, but can also denote a fatality. Hope was contacting KAF to demand a helicopter medevac when word came that she was Priority Four only because she was vital signs absent (VSA). The entire radio net fell quiet. Hope walked over to Major Steve Gallagher, whose vehicle sat behind his. Gallagher had been busy on the artillery radio and had not heard what had happened. Hope delivered the bad news: "It's Nich. She's dead," was all that he said. Gallagher and battery sergeant Major Paul Parsons stared at him in stunned silence.

Throughout the day, both Andrew Nicholson and Bob Meade had listened in on the battle. From a base in the mountains north of Kandahar, Andrew smiled to himself as he recalled Nich's frustration only days earlier about being stuck within the confines of KAF. There she is, calling in great engagements, he thought. Hours later, when he first heard the report of a casualty, he figured it was infantry. When Gallagher called him on the satellite phone, Andrew assumed he was organizing reinforcements for the next day's battle. "Put me in the fight, coach," he said. "Nichola's dead," Gallagher told him. "What? Say again?" "Nich's dead, Andrew." Bob, at Gumbad Platoon House, heard the VSA report come in over the radio that evening. Knowing the statistics, he too assumed it was infantry. It would be several hours before he heard the name of his colleague and close friend's wife confirmed as the fatality.

■ ■ ■

As the bruised and battered Golf One Three finally made its way up to the support personnel, Jeff was half hanging out of the LAV, screaming for a medic. One came over, climbed up and peered in. She looked down at Nich, looked at Jeff and left without a word. Jeff's grief and fear now had a new companion: rage—an emotion Chris shared. It would take both men months before they came to understand that the medic, in performing a rapid triage and moving to the next case, had realized instantly what they had yet to admit to themselves: there was no helping their young commander, and there were other wounded to tend to. A few moments later, an interpreter working with the CIMIC officers ran up to the LAV. He helped Chris and Jeff lift Nich out through the top of the turret. The men laid her on the LAV's back ramp, and Chris covered her body with one of the Ranger blankets used as ground cover for the nights they'd slept beside the LAV. As sporadic fire erupted once again, Jeff kneeled down and grabbed his weapon, emptying an entire clip (thirty rounds) into the direction of the gunfire, feeling for the first time in his life "just pure hatred and anger."

Over the next hour and a half, sporadic enemy fire continued as the night sky cast a black shroud over the landscape. Jeff kept watch from the turret, scanning the area with his rifle and thermal sights. Clint stayed in his driver's seat, prepared to move again at a moment's notice. Chris was in the back on his radios, also scanning with his rifle. Jeff instructed Chris to raise the ramp so the enemy couldn't see the lights of the vehicle. "I can't," he told Jeff. "What the hell do you mean you can't?" Jeff barked back. "Nich's body is still on the ramp," answered Chris. Jeff, thinking the medics had long since removed her from the LAV, felt a mix of shock and renewed anger wash over him. "We still have to ramp up," he said. With the interpreter's help, Chris carried Nich into the LAV and put her on the bench. Forty-five minutes later, the medics finally arrived with a body bag.

Once Clint managed to get them over to the White Schoolhouse, where the rest of the battle group was gathering, Jeff grabbed his map to go see Adair. Despite the chaos of the past several hours, there was still work to do, and Jeff needed his instructions for the night and day ahead. "Who are you?" Adair asked Jeff. "I'm Golf One Three," he responded. "I'm in Nich's crew, but I guess I'm the boss now." Adair shooed away his crew members and directed Jeff into his LAV. Flipping the light on, he stared at the battle-weary soldier with an expression of alarm. Jeff looked down: he was covered in blood. In "full zombie mode," he was directed immediately to the medics for examination. Although Jeff tried to argue otherwise—he was still clutching on to the military adage that "when your boss is down, everybody steps up"—Adair made it clear that he and the rest of his team were done for now. They'd be heading back to KAF at the first possible opportunity to rest and recuperate until they were sent out on another operation. Each was allowed to phone family back in Canada on the medics' satellite phone; they could reassure their loved ones that they were okay, but couldn't provide any more information on what had just transpired. Jeff first tried his brother Rod in Victoria; he wasn't ready for an emotional conversation with mom Margaret back in Manitoba. Still, it was a necessary call: once Nich's name was released to the media, his relatives back home would be sent into a flurry of panic, fearing that he too might have been seriously injured. But Rod wasn't answering. Jeff called his mother: "Mom, something's happened," he told her. She knew the FOO team, and started asking about everyone by name. "I'm okay, but I can't speak for anyone else." Margaret continued to ask about Nich, Clint and Chris. "I can only tell you I'm okay, Mom."

The medics returned to Nich's LAV to inform the surviving crew members that her body had been laid out, and was under guard, in a room in the White Schoolhouse. In another room, the ANA were guarding 32 Taliban captured during the day-long battle. If any of her FOO party wanted to pay their last respects, this was their opportunity. Clint and Jeff declined. I want to remember her the way she was, Jeff said to himself. I want to remember her smiling and just being Nich, not as a body in a bag. Chris, the soldier Nich knew as the toughest in the bunch, was the only one to take up the offer. As he made his way to the building, the night sky lit up with a series of flashes. A precision-guided, 500-pound bomb dropped by a U.S. Air Force bomber high overhead—directed by the grid references for the Taliban group that had ambushed Nich's FOO team—followed. An embedded American journalist later described the impact that turned everything in its wake to dust, "like the hand of God slapping down and smashing everything." The deafening explosion—its dramatic display of force and rage ordered by Lieutenant-Colonel Ian Hope— silenced the enemy and served a dual purpose: to let the Taliban know they'd be back the next day, stronger than ever, and to repair the morale of a shaken and exhausted battle group that had just lost one of its leaders.

Chris kneeled down on the dirt floor of the White Schoolhouse and looked at the unscathed face of Captain Nich Goddard, her body bag unzipped to just below the shoulders. He thought about how she'd just shared with him his greatest day as a soldier, of how over the past three months she'd worn him down, earning his loyalty, trust and friendship.

"I'm sorry this had to happen to you," he said to the soldier who had, these past three months, put the safety of her crew and fellow soldiers first in one of the most dangerous places on the planet.

"Rest in peace. See you on the other side."

PART IV

CANADA'S DAUGHTER

SIXTEEN

The "Lady from Canada"

Hi everyone,

I am sorry to have to tell you this via email, but I figured it would be the fastest way to get a hold of all of you.

Nichola was killed in Afghanistan earlier on today. Details are still vague. So far all that I know is that she was involved in a firefight with enemy forces when she was killed. She was the only Canadian casualty at the time.

Details should be released to the media shortly.
Jay

— mass email, morning of May 17, 2006

PULLING UP TO THE DUSTY FRONT GATES of KAF in the late-night hours of May 17, the FOO team of Golf One Three was exhausted, dejected and still in the zombie state that had shielded them from the full force of the trauma coursing its way through their bodies. Their blunted emotions helped them to focus on the goal ahead: the post-battle clean-up. The LAV would have to be completely gutted of its contents, with anything deemed a bio-hazard—clothing and personal items covered in blood and human tissue—destroyed by burning. As they prepared for the solemn task, their main concern was protecting the privacy and dignity of their boss, Captain Nich Goddard. Jeff stopped in at the command centre for permission to park the LAV somewhere far from the prying eyes of the curious. "The less people that have to see the inside of it," he told one of the officers there, "the better." The officer, startled at the sight of the soldier wearing fatigues covered in dried blood, eyed him with suspicion. "What's going on with you guys?" he asked. "Nothing's going on with us," Jeff responded with a blank expression. The officer nodded his head. Then he pointed, to Jeff's relief, in the direc-tion of a quiet lot filled with other large vehicles and equipment. As they pulled into the designated spot, Jeff and Chris looked around warily for any rubberneckers clutching a camera, hop-ing to snap a photo of the damaged vehicle. A soldier wandered up and offered his services. "You do not need to see what's in this LAV," Jeff told him matter-of-factly. "Just politely fuck off."

As the new boss of Golf One Three, Jeff set out the rules before they started the job. "Nobody go into that turret except me," he told Clint and Chris, "because no one else has to see it." While he gathered up various items from the turret, Chris and Clint formed four piles of individual possessions, along with the ones to be burned. At that point, Jeff thought to himself, Nothing would faze us. They were nonchalant, almost sarcastic as they held up each item to determine which pile it belonged in. "This is fucked," said Chris, brandishing Nich's shrapnel-shredded gun that had been sitting atop the LAV. "This one has holes," said Clint of a T-shirt, which he then tossed into the discard pile along with a pile of papers. They were all glad that Nich's camera was still salvageable, but Chris, seeing that his was "pretty well blown up," threw it in the destroy pile. Jeff grabbed a helmet lying on the ground. Turning it over, he saw its back torn apart by shrapnel and still covered in blood and brain matter. He stopped in his tracks, trying to catch his breath. The tears began to flow and he doubled over, his body heaving as he sobbed quietly for what felt to him an eternity, but was probably only a minute or two.

Once he snapped back to his previous numb condition, Jeff looked at the helmet one more time, and placed it atop the burn pile. When they were done, another soldier came and threw a tarp over the LAV. Jeff felt a brief twinge of satisfaction: they'd got the job done, and no one had snapped so much as a single digital image. As they walked to the showers to scrub off nearly twenty-four hours' worth of sweat, dust, grime and blood, they didn't speak. They had just returned from the first face-to-face battle between Canadians and enemy combatants in more than fifty years, and they had just lost one of their own. They were in no mood to talk.

■ ■ ■

Not long after the three surviving members of Golf One Three had landed back at KAF, Major Bill Fletcher, who was waiting for a flight out of Camp Mirage to Thailand where he'd be meeting his wife, Daria, for his leave, got word that a female soldier had been killed in the fight at Bayanzi. He knew that there were only two women from Charlie Company in the operation, and one was a medic. His parting words to Nich had been "Good luck, take care, come back safe." He "didn't think anything of" this latest operation, since there still weren't any solid indications of significant Taliban presence in the area. The enemy had popped out only on occasion, never appearing long enough to spur a full-on confrontation. Hearing about the death, Fletcher had a sick feeling in his stomach. Nich's job was to be at the front of the front lines, as close to the enemy as possible in order to adeptly assist the soldiers on the ground. If things had heated up, she'd have been in the direct line of fire. When it was confirmed that he had lost his FOO, Fletcher's heart sank. He felt "so frustrated to hear something like that on the radio, and not be there." But Fletcher, much respected by his soldiers for commanding from the front, knew his presence on the battlefield "would not have made a difference—they did everything they were supposed to do."

North of Kandahar City, Andrew Nicholson was trying to absorb the reality that his close friend, whose personal and professional life had been intertwined with his own for the past four years, was gone. He couldn't phone Liane back home and let her know her beloved Nich had just died; the news hadn't yet made its way to the thousands of soldiers watching the Can-Con "morale-boosting" variety show at KAF that evening. He tried to console himself with the fact she hadn't suffered: the medics on the scene had determined that the blow to the back of her head was devastating enough to have caused instantaneous death. Desperate to the point he would have "stuck out my thumb and hitched a ride back," Andrew called his superiors and asked if he could return to KAF for the ramp ceremony. His boss approved, but there were no convoys or helicopters leaving soon enough. He would have to find his own way to say goodbye.

More than 10,000 kilometres away, CFB Shilo was basking in an almost summer-like spring heat wave. At just before 11:00 a.m., Jay Beam was sitting at his computer scanning the house listings for Wainwright and awaiting mortgage-approval papers over the fax line. There was one house he thought would be perfect for their first real home as a family: it was out in the countryside, so there was plenty of room for dogs Sam and Bill to roam, and it had Internet service, a definite must for the computer-savvy Jay. He couldn't wait to tell Nich. He heard a noise coming from downstairs, like someone stuffing flyers between the front and screen doors. Jay turned back to his computer screen. A moment later, there was a soft knock. He made his way down the stairs, and opened the door to find Acting Commanding Officer Liam McGarry and Captain Dave Wilson, the base's padre, standing outside. There was only one reason why these two men would be together on his front porch. Jay took a deep breath, offered an empathetic smile and said, "Just wait a second, I'll let the dogs out the back." He calmly walked to the back door and opened it into the morning sunshine as Sam and Bill rushed past. He returned, and invited the men to enter the living room. "Please, sit down," he heard one tell him. Jay knew what they were going to say, and felt sad for their unenviable task. "Were there other casualties?" he asked, knowing that they probably couldn't tell him. McGarry stepped outside for a moment; Jay could see he was on his cellphone, and assumed he was informing his higher-ups that Nich's official next of kin had been notified. He'd spent time with the padre a few months earlier as part of Nich's pre-deployment interviews. On this day, he sat across from the man in silence, his eyes cast down at the floor as his mind raced a hundred miles an hour. He was twenty-six years old. He was a widower.

He'd heard from his wife only twenty-four hours earlier. She'd managed to dash off one last email from the PRT the night before heading out. She wasn't sure "why we were rushed out here," but was happy to report that "the food here is amazing." She was in good spirits, encouraging him about his computer courses and sharing plans to pull a prank on Sergeant Dave Redford when he returned from leave. She wrote, as she had so many times before, "I hope that you have a great day," and signed off her note with her usual "All my love, always." And now, Jay was standing in the home they shared, unable to still his trembling hands as he dialled the phone number to Tim and Sally's home in Calgary. The call went straight to voicemail. He left a message, trying his best to sound calm as he asked them to call him back.

■ ■ ■

At ten o'clock in the morning mountain time, Tim Goddard found himself puttering around alone in the split-level he had called home in Calgary for the past seven years. It was the longest he and Sally had ever stayed in one place, prompting them to unpack nearly all the artifacts of their three decades together: Inuit sketches hung on the living room walls beside brightly coloured Papua New Guinea paintings; tables and shelves were crowded with ebony bowls from Trobriand Island carvers and knick-knacks Tim had picked up on countless trips to Eastern Europe and the Middle East. He had strolled into the house from the backyard deck, where he'd spent the past half hour reading the first dozen or so pages of Leonard Cohen's new poetry collection, *Book of Longing*. It was a gift from Sally for his fifty-third birthday. Along with Kate, who'd just returned from four months studying in France, the couple had celebrated earlier that morning over breakfast before Sally went to work and Kate to school. Sally was part of a University of Calgary research project on the effects of dual-language books in English and Farsi, and working out of an elementary school in a northeast suburb known as Little India. Kate was just a few blocks from home, enrolled in grade eleven at William Aberhart High School. Tim had booked the day off from his job as the University of Calgary's vice-provost (international) to enjoy his birthday, making time for just one meeting with a scholar visiting from overseas. He knew he'd be getting a call from Wales; Victoria, who had been travelling the past few weeks through Europe, had just arrived there to visit grandmother Betty and wait for a replacement credit card. Her intention was to stay a few days with Betty, then resume her travels for the next several months.

He didn't expect, however, to hear from his eldest daughter: Nich, letting him know she'd likely be "out for coffee" on his birthday, had made certain to relay her wishes two days earlier. He'd put the book down and went in the house to make one work-related call. While he was on the line, the light indicating a new voicemail came on. As he listened to Jay's subdued voice, Tim shuddered. The message wasn't a birthday greeting, and Jay, despite his best efforts, didn't sound very cheery for a man calling his father-in-law on his birthday. "Hi, Jay, is everything all right?" he asked tentatively when Jay answered. "No, I'm afraid not," he replied softly. "Nichola's been killed in Afghanistan."

Tim let out a cry of anguish, regaining his composure just long enough to utter an abrupt goodbye.

In a fog of shock and sorrow, he stumbled out of the house and over to the coffee shop a couple of blocks away, where he was to meet his overseas visitor. He walked up to the front counter. "Are you okay?" the barista asked as she looked at the crying man in front of her. "No, I just heard my daughter's been killed in Afghanistan." His appointment walked in moments later, and he delivered the sad news before racing back to his house. Desperate for an explanation of any kind, he called Jay again, but there was no new information; all he could tell Tim for certain was that now that next of kin had been notified, it was only a matter of time before the news of Nichola's death hit the national news broadcasts.

The wheels have fallen off now, Tim thought to himself as he jumped in his car and tore up to the two schools where his wife and daughter were. He first picked up Kate, who sat in the front passenger seat as her father raced to the other side of town. When a school official came to summon Sally, she was sitting down to coffee with a group of student teachers. They were talking about a woman they knew whose son had committed suicide two weeks earlier. "We're so ill-prepared to deal with death," Sally told them. "How awful it must have been for his mother to find out on Mother's Day." When she walked into the conference room minutes later, Sally found Tim waiting with an expression on his face she'd never seen before. "She's gone, she's gone," was all he could say before embracing his disbelieving wife and youngest daughter. "What are we going to do?" asked Sally as she felt the floor underneath her feet almost give way.

There was no time to collapse into grief. Sally's mom, Kathleen, kept the television in her and Michael's Sault Ste. Marie home tuned in to CBC Newsworld all day long; Victoria didn't yet know, and between husband and wife, there were eight siblings and their families. Their desperate dash, hoping against hope that no one in Nich's inner circle would hear the news from the radio or television, kept them focused and determined. After phoning Sally's parents, they called Tim's mother and Victoria, who was just sitting down to dinner with her grandmother. Betty picked up the phone. Victoria watched in stunned silence as the older woman's face fell. After a moment or two of whispered conversation, she handed her the phone. Just before she did, Betty said, "Tory, I'm afraid we've lost your sister."

After he got off the phone with Tim, Jay paced around his living room, trying to keep his wits about him as he thought of whom else he needed to notify. It was a burden no one expected him to bear. While Jay sat down to write the mass email informing scores of friends of Nich's death—calling up the same mailing list used for distributing her weekly dispatches from Afghanistan—the padre called Sergeant Dave Redford, who was just wrapping up his leave in Dauphin, Manitoba, where his wife was stationed as an RCMP officer. Dave was flying out that very day for the long trip back to KAF. He was getting into the shower when he heard his phone ring. He decided to answer rather than let it go to voicemail. "I've got some tragic news," Wilson told Dave. "There's been a firefight and Captain Goddard was killed." As he stood holding the phone, Dave couldn't get out any words at first. All he could think was, Why wasn't I there? Like Nich, he feared something happening to his crew when he wasn't there to help. "What should I do?" he asked the padre.

"Stay in Canada, or go back over there?" The padre replied, "Your troops need you. Carry on with your mission." The pragmatic soldier paused for a brief moment. "Good point," he said, and hung up the phone to prepare for his drive to the airport. On his way there, Dave thought about his smart and funny friend, the best officer with whom he'd ever worked. He decided that as soon as he got on that plane, he'd drink himself into a stupor. As he raced to the airport in the early afternoon, the first news report of Nich's death came over the car radio. "First female, first female," he muttered under his breath, shaking his head as he repeated the main thrust of the news reports. "That would have driven her absolutely berserk."

Gundy Goutouski had spent the morning shopping for groceries and, basking in the warm sun shining down on all three prairie provinces, she celebrated the season by picking up a cartful of annuals to put into garden pots over the upcoming Victoria Day weekend. When she got home, she unpacked her groceries and wrote down some items she'd forgotten for next time. On the list were soaps and licorice, part of her next parcel to Nich in Afghanistan. After not hearing from her young friend all of April, the phone call on her fifty-ninth birthday had been the best gift Gundy could have hoped for. She was still on a high from their nearly hour-long chat. She'd written a long thank-you note to Nich and had popped it in the mail a few days earlier. When she saw the familiar Manitoba number on the call display, she picked up the receiver with anticipation; Jay would by now have finalized his and Nich's itinerary for June, when they'd be coming through Cold Lake en route to Wainwright and house-hunting. The call was short and simple; Jay, like Tim and Sally, was working against the clock, ticking off in his mind the people who should hear the news from him. Gundy called Bryan at CFB Cold Lake. "You need to come home right now," she said, not saying why. As sweet and loving as his wife was, Bryan knew Gundy was a strong and resilient woman. She never called him during work hours, let alone asked him to come home. As he drove home from the base, he was certain the worst had happened. Nich, he thought. It has to be Nich.

Just before lunch, Julianne Charchuk rang Jay on his cellphone. She was worried about her little Yorkie, Howitzer. With Andrew away on his FAC course in Gagetown, New Brunswick, the same course Nich hadn't had time to attend before her Afghanistan tour, the two friends and Packway neighbours relied on each other for companionship and life's day-to-day basics. "Hey, Jay, it's Jules. Could you do me a favour and bring Howitzer in to the vet clinic today?" she asked. "No, I don't think so," Jay replied in almost a whisper. "I just found out Nichola's been killed." After a momentary pause, Julianne responded. "I'm sorry, I don't understand." But she did. Before hanging up, she assured Jay she'd let the other two members of Nich's innermost Shilo friendship circle know. "Thanks, Jules, that would be good," he said.

Within minutes, Julianne was at Liane Nicholson's home in Brandon. They couldn't locate Chantal Hatton, who was now living in Kingston; she was supposed to be in mid-air, on a flight to Arizona to visit family. The plane was stuck on the tarmac for a good hour, so Chantal kept her cellphone on while she waited. Sonny, a fellow artillery officer at Shilo, was at the Royal Military College studying for his master's degree. He'd been told of Nich's death by Major Anne Reiffenstein, who knew they were close friends, and he caught his wife before takeoff. Chantal sat frozen in her seat, thinking of the Packway friend who'd brought an

extra Therm-a-Rest mattress along on their camping trips together, so dogs Sam and Bill would be more comfortable.

"Are you afraid of flying?" a man in a nearby seat asked.

■ ■ ■

In the early afternoon of May 17, moments before a vote on extending Canada's Afghanistan mission by two years, Prime
Minister Stephen Harper stood in the House of Commons to
announce that a female soldier had been killed in combat. Not
long after, the Prime Minister's Office (PMO) would release a
statement confirming the identity of that soldier, and that history had been made on that day: Canada had lost its first female
soldier in a combat role. "On behalf of all Canadians, I wish to
express our profound regret and sadness at the news of the death
of Captain Nichola Goddard. Captain Goddard died while helping to bring peace, stability and democracy to a troubled region
of the world. She, and the other men and women who serve in
Afghanistan, are involved in a difficult and dangerous mission.
They are serving our country and its people with distinction.
Our nation will not forget their sacrifice. I wish to extend our
deepest condolences to Captain Goddard's family, friends and
co-workers—particularly those at her home base of 1st Royal
Canadian Horse Artillery in Shilo, Manitoba. Our thoughts and
prayers are with them and with the families and loved ones of all
those serving in Afghanistan."

Within seconds of Harper's public statement, all of the
country's major radio and television news networks were leading their reports by announcing the sixteenth Canadian soldier
to die in Afghanistan, and the first female soldier to die in a

combat role in the nation's history: Captain Nichola Kathleen Sarah Goddard. Goddard, the reports said, was assisting Afghan security forces in an area west of Kandahar City when her battle group was ambushed.

Over the coming hours, the at-first-sketchy reports would be regularly updated to include the gathering biographical details. She was twenty-six, an officer, was married and had no children. Calgary, a city in which she'd never lived but regularly visited after her parents moved there in 1999, was named as her hometown—an oft-repeated simplification of the fact that she had lived all over the country but had never stayed anywhere for longer than four years. She was killed by RPG shrapnel ricocheting against the body of the light armoured vehicle she commanded; in what commanding officers and army brass would later describe as a miracle, she was the lone Canadian to die. An ANA soldier had also died, and the Taliban death count was, the army estimated, significant. In the first reports, it was eighteen, though the number would eventually settle at between twenty and twenty-five, along with thirty-two insurgents detained. "Our thoughts and prayers are with Captain Goddard's loved ones," said Defence Minister Gordon O'Connor in an official statement released later that day. "She will be sorely missed, and while we mourn her loss, we can take comfort in knowing her sacrifice will not have been made in vain." No mention was made of Nich and her FOO team calling in the first artillery fire against an enemy combatant since Korea. It was Nich's gender that led all of the stories: Goddard, one of about 230 female soldiers serving in Afghanistan, and one of only a fraction serving in combat roles, had, in death, broken through one of the last remaining barriers to gender parity.

Later that day, the House of Commons voted by a slim margin—149 in favour, 145 against—to extend Canada's mission in Afghanistan to February 2009. Harper also promised to commit Canada to taking on the leadership of the NATO force in Afghanistan for one year, beginning in February 2008, and approved $310 million in new development spending for Afghanistan. "This government is not in a position to simply walk away or to run away," said Harper, who vowed before the vote to go ahead with extending the mission at least another year regardless of the outcome.

■ ■ ■

In a quiet new subdivision of Brandon, Manitoba, Liane Nicholson turned on the television in her living room to see the face of her friend Nich Goddard smiling back at her. Julianne sat on one side of Liane, and neighbour Paula Nelson, whose officer husband Howie was also in Afghanistan, sat on the other. When the name "Captain Nicola Goddard" ran across the ticker tape at the bottom of the screen, the women screamed out. "Oh no, they've spelled her name wrong," said Julianne. "She'd be furious." Liane grabbed the phone and dialled the local affiliate of the national news broadcaster they were watching. Minutes later, the newscast had added the "h" in Nichola. The young women felt a momentary sense of accomplishment. They could do at least this.

While the Brandon trio sat in Liane's living room transfixed on the television screen, in Toronto, Alison West-Armstrong was holding a yoga pose on the floor of her hotel room. Alison had travelled from her home in Arnprior, a bedroom community of Ottawa, to attend an academic conference. Sally, who had been trying for hours to track down her sister, would later lament the fact she had to hear the news on the radio playing softly in her room as she enjoyed a peaceful moment. *My poor sister, will she survive this?* was the first thought that ran through Alison's mind as she stopped and listened intently. *How are my parents going to survive this?*

Others on Jay's email distribution list, busy going about a normal day, had not yet logged on to their personal accounts. Shanon Archibald, Nich's high school friend from Antigonish, was sitting on a Greyhound bus heading to Ottawa when the words "Nichola Goddard" came over the French channel of CBC Radio playing next to the driver. "Does anybody have a phone, or a BlackBerry, I could use?" she asked the strangers around her. "I think my friend just died."

In Halifax, Krista MacEachern had just come home from work. The beautiful spring day had put her in a celebratory mood. Her phone rang. It was her cousin on the other end of the line. "Have you seen the news?" she asked Nich's best friend and maid of honour. Krista refused to believe it. She spent the next hour pacing the apartment, unable to feel anything but panic and confusion. The two had drifted apart the last couple of years, mostly because of Krista's growing discomfort with Nich's decision to stay in the military. Krista had struggled with reconciling the sensitive young woman she knew and loved with a warrior trained to kill. Now the unspoken rift would never be healed; there'd be no second chances. Waves of guilt and regret washed over her. *Does Sally want to hear from me?* she wondered. A while later, the phone rang. It was Tim: yes, they would love it if she came to Calgary for the funeral, he told her. Krista spent the rest of the day and evening watching the newscasts, rage growing in her chest. "She's not a news piece," she cried out at out the flickering television as she stood alone in her home. "Don't say her name wrong, don't say she's the first female."

Allison Alvi, Nich's RMC roommate, with whom she had stayed in touch after graduation, was driving with her husband, Hasan, to a Halifax department store to buy some clothes. The couple had just been posted to Ottawa, and was only a day or two away from beginning the road trip to their new home. Allison was scanning radio stations when she heard Nich's name. She sat frozen as she listened to the "nearly incomprehensible" news report. Fellow RMC buddy Mitch Rivest was on a course in Victoria when he was summoned out of class to take an emergency call from his mother. The best man at Nich and Jay's wedding was inconsolable. The warrior poet, who could dance, sing, write, fight, run and jump, Mitch cried to himself, was no longer.

Over the course of the day, the news wound its way to many of the places Nich had lived, worked or trained throughout Canada, to the people whose lives she had touched and who had never forgotten her. At Dr. John Hugh Gillis High School in Antigonish, Nova Scotia, Louise Loriface arrived early to her global studies class to prepare the afternoon lecture. She started each class with a look at the "pictures of the day" on the CBC's website, connecting her computer to a large screen at the front of the room. The first photograph that flashed on the screen was her former student, that unmistakable gap-toothed smile taking her back a decade in time. When her students filtered in, the staunchly anti-war educator kept the image up on the screen. "This was one of my students," she told the class as reporters and TV news cameras gathered outside to interview Nich's former teachers.

While Louise was grappling with her anger, Sylvia Berg was "feeling devastated" after hearing on her car radio about the death of her brilliant former Renaissance studies student at RMC. Major Anne Reiffenstein, who was at the college for the year working as a division commander of 400 cadets, tried to assuage her shock by relying on her soldiering instincts, reminding herself of the fact "She was at war." Up in his third-floor office with the Buddhist statues and other talismans from his world travels, Michael Hurley quietly told himself this was not a tragedy. This life makes sense, it has coherence, it has shape, Nich's former world literature instructor said to himself. He knew Nich had seen the beauty in the mud houses of that foreign country, but also the danger. "Well done, Nichola," he said as he pulled out the collage she had created for him four years earlier. He had kept it just behind his desk, occasionally showing it to other students. "You came into this incarnation, passed your blessings on to us and moved on."

For those closest to Nich, such calm reflection would have to wait. On this day, time stood still while the world swirled around them like an out-of-control carousel. In between phoning relatives and answering the door to scores of well-meaning friends carrying plates of food and cooked chickens from a nearby grocery store, it was all Tim and Sally could do to stay steady on their feet.

By mid-afternoon Jay had been joined by Tim Haveman, CFB Shilo's homefront officer. The fellow officer and his wife, Lisa, had lived for a time across the street from Nich and Jay, but being a couple that kept mostly to themselves, never got to know them well. Haveman had recently been handed a binder outlining his duties in the event of a soldier's death. After Timothy

Wilson and Paul Davis from CFB Shilo were killed when their LAV was in an accident on March 2, it had become obvious that a more formal process was needed to deal with the renewed reality of combat death. Haveman, unable to serve overseas after being diagnosed with celiac disease, was both nervous and enthusiastic about his new role. Death wasn't familiar to him; he'd lost only one person in his life, a grandfather. But he knew he could make a difference helping out next of kin. He let Jay know that he was now at his beck and call; anything he needed done over the next few weeks, all he had to do was ask. The need for Tim's assistance was felt immediately, as he fielded phone calls from journalists and shooed away an officer's wife who came by with a bottle of hard liquor. A few hours later, Jay packed the dogs in his SUV for a drive to a kennel in nearby Portage La Prairie. The next few days of memorials and other official services would keep Jay constantly on the move. He drove out of the base and was met by a wall of reporters and TV cameras at its gate. Jay drove past the crowd. Oh, what the heck, he said to himself and turned the car around. "Sorry, I'm just not ready to talk to you right now," said the ever-polite young man, as though an apology was required. "But I will tomorrow."

The following morning, Jay was awakened at just after eight by the whirring of his fax machine. He stumbled out of bed to see what it was printing. It was from the bank, the approval for a mortgage. He looked numbly at the fax machine, and then walked over to his computer. He wanted to see if there was a new email from Nich. Please let there be a note from her, he thought. His in-box was filled with new messages, all of them condolences. He collapsed on to the floor and, for the first time since hearing his love and best friend of nearly a decade was dead, began to cry.

■ ■ ■

As Nich's family and friends back home stumbled into their beds that night, their bodies aching from absorbing the unthinkable, the soldiers at KAF were waking to the official news that had made its way through the rumour mill the night before, after the Can-Con show had been interrupted for a brief announcement by Major Tod Strickland, deputy commanding officer of Task Force Orion. A hush fell over the crowd when he told them there had been a fierce firefight in the Panjwayi that day and that Canadians, as well as ANA, had been killed and wounded in action. Later that night, Brigadier-General David Fraser, head of Regional Command (South), confirmed the dead soldier was the young female officer known for her unflappable demeanour and upbeat personality. "Our hearts, our prayers and our sympathies go out to the family of Nichola Goddard," said Fraser as he stood in front of a Canadian flag at half-staff.

The next day, May 18, Afghan president Hamid Karzai visited the capital of eastern Kunar Province, another area favoured by insurgents. He angrily denounced the new violence raging in Kandahar Province as the work of religious extremists, aided by intelligence services in neighbouring Pakistan. He took the opportunity to speak of his alarm over the death of Captain Nichola Goddard of Task Force Orion: "Our land is being protected by a lady from Canada, when we should be protecting her as a guest."

Less than 50 kilometres down an IED-ridden, pothole-pocked highway, in a village few back at KAF had even heard of, the soldiers of Operation Bravo Guardian had at first light rolled up the sleeping bags that had been their beds on the ground for only a few short hours. All three platoons were well into the day's sweep of the village as dawn broke over the Panjwayi. Over the next few hours, they would capture a handful of Taliban hiding in the nooks and crannies of the confounding terrain. But by and large, their enemy had slipped away during the night. Assessing the events of the previous twenty-four hours, Ian Hope considered the implications. His battle group would soon be returning to KAF, ordered by mid-afternoon to temporarily leave the area because U.S. Special Forces, who were responsible for the bulk of the high-value-target missions, were going in to hit a Taliban group.

Looking out on the jumble of trees, vines, mud-brick walls and labyrinth-like paths, well aware it was a terrain he would soon come to know well, Hope thought, We've stirred up a hornet's nest.

SEVENTEEN
Stand Easy

"I didn't try to lead the charge, but sometimes it just happens.
Strength and Honour, Nich"
 — final line in Captain Nichola Goddard's just-in-case letter

TAKING HIS PLACE on the left side of his boss's funeral casket on the morning of May 19, 2006, Jeff Fehr realized he'd be passing directly in front of his comrades from Shilo's A Battery. As his eyes scanned the sea of familiar faces, he nearly bit through his bottom lip trying not to break down. But just as he hadn't wanted anyone else to see the inside of the turret, he knew that carrying his fallen commander was the job of her men. Even the superstitious Chris, who had earlier turned down a pallbearer role for another soldier friend because it "might create bad juju," agreed. Not long after returning from the battle at Bayanzi, Jeff had submitted two requests up through the chain of command: the first was that one of the three surviving FOO team members would accompany Nich's body on its long trip back to Canada; the second was that they be pallbearers for the ramp ceremony. His first request was denied, but they got their wish to be pallbearers.

Having hardly slept the past three days, the trio was still running on adrenaline as they took their places with five other members of the Canadian Royal Horse Artillery that included Captain Bob Meade, just returned from Gumbad, along with Shilo friends and A Battery comrades Captain Howie Nelson, Captain Sean Tremblay, Bombardier James Clark and Bombardier Steve Adams. Carrying Nich's beret was Captain Howard Han, a Packway neighbour and the officer chosen to accompany Nich's body back home. The eight soldiers removed the coffin from the LAV that served as her hearse, struggling as they hoisted the heavy flag-draped casket that was further weighted down by about 90 pounds of dry ice. Nich's men were doing their best to give their beloved commander a proper sendoff. This is nearly killing us, Jeff thought to himself. She was the best officer I ever worked for.

As the pallbearers made the slow, steady procession across the tarmac, they were joined by hundreds of troops from at least seven countries, along with several ANA soldiers, lining the path that led to the back of a waiting Hercules transport plane. Piper Master Corporal Callum Campbell of Victoria played the haunting "Flowers of the Forest," an ancient Scottish folk tune familiar to Canadians each year on Remembrance Day. The casket passed under an arch formed by the barrels of a pair of 155-mm howitzers, the type of gun Nich knew so well and had been directing just two days earlier in the foreign terrain of the Panjwayi. "Task Force Afghanistan, to our fallen comrade, salute," an officer yelled out as the mass of camouflage-wearing soldiers simultaneously raised their right hands to their temples. The pallbearers then lifted the coffin onto the plane, where a large Canadian flag hung in the cargo hold. The first stop would be Camp Mirage, where the casket would be transferred onto a Canadian Forces Airbus. Several of the pallbearers, now out of sight of their fellow soldiers, broke down as a trio of padres spoke about Nich. Brigadier-General David Fraser paid his last respects inside the plane's cargo hold before it jetted off and disappeared into the mist of clouds en route to the Persian Gulf. Later in the day, Fraser would say that while May 17 was a tragic day for the loved ones of Captain Nichola Goddard, it was, in the context of operations in Afghanistan, a success: "The intelligence was bang-on, the operation involving Afghan and Canadian forces reportedly well synchronized and, in the harsh battlefield scorecard, the coalition forces came out ahead."

At about the same time the pallbearers were taking their slow, deliberate steps to the Herc, 100 kilometres north of KAF another smaller ceremony was being held in Nich's honour. Andrew Nicholson gathered the troops around one of the M777 howitzers to say a few words about his friend followed by two minutes of silence. Firing what he called "Captain Goddard's last round," the big gun performed a direct shoot into a nearby mountainside, its thunderous explosion echoing throughout the valley. *Jay, I wish I could be there for you,* Andrew thought of his friend back home at Shilo. *I can't even fathom what you're going through right now.*

Later that day, Lieutenant-Colonel Ian Hope sat down with Brigadier-General Fraser and other senior officials at KAF's command centre. "I have a bit of a problem I need to confess to you," he told the men. "I think Captain Goddard was outstandingly brave, and we need to recognize that. But I think as soon as we put forward a bravery nomination, there will be an automatic reaction that it's only because she's a woman." Hope knew that such days should have been long over, and that for an army that had been mostly a peacekeeping one for the past half century, the criteria for what constituted valour was brand new. He also knew that it would take some time and effort to accomplish his goal of recognizing Nich's accomplishments, but he wasn't going to accept anything less than a yes. He'd wait it out, and do the legwork required to make sure one of the best officers he'd ever known would get her due.

■ ■ ■

As the coffin holding her body was beginning its 10,000-kilometre journey, in Canada Nichola's name was now familiar to all her fellow citizens. Every single newspaper in the country led the day's news with her death, her gap-toothed smile beaming out from the front pages. In Alberta, she was described as a Calgarian; in Nova Scotia, her high school years were detailed; in Saskatchewan and Manitoba, she was celebrated as one of their own. These claims on the young woman now being heralded as "Canada's Daughter" all had a ring of legitimacy: Nich's travels with her family and later as a soldier took her to every single province, as well as the Northwest Territories. By week's end, her name would appear no less than six hundred times in print and broadcast media, making her a Canadian soldier whose fame was now approaching that of World War I flying ace Billy Bishop. It was a fame, say her friends, comrades and family, she would never have wanted, and would know came only because of her gender. Along with the tributes came scores of editorial columns and letters decrying the loss of a female soldier, along with arguments for and against allowing women on the front lines.

It would be months before Tim and Sally had time to read the various news stories about their daughter. From the moment of her death, they, along with Jay, were swept up in the very public process of grieving. On May 18, they held a press conference at the University of Calgary, hoping that would be enough to quell the constant ringing of their telephone with requests from media outlets all over the world. Struggling to keep from breaking down, they told a packed room of TV cameras and reporters that Nich died "doing the work she loved," and of her being "far happier in the hills . . . keen to get on with the job." When asked if she and Tim had tried to brace themselves for the possibility she could die in Afghanistan, Sally did her best to answer without succumbing to tears. "I don't think anybody is ever prepared," she said. "It's devastating, and it's going to take us a while to come to grips with it." That same day, Jay sat down with a CBC camera crew to field questions. He immediately addressed the elephant in the middle of the room. "I don't think she wanted to be perceived as a female doing a job," Jay said in his soft-spoken manner. "She felt she was just like one of the other soldiers and wanted to come across that way." He also reinforced his support of all soldiers doing the dirty work of fighting the Taliban: "I don't think we should be backing out just because there's been a couple of Canadian casualties. We shouldn't tuck our tails behind our legs and run or anything like that," he said. "Even though you lost your wife?" asked the reporter. "I still strongly believe we should still be over there," Jay replied.

As Nichola's husband and immediate family prepared to leave for Trenton to meet her coffin on the evening of May 19, the tributes and condolences continued to pour in. Prime Minister

Stephen Harper called the Goddards to pay his respects, as did Governor General Michaëlle Jean, the commander-in-chief of the country's military. Harper, Jean and Defence Minister Gordon O'Connor called Jay, and General Rick Hillier, chief of the defence staff, publicly described Nich as "a true daughter of our country."

The morning after they arrived in Toronto, Tim, Sally, Kate, Jay and Victoria, newly returned from Europe, visited the funeral home where Nich's body was sent after the repatriation ceremony. The staff advised the family that while Nich's brain stem had been severed by the blast, her face and the rest of her body were intact. Would they like to view the body when it arrived in Toronto? Like Jeff Fehr, Jay and the Goddard family decided they wanted to remember Nich as she was, and declined the offer. They didn't have to decide on how to deal with Nich's funeral arrangements: she had left clear instructions that she wished to be cremated. They headed off for the two-and-a-half-hour limousine ride, Jay accompanied by his family and Tim Haveman, the homefront officer from Shilo. At just before midnight, they were directed to a reception room at the base, where a group that included Defence Minister Gordon O'Connor, General Hillier and Major Anne Reiffenstein, along with family and friends who had come from other parts of Ontario to be with them, had gathered.

"This is the hard part, Sally," said Hillier to the grieving mother as they were given the green light to head to the tarmac. As the TV cameras and reporters strained behind the barbed-wire fence of the base, several hundred metres away the plane's back ramp opened as 300 soldiers simultaneously raised their arms in salute, creating a sound Sally would liken to the ripple of a large ocean wave. The entire ceremony lasted less than ten minutes, as Nichola's coffin, accompanied by the strains of a lone bagpiper, was carried from the plane to the waiting hearse. The return trip, aided by police escorts on motorcycle, took just over an hour as they sped down Highway 401. By August 2007, this same stretch of road would be renamed the Highway of Heroes, and fifty more families would follow, in just one year, Jay's and the Goddards' sad journey.

Over that first week, news of Nichola's death continued to wind its way around the world, finally reaching into the heart of one of its most remote corners. Sister Helen was instructing teachers on sex education at a Catholic mission deep in the bush, at the foot of a mountain in Papua New Guinea's Goilala District. A man walked in with a note that had taken a few days to be delivered. "Nichola killed in Afghanistan yesterday," was all it said. She dropped into a chair as her teacher students rushed to her aid. "A good friend has been killed in Afghanistan," she said. Not able to get a message out until she returned to Port Moresby, Sister Helen that night fell into her bed and cried for Tim and Sally.

Jacqueline Patterson was walking to the class she taught at Kiriwina High School when someone ran up to her with a copy of *The National* newspaper from Port Moresby, a few copies of which had been sent from the mainland by Tim's former student Serah Clark. "Papua New Guinea Born Soldier Dies in Afghanistan," read the headline. Jacqueline burst into tears seeing Nichola's name; she'd never forgotten the adorable little girl she babysat in the main-island town of Wewak more than twenty years earlier. She raced home and pulled from a shelf a box containing several photographs. She found the one of Nichola sporting a pout and a grass skirt, her little face painted with bright tribal colours. She sat her children down, and through tears, talked about the young girl from Papua New Guinea: "Even though she has a different-coloured skin, she was one of us," she explained. "And we have lost her."

While Sister Helen would have moved heaven and earth to be at Nichola's May 26 funeral in Calgary—just as she had hoped three years earlier to come to her wedding in the very same church—it was not to be. Just about everyone else who could make it, though, was there in the pews as the Canadian flag-draped, maple coffin holding Nichola's cremains was wheeled across the same cream-and-white-tiled floor where she had last walked as a beaming bride on the arm of her smiling father. Along with family that had come from as far as England and Qatar, the gathered throng was a who's who of Nichola's too-short life: childhood friends Krista MacEachern, Shanon Archibald and Zeph Williams; RMC buddies Allison and Hasan Alvi, and Mitch Rivest, along with teacher Michael Hurley; Shilo friends Liane Nicholson, Julianne Charchuk (whose husband, Andrew, was preparing to replace his friend and fellow captain in Afghanistan), and Bryan and Gundy Goutouski, joined by Major Anne Reiffenstein and scores of others from Nichola's military life. Nearly all of those friends would, in the coming days, return home to find upbeat letters from Nich in their mailboxes, written on her birthday and mailed just a few days before leaving the wire for the last time.

When she had walked into the memorial service the night before the funeral, Krista was still struggling with an overwhelming sense of anger. As she waited in line to pay her respects to the closed casket that sat next to an easel that held a large photograph of Nichola, two men in front of her chatted about farming. That's my best friend in there, she found herself screaming inside her head. How can you be talking about farming at a time like this? She walked up to the casket and put one hand on it. The dam finally broke, and she was helpless to stop it. Seeing she was on the verge of collapse, Irene Carter and Rosa Whitstone from Onion Lake First Nation—part of a group that performed a Cree Honour Song in Nichola's memory—guided her to a chair and sat the sobbing young woman down, embracing her as she gave in to her grief. They were, Krista would later remember, like angels coming to her rescue.

After a video montage showing Nichola beside shimmering Canadian lakes, playing in the snow, her eyes squinting under the constant sunshine of the great outdoors, Major Liam McGarry, commanding officer of the 1st Regiment, Royal Canadian Horse Artillery from CFB Shilo, approached the podium to pay his official respects on behalf of the Canadian Forces. "Captain Goddard was an outstanding leader and soldier," he said, "who approached every task, whether in combat or training, with tireless passion and continually produced exceptional results. Captain Goddard's dedication to both soldiers under her command and the units she was supporting was unwavering, and her calm character and persona were always present regardless of the task . . . Nich, end of mission, stand easy."

Jay kept his remarks short. Wearing the Silver Cross pinned to his chest—in another sign of the ever-narrowing gender gap, Jay had become the first widower to receive the award traditionally given to mothers and wives of fallen Canadian soldiers—he talked of meeting the gregarious young army recruit while at training at Saint-Jean-sur-Richelieu. "She introduced herself as Goddard, and I responded with 'I'm

Beam,'" he said, making the gathered mourners laugh when he pointed out that he was clueless to her immediate interest. "I never thought that two-second conversation would turn into the fabulous relationship we had." He came close to joining some of the crying mourners, though, as he said his final words. "I still can't believe you are gone," he said. "I'm going to miss your laugh, your smile and your company. But mostly I'm going to miss having my best friend to share life with." When he finished, he put two trembling fingers to his lips and then placed the kiss on her casket.

"We are a family of storytellers," began Tim in a rousing twenty-minute eulogy that brought up memories both amusing and poignant of a life that reached the four corners of the world. "We sit around the dining table for hours after a meal, with a bottle of wine or some coffee or whatever and tell stories. This morning I'm going to tell you some stories, but I know we don't have very long, so as Nichola would say, 'Come on, Daddy, spit it out!' So I'll try."

He conjured images of his bright and beautiful daughter: as a barefoot baby in the Trobs who learned to hack open a coconut with a machete; as a Dene speaker in Black Lake; of earning the nickname Care Bear after coming to the aid of a fallen competitor in a high school cross-country race; and of her polar bear swim in Wales the previous Christmas. He spoke of the one thing that always managed to elicit a furrowed brow: it was Nich or Nichola, never Nicky. "Only one person ever called her Nicky and lived to tell the tale, and that was Lieutenant-Colonel Ian Hope, her commander in Afghanistan," he said to a chorus of tearful laughter. "She never had the nerve to tell him that she hated it—'I'll wait until I outrank him,' she joked. I guess that won't happen now, so I'll take it as a father's duty to pass the message along."

He talked about the public nature of their private loss, and urged them to remember Nichola not just as a soldier, "not just as the first Canadian woman to be killed in combat, but as a person with passion, one with a great enthusiasm for life." He made sure to thank a number of people who had helped in their darkest hours, and gave a nod to Hope's Task Force Orion, "who responded to her death with great vigour and imposed an almost biblical wrath" on the Taliban. "Yours was a short life, but a good one. You had so much promise, so much potential, and the world is a far lesser place with your passing. You wore your uniform so proudly, and from the earliest days of RMC had wanted to serve in the First Regiment. So now, as your journey continues, we remember the words on the cap badge of the artillery beret: *Quo fas et gloria ducunt*—'Whither right and glory lead.'"

It was a riveting eulogy worthy of a man who had spent three decades honing his oratorial skills in classrooms around the world. But what caught the country's attention was his admonishment to the Canadian government for not allowing the media inside for the repatriation ceremony at CFB Trenton a week earlier. Corporal Matthew Dinning had died on April 22 with three other soldiers after an IED hit his armoured vehicle. His father, Lincoln, stood up at his son's funeral and criticized the government's banning of journalists at repatriation ceremonies, along with its decision to stop lowering flags on Parliament Hill to half-staff upon the death of a soldier. No one who knew Tim Goddard was surprised that he would follow suit: "I find it troubling that the privacy decision means we are keeping the press outside the wire, where the bad guys are," he said. "I would like to think that Nichola died to protect our freedoms, not to restrict them."

Mere hours after that portion of Tim's eulogy hit the national television and radio news broadcasts, the federal government did an about-face on its new policy to keep the press away from the repatriation ceremonies. "I had given fairly clear instructions that, when bodies were to come home, families were to be consulted," Prime Minister Harper said at a news conference in Victoria. "And if all families were agreed on making that particular ceremony public, that our government should have no difficulty with that. I'm not sure what happened in this case."

A week later, the family was in Ottawa, burying most of Nichola's ashes—a small portion was set aside for burial at St. Barnabas Anglican Church in Calgary—at the National Military Cemetery, the former Beechwood Cemetery and newly established Canadian equivalent of the American military grounds in Arlington, West Virginia. In yet another first, Nich was to be the first soldier killed in Afghanistan to be buried here; the fifteen who came before her were all laid to rest in their hometowns.

While the official farewells were going on half a world away, Lieutenant-Colonel Ian Hope and the soldiers of Task Force Orion were back outside the wire. The man who had taught Nich the "strength and honour" quote she'd used in her just-in-case letter sat across from a group of thirty elders at a large shura involving two districts of the Panjwayi. Having conducted dozens of these meetings, Hope knew what to expect. On this day, though, they wanted to talk about something else: Captain Nich Goddard. "We just want to tell you how profoundly thankful we are that you in Canada . . . think Afghanistan is so important that you're willing to allow your women to fight," said one of the elders, his voice breaking with emotion. Hope knew that for those who'd spent their lives immersed in Pashtun culture, the thought of a woman bearing arms was nearly impossible to imagine. The elder went on to tell Hope that the Afghans were comparing the young Canadian officer to Malali of Maiwand, the mythical female warrior said to have died in battle against the invading British army in the nineteenth century. Malali's place of death was less than 50 kilometres from where Nich had been felled. Perhaps this Canadian woman was Malali returned to them, or her daughter, they told Hope. Mere days after Nich's death, federal defence minister Gordon O'Connor had told Canadians, "I just don't consider this to be war." The Afghan elders knew differently. The coalition forces knew differently, too. That week, U.S. warplanes bombed a religious school and homes near Bayanzi, killing dozens of suspected insurgents, but also seventeen civilians, some of them children. The operation, which did not involve Canadian soldiers, was one of the deadliest since American troops arrived there in 2001.

Chris Gauthier also knew it was war. On May 28, while out on patrol in the Zhari district, the tough native Montrealer was part of a convoy ambushed by insurgents. The flying shrapnel of an RPG injured five soldiers, including Chris. Seconds after being hit, he looked down at his left hand, which had been torn apart by the blast. The left-handed soldier did the one thing that came naturally: he laughed.

Epilogue

"A brave captain is as a root, out of which, as branches, the courage of his soldiers doth spring."

> — *Sir Philip Sidney, sixteenth-century soldier and author of* In Defence of Poetry

ON A BRIGHT MORNING in the summer of 2008, Tim and Sally Goddard cast their eyes on a familiar sight: tribesmen holding intricately carved walking sticks, curious women balancing baskets atop their heads and excited children being shooed off an airplane landing strip. In their first visit back to Papua New Guinea in more than a quarter century, the pair was treated as returning royalty. Old friends like Sister Helen and Serah Clark were there to greet them at various stops in the country; reporters from Papua New Guinea's two national newspapers waited to interview them in the capital city of Port Moresby; and the people of the Trobriand Islands feted them in a ceremony complete with grass-skirted dancers performing traditional songs of sorrow and reverence.

Their journey back to the country where they'd met and married had begun nearly two years earlier, in the fall of 2006.

David Irvine-Halliday, the founder of the international Light Up the World Foundation, met with them to talk about ways in which they could honour Nichola's memory. Irvine-Halliday's solar-powered LED lights, which have been installed in numerous Third World countries, seemed like the right fit—and Papua New Guinea the best recipient. Not long after, the couple was invited to the United Nations in New York City, to accept condolences from the people of Papua New Guinea. They also received Independence Day medals from Papua New Guinea's prime minister, Michael Somare, in honour of their contributions to the education of the people of that country. Tim let Somare's chief of staff, Leonard Louma, know that he and Sally were thinking of bringing the lights to the first-aid posts in the Trobriand Islands. "Why not all of Papua New Guinea?" asked Louma. Less than two years after that meeting, Tim and Sally, backed up by a team of technicians, were on hand to see the first of PNG's 1,100 health centres and aid posts receive the lights as the first project of the Nichola Goddard Foundation.

Along with her parents' ongoing humanitarian work, Nichola's memory has been honoured in a number of ways. In November 2006, her colleagues at CFB Shilo dedicated a trig marker—a survey point that fixes one's location and orientation and is used for navigation—on the base to Nichola in a ceremony attended by more than 600 soldiers. Trig Goddard would serve as a constant reminder of Nichola's sacrifice. "By naming one of these markers after Nichola we will be using the memory of our friend, and of her sacrifice," wrote Captain Sean Tremblay, "to help us fix our path as we try to make moral decisions and just actions, to guide us and help us keep doing what is right and good."

Jay Beam accepted on Nichola's behalf the Meritorious Service Medal, for "her exemplary service in Afghanistan . . . her spirit and unfaltering dedication were without equal." In late 2009, Nichola was among several soldiers and officers recognized with the Sacrifice Medal, for CF members injured or killed "under honourable circumstances as a direct result of a hostile action or action intended for a hostile force." The Captain Nichola K. S. Goddard Memorial Scholarship is administered by the University of Calgary; the Captain Nichola Goddard Scholarship in International Education is awarded at the University of Prince Edward Island; the Captain Nichola K. S. Goddard Memorial Sword is presented each year to the best Regular Officer Training Plan artillery senior cadet at Royal Military College; as well, numerous other tributes, such as the Captain Nichola Goddard Park in Sault Ste. Marie, and the Goddard Peace Summit in Indian Harbour, Nova Scotia, have also been established in her name.

Today, Tim is dean of education at the University of Prince Edward Island in Charlottetown. Sally continues her involvement with the Onion Lake First Nation in northern Saskatchewan in her work as a curriculum consultant. Victoria Goddard is working on her PhD at the University of Toronto, while Kate Goddard is pursuing conflict studies at the University of Ottawa.

■ ▨ ▨

Before their return home to Canada in the late summer of 2006, the soldiers of Operation Archer continued to be confronted by the Taliban. May 17, 2006, was a watershed for Canada's

Afghanistan mission: over the next three months, the tour would distinguish itself as the first sustained combat of Canadian soldiers in more than a half century. TF Orion's final tally was more than a hundred contacts with the Taliban, half of those involving intensive firefights; nearly 500 insurgents were counted among the dead, while Roto 1, those 1,000 fighters who made up Task Force Orion, lost 19 soldiers between February 1 and September 1, 2006.

The Canadians returned time and again to the area of the White Schoolhouse, the place where Nichola's body had been laid out for her final goodbyes. Captain Massoud's warnings of a massive Taliban build-up in the south of the country had indeed been no exaggeration: on August 19, 2006, Afghan Independence Day, an estimated 400 insurgents encircled the Panjwayi District Centre. Their initial aim was to overtake Kandahar City, but between August 2 and 11, TF Orion soldiers stymied their efforts by reducing their combat capacity. Instead, they set their sights on the restive area 15 kilometres away. With the help of ANA soldiers and members of the ANP, the Canadians were able to stave off the capture of the town; the Taliban withdrew from the fight after losing 50 of their men.

A point of pride for the Canadians was that no civilian casualties were incurred over the tour, and that their work prevented Kandahar City from falling into Taliban hands during the heated summer of 2006. Almost exactly one year after Captain Nichola Goddard was killed in the dusty village of Bayanzi, U.S. Special Forces in nearby Helmand Province killed Mullah Dadullah. The media-friendly, top-operational Taliban commander for southern Afghanistan was tracked down and killed after conducting a videotaped interview a day earlier. The more elusive

Mullah Omar, head of the Taliban, and Osama bin Laden, recognized as the leader of al Qaeda, have to date survived numerous attempts by the American Special Forces to hunt them down.

In his book *Dancing with the Dushman*, written for the Canadian Defence Academy, Lieutenant-Colonel Ian Hope wrote that Task Force Orion succeeded in "elevating the credibility of the Canadian Forces and the nation to its highest level in generations. By all counts, this was a successful mission."

Yet, as Chris Wattie wrote in *Contact Charlie: The Canadian Army, the Taliban and the Battle for Afghanistan*, the battle in the Panjwayi caught most by surprise: "Even many senior Canadian and U.S. generals did not realize what their troops were involved in until well after the fact. The only Canadians that did recognize what was happening on the ground in the orchards and villages of Panjwayi during that long, hot summer were the soldiers of Task Force Orion—the sergeants, corporals and captains who fought the Taliban at places like Bayanzi, Seyyedin, Pashmul, Nalgham and the White Schoolhouse."

In time, though, the soldiers and officers of Task Force Orion were given their due. Hope—the last member of TF Orion to return to the comfort of inside the wire at KAF on August 23, 2006—received the Meritorious Service Cross for combat leadership; Major William Fletcher, now Lieutenant-Colonel William Fletcher, was awarded the Star of Military Valour. Sergeant Michael Denine, who was deployed with 8 Platoon of Charlie Company, received the Medal of Military Valour for his efforts in the May 17, 2006, fight in the Panjwayi, after manning his vehicle's exterior machine gun when the main cannon and machine gun malfunctioned. Captain Jon Snyder, who served so often beside Nich for those long months, won the Star of Military

Valour shortly before his own death in 2008. Captain Jason Adair, now Major Adair—a man Hope credits with taking firm control of his company on May 17 while personally being under fire—completed his third tour in Afghanistan as operations officer for 2 PPCLI in 2008 and has since been promoted to officer commanding of Charlie Company.

Despite several efforts, Hope has not been able to determine if Captain Massoud, his ally in the Afghan National Police, is alive or dead. "I must confess I fear for him," he says. "Some people thought that he was involved in an attempt to kill me—as I was targeted on four occasions for specific suicide bombings and mortar attacks, and on all occasions the Afghan National Police were the common link." He doesn't believe Massoud was involved. "He tipped me off about danger so many times, and he fought at my side enough that I trusted him. I think of him often."

■ ■ ■

For a new generation of Canadians, this twenty-first century conflict has been a jarring wake-up call. Our sometimes smug self-image as a nation of pacifists has been decimated by nearly a decade of war and the return of more than 150 coffins. The image of the blue-beret-wearing peacekeeper, which many have described as a myth at the best of times, has once and for all been put to rest. This isn't, however, a minor conceit we can reconcile easily: our peacekeeping role lies at the very heart of our national identity, reflecting our fundamental beliefs. Although more than 100 Canadian soldiers have lost their lives in so-called peacekeeping missions over the past half century, their sacrifices have been largely ignored; we don't seem to want reminders that the concept of peacekeeping hasn't kept up with our role in the international community.

Afghanistan, then, has represented a loss of innocence, or of blissful ignorance. No longer can we pretend we are different from countries like the United States; we too require our soldiers to be warriors, trained to kill, and willing to risk being killed in the process.

The story of Captain Nichola Goddard has only compounded the necessary awakening to our new status. The death of a female soldier on the front lines was a shock to many. Canadian women have, as far back as the Northwest Rebellion of 1885, been willing to put themselves in harm's way as our nation went to war in various parts of the world. Enemy action during World War I killed 29 Canadian military women; in World War II, women held a wide variety of jobs, from nurses and cooks to parachute riggers and heavy mobile equipment drivers. Female infantry soldiers began joining men in peacekeeping missions nearly two decades ago.

Still, the number of Canadian women soldiers in combat roles, one of the most respected elements of the military, accounts for less than 2 per cent of our forces. One leading a battle group of more than 200 men, as Nichola did on May 17, 2006, represents but a fraction of that. Her presence on the battlefield was a historic one. Although it has now been more than twenty years since women were allowed into the combat trades in the Canadian Forces, Afghanistan was the first test of our determination to lead the world in terms of full-scale gender equality. Nichola matched her men when it came to physical toughness, dedication and professional competency. She served "as an example of what an officer should become in the Canadian

Forces," says Hope. Her willingness to kill, and risk being killed, also made her a true warrior.

■ ■ ■

After the death of their commander, the FOO team of Golf One Three was back on the job in a matter of days, venturing outside the wire on numerous occasions. With the exception of injured Bombardier Chris Gauthier, they stayed until the end of their tour in August. A year after his return to Canada, Master Bombardier Jeff Fehr received a Mention in Dispatches for his work in Afghanistan over the spring and summer of 2006. He also received a surprise from his friend Jay Beam: Jay had gone through Nich's camera and found images of her and her crew, including the celebratory ones of Jeff holding up the historic fire mission of May 17, 2006. Jay emailed them to Jeff, who had long forgotten that the camera had been one of Nich's few salvageable possessions after the deadly ambush. "When I opened it up and saw what it was," says Jeff of the email attachment, "it shook me up quite a bit." The loss of his friend continues to haunt him. "I knew I'd done all I could for her," says Jeff, who is still in the military and lives near CFB Shilo. "The fact I literally walked away without a scratch . . . to this day I have a hard time dealing with that. Losing Nich was like losing a member of my family." And while he still believes that TF Orion did a good job, he admits that he's turned down opportunities to return to Afghanistan. "The government decided to pull out in 2011," rendering the mission, in his view, "a joke now—we're just sending people over there to die. We should be in there for the long run."

Like Jeff, now master bombardier Clint Gingrich admits to dealing with issues of survivor guilt. "She did far more than I did, and I came back with not a scratch on me," says Clint, whose partner, Nicole, gave birth to their first child, Elizabeth, on November 8, 2007. "It's just not fair."

Sergeant Dave Redford was recently posted to the Canadian Ranger Patrol Group (1CRPG) in Yellowknife, Northwest Territories, flying into communities across the north to conduct training with ranger detachments. His marriage ended not long after his return from Afghanistan, and today he lives with his partner, Cindy Rey. "Nich would be a person I'd call up now and say, 'You'd never believe what's going on in the regiment,'" says Dave, whose toughest moment post-tour was meeting Tim and Sally Goddard at the trig ceremony for Nich in November 2006 at CFB Shilo: he "pulled a fast one" after the ceremony, giving the couple a ride in a LAV. "Nich would have been fascinated" with a book about a soldier's experience in Afghanistan, he says, "but she wouldn't have been thrilled it was about her."

After years of physical therapy and ten surgeries to repair his injured left hand, now master bombardier Chris Gauthier can use it for a variety of tasks, "despite losing my trigger finger" and part of his thumb. He fought to stay in the army after his injury, though in true Chris fashion, attributes that more to being "an idiot" than any other reason. Still, he says, "I don't have any regrets" (about his career choice), and is looking forward to the challenges ahead: around the same time he was informed he'd been posted to CFB Edmonton to work in its detention barracks, he also learned that his wife, Lauren, was pregnant for the first time, with twins. "Damn, I got lucky," says Chris of an injury that would devastate the average person.

"I'd still go back, but I'd be a bit leery about going out and doing patrols."

Her fellow soldiers and officers say that while they'll never forget Nich or the other friends and comrades they lost during the Afghanistan mission, most remain confident of the rightness of the fight. "I'd far rather play in their backyard than let them play in ours," says now captain Andrew Nicholson, who completed a second Afghanistan tour in early 2010. "We are doing a very good job over there, and we do have a reason to be there." Captain Bob Meade, now posted to Canadian Forces Joint Headquarters in Kingston, Ontario, agrees. "I feel that we were right to go in with as strong a battle group as we did," he says. "I was very proud to be among them." Still, it doesn't take away the pain of fallen comrades. "Nich was a great person who loved life, was always smiling and was a great friend," says Bob.

Her superiors will never forget the capable and competent officer they were preparing for promotion when she was felled by enemy fire. "I'll always remember the grin," says Lieutenant-Colonel Fletcher. "Nich stands out for me because you get to know everybody, but as the company commander you get to know the officers a little better." Fletcher, who admits he'd go back to Afghanistan in a heartbeat, says Nich approached everything with joy and enthusiasm, and was "an absolutely brilliant FOO." Hope, who is currently instructing at the Royal Military College, remembers Nichola as the best artillery officer he'd ever seen. "Her willingness to volunteer for dangerous tasks, her acceptance of risk in the continual presence of the enemy and her continuous demonstration of the highest leadership skills parallel the highest manifestations of leadership and courage in Canadian military history."

■ ■ ■

While time has marched on for her close friends—the Shilo circle of Julianne Charchuk, Chantal Hatton and Liane Nicholson now includes three more children—the loss of Nich has transformed many lives. Krista MacEachern, who has relocated to Halifax, Nova Scotia, re-established her ties with the Goddards after Nich's death. The young woman Sally likes to call "our fourth daughter" also educated herself on the Afghanistan mission. "Before, I would hear that someone died and think 'Oh, that's horrible, and I feel really bad for the families,'" she says. "But when it happened to Nichola, I suddenly thought of all the people those deaths have affected." Educating herself on the mission has helped in her grieving process. "I wanted to know why this happened." While she supports the troops, Krista doesn't support the mission. "But I feel like I'm betraying Nichola in a way, because she believed strongly in the mission."

Friends Gundy and Bryan Goutouski find solace in the fact that Nichola died having lived an examined life, and was secure in her choices. "She had a mature understanding," says Bryan, now retired from military service and back with his wife in Ontario's orchard country south of Toronto. "She was a model of respect, understanding and the communication with the Afghan people—so way beyond what you'd expect from a young captain."

Three years after the death of his wife, Jay Beam moved into his new bungalow on an acreage not far from CFB Shilo. His dogs, Bill and Sam, ran away one day through a hole in a fence set up for construction. After months of searching, Jay finally gave up on finding Nichola's beloved pets. Despite everything that has happened, he remains hopeful about the future as he looks around his modest but charming 1,600-square-foot, four-bedroom home. "I didn't build my house for a single guy," he says. Jay, who still hasn't decided on a set career path, quietly admits to having started back on the dating scene, and that in time he hopes to marry and start a family. "I still think of her quite often, and miss her like crazy," says Jay. "Every now and then I still have a 'bad day,' when I feel down or upset about the events of May 17, 2006, but those days seem to be getting further and further apart."

Despite the loss of his beloved wife, Jay stands behind the statements he made in the wake of her death. "I still support the mission that the Canadian and other international troops are doing in Afghanistan. I have many friends who continue to go on tours to Afghanistan. I worry for their safety while they are over there, along with the many other troops that are currently serving. I am glad that they are over there, and do believe that they are making a difference in the lives of Afghans."

Not long after her death, Captain Nichola Kathleen Sarah Goddard's name was etched into the Memorial Arch at Royal Military College in Kingston, Ontario, under which, less than a decade earlier, she and her new friend Jay Beam walked, two eighteen-year-olds not sure what the future would hold, but already certain that they would face it together.

Acknowledgements

THE BEGINNINGS OF *Sunray* were sown in the fall of 2006, in an office at the University of Calgary. Over the course of three days, Tim and Sally Goddard shared with me the stories of their daughter's unique upbringing and unlikely choice of the soldiering life. The result of those many hours, filled with tears and occasional laughter, became a two-day *Calgary Herald* series that November.

Nearly two years later, I accompanied Tim and Sally's team of installers, a university media liaison and a photographer to Papua New Guinea, a wild adventure that marked both the true start of this book and of a cherished friendship with a remarkable family. Without Sally's early support and openness, *Sunray* might have ended up like so many incredible life stories— known by intimates, but never put down on paper.

The generosity of spirit and time offered by the Goddard and West families—Sally, Tim, Victoria, Kate and other extended family members—has brought the young Nichola to life in all her youthful, idealistic splendour. Her gentle husband Jason Beam, in sharing his beloved wife's most private, intimate correspondence, allowed Nichola to speak to us directly. Her friends in civilian life and the military, some who appear in this book and others whose stories helped to provide me with a strong understanding of this complex woman, further rounded out Nichola's story.

As a typical Canadian, I had little knowledge of the workings of military life before embarking on this ambitious project. I could not have written the chapters on Nichola's military education and training without the patience and generosity of so many, most notably Lieutenant-Colonel Ian Hope, Major Anne Reiffenstein and Captain Bob Meade.

In the years after Nichola's death, the four men who made up her Forward Observation Officer team—Sergeant Dave Redford, Master Bombardier Jeff Fehr, Master Bombardier Chris Gauthier and Master Bombardier Clint Gingrich—had remained protective of Nichola, and had not spoken a word publicly about their time together in Afghanistan, or the historic battle that took her life. Knowing the story had the blessing of her closest loved ones, they decided, as Dave Redford told me, "to put in our two cents—we'll do it for Nich." Their candour about their collective adventures and misadventures, and willingness to revisit the trauma of battle and the loss of their commander, have allowed me to experience Afghanistan from the perspective of those soldiers who have had their boots on the ground these past eight years.

My agent, Denise Bukowski, and my editor, Linda Pruessen at Key Porter, took on this first-time author without hesitation; their ongoing optimism and coaching helped me through those long months of painstaking research, interviewing and writing, as did the incomparable Anne Green, with her book and life wisdom. Harry Vandervlist's coaching and Dianne Bos' help navigating Papua New Guinea saw me through the entire journey, and fellow journalists Jennifer Allford and Janet Naclia were also on hand as sounding boards and critics. To my shining star, Shelley Boettcher—thanks for making me a part of your family.

To my tribe of passionate females, I offer thanks: Shelley Arnusch, Valerie Berenyi, Louise Castonguay, Kim Gray, Fran Humphreys-Watson, Romi Lagadin, Jacquie Moore, Liz Tompkins, Shelley Youngblut, Catherine Wood. The lifetime crew, Louise Lage, Joanne Onerheim and Doris Cowley, who've hung in there twenty years and longer. To my friend of thirty years Brent Piaskoski, and his wife Barb Haynes, thanks for opening your home to me and letting me write far away from the Calgary winter.

As always, my family came through with flying colours: my siblings Denise Fortney and Doug Fortney, and my mother-in-law Terttu Majamaa, who made sure my mutt Sasha was walked on those long days of holing myself up in the house to write. For my late mother Patricia Fortney, my first teacher, I hope I have made you proud.

To my wonderful husband, Robert Majamaa, this book is as much yours as it is mine: for all those nights you read and critiqued draft after draft, for your unwavering love and support, and for agreeing with me that a month in Maui doing final drafts would be good for both body and soul.

In 2006, my boss at the *Calgary Herald*, editor-in-chief Lorne Motley, decided I would be the right journalist to tackle this tough assignment; without that opportunity I would never have known what riches were to be discovered in Nichola's story. I'm indebted to my professional mentors, Monica Zurowski, Eric Dawson, Malcolm Kirk and Gerry Nott, for showing me how it's done with professionalism and integrity. Sydney Sharpe and Rebecca Eckler steered me in the right direction when I had no idea what my first step would be. Also, thanks to the Canada Council for the Arts for helping to make it possible to take the time to do the heavy lifting.

As I was putting the finishing touches on the final chapters of this book, two people for whom I have the utmost respect and admiration left us much too early: on December 30, 2009, thirty-four-year-old Michelle Lang, a *Calgary Herald* colleague who was in Afghanistan as an embedded journalist representing CanWest News Service, died along with four Canadian soldiers when the LAV they were riding in was struck by an IED; sometime on or around January 12, 2010, fifty-seven-year-old Walt Ratterman, the lead light installer on the Papua New Guinea project in 2008, perished in the Haiti earthquake. As he had in places like Rwanda and Afghanistan, Walt was in Haiti to do humanitarian work, installing solar lighting systems in remote medical clinics across the country. This book is also dedicated to the memories of these two brave and selfless people, whose deaths once again serve as a reminder that making a difference in the world often comes with great sacrifice, and risk.

Ultimately, the person who can take the most credit for *Sunray* is Nichola Goddard. By leaving a most prolific collection of letters, she has not only let us into her heart and soul, but provided a collective voice to her fellow Canadian soldiers, our nation's twenty-first-century warriors.

Index